SUSPECTED
HIPPIE
IN TRANSIT

sex, drugs, rock 'n' roll,
and the search for higher consciousness
on the international trail, 1971–1977

VOLUME 1

MARTIN FRUMKIN

BALSAM PRESS LLC
Denver, Colorado

Balsam Press LLC
Denver, CO
MartinFrumkin@gmail.com

Printed in the United States of America
27 26 25 24 23 22   1 2 3 4 5 6 7 8

Cover photograph: Martin Frumkin
Book and cover design: Sandra Jonas

Publisher's Cataloging-in-Publication Data
Names: Frumkin, Martin, 1948–.
Title: Suspected Hippie in Transit : Sex, Drugs, Rock 'n' Roll, and Search for
    Higher Consciousness on the International Trail, 1971–1977 /
    Martin Frumkin.
Description: Denver, Colorado : Balsam Press LLC, 2022. | Includes bibli-
    ographical references.
Identifiers: LCCN 2020905319 | ISBN 9781734800012
Subjects: LCSH: Hippies—Religious life. | Spiritual biography. | Autobiography.
    | International travel. | Nineteen seventies. | LCGFT: Autobiographies. |
    BISAC: BIOGRAPHY & AUTOBIOGRAPHY / Personal Memoirs.
Classification: LCC CT275 .F78 2021 | DDC 305.568092 — dc23
LC record available at http://lccn.loc.gov/2020905319

To Grandma Lena, Grandpa Max,
Anna "Chanshi," Babi Clara,
"Tex" Solomon, and Wolf Duvid,
and to Jane, Joanie and Leah,
and to Zeyda Yacov,
who loved me and supported my travels—
even after he forgot my name.

And to dear Patti Buum, my Norwegian friend,
and her twenty-four-year-old "memory."

Contents

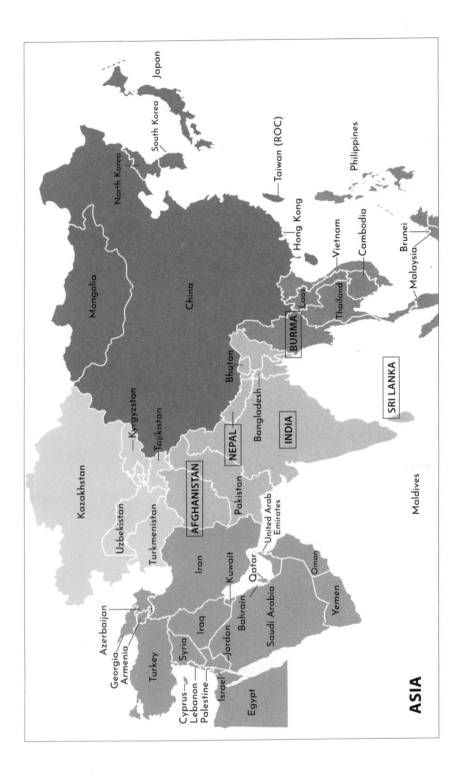

ASIA

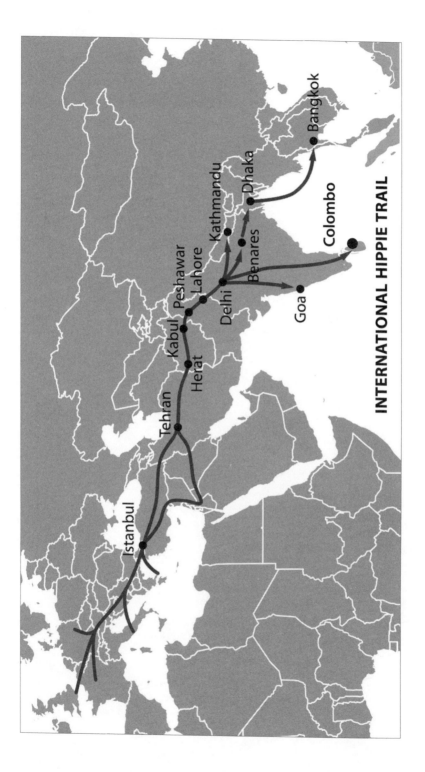

INTERNATIONAL HIPPIE TRAIL

Author's Note

Crossing the overland frontier from the fierce jungles of southern Thailand onto the sudden smooth blacktop of northern Malaysia became a comedy for some, a tragedy for others. Clearly posted during early April 1976 was the following:

Malaysia welcomes bona fide tourists but not hippies. You are therefore advised at all times to dress, behave, and live decently in hotels as becoming a bona fide tourist.

If you are found in shabby, dirty, or indecent cloths, or living in temporary or makeshift shelters, you will be deemed a hippie.

Your visit pass will be canceled and you will be ordered to leave Malaysia within 24 hours, failing which you will be prosecuted under the immigration laws.

Apparently, being a hippie is a crime in itself. Hidden meaning? The hippie species has been banned in Malaysia. But sometimes, Malaysian immigration isn't sure who or what is a hippie.

The solution to this vexing national security dilemma? "S.H.I.T." is stamped in the passports of those unfortunate souls who lack a designated identity: "Suspected Hippie in Transit."

Confessions of a Perennial Peripatetic

Virtually all my life I have tried to remain under the radar. So why did I write *Suspected Hippie in Transit*? Why does anyone share his or her thoughts and feelings, behaviors and intimate songs and dances of fear and struggle, of trial and triumph? Because it is human propensity, a survival property of Dr. Freud's animalistic id. I wanted to share with others what I anticipated would be unique adventures beyond their experience.

I began by reviewing a score of tattered notebooks I had filled under wanting conditions, followed by self-editing thousands of pages of longhand copy in a laborious and questionable attempt to accurately and sequentially record spontaneous events. I resisted temptations to modify or delete those hypocritical, crude, and perhaps undeveloped notions to which I no longer subscribe, and chose not to delete vignettes in which I took myself far too seriously. It is important to me that *Suspected* reflect my fluctuating, emotionally charged musings, internal conflicts, embarrassments, and, alas, failures—at the time they were written.

My writings and journeys were experiments, I the subject of investigation. Various writing styles—from playful street-jargon scratch and scribble to pseudo academia—are ascribed to cutting college classes and denying unhinged mood swings. The book unfolds in real time in diary format. On occasion, I describe one locale while rooted in another. No doubt, when on the road, you must take advantage of immediate opportunity, like squatting to take a shit in a muddy hole in the ground.

My experiences often turned out to be far different than what I had originally anticipated. As for the disparate local spellings of remarkable foreign destinations and words to which I was exposed, I have used those most popularly accepted at the time.

It was only after I had crossed into countries that I was able to clarify my vague mental images of where they were geographically located. I had read little about them. Silver lining? *Without* expectations, I was simply blown away. My unsolicited advice? Get off your ass and smart phones and try it.

Free of expectations, I encountered and flirted with a great deal of cosmic philosophy, literature, and music—from scholarly works to nonsensical barbs. I have woven those items into the text, along with events that either substantially influenced me or shed light on this world we live in.

My experiences didn't significantly differ from those of most people I met on the international hippie trail (IHT), a culture unto itself. The difference? I wrote them down. However, interpretation of same by my often capricious colleagues, I strong suspect, remain subject to wide discrepancy. What some loved others hated. No matter, my writing became a predominantly pleasurable habit that eventually bordered on neurotic and psychotic obsession and compulsion.

Feng shui, a metaphysical Chinese art, purports to orient placement of temples, buildings, furniture, and other worldly items in an auspicious manner based on "invisible forces" defined as bodies of water, the stars, and the like. In essence, such placements must *feel* "right," "balanced," "complete," and "comfortable." Applying the same practice to writing on the road seemed natural. I was usually in the mood. Not so when applying feng shui to publication. No parallel process. Creativity is soulful. The delivery system sucks.

Running away from home for whatever reason describes many I met on the trail. In fact, I often found myself more comfortable—and safer—with local Asian populations than with those from "civilized" Europe. And little did I know that my momentary encounters on the IHT would duplicate today's fleeting brushes with intimacy and fame on social media.

From where did my motivations to seek another way, another *Tao,* originate? Dissatisfaction and restlessness with life at home, adventure, rebelliousness, and the free-spirited 1960s counterculture's fascination with Indian mysticism and the East? The Beatles and "Sexy Sadie"? The Beats of the 1950s? The Aquarian Age and Woodstock? An age-specific developmental stage that caused me to pursue who the fuck I was and why I existed?

When adding centuries of rabbinical DNA to the mix, I became a "second-generation" flower child searching for nirvana as depicted in Ram Dass's *Be Here Now* (1971) and Parvati Markus's *Love Everyone* (2015). Could ingestion of LSD, mescaline, and psilocybin have played a role? Actually, in hindsight, I was fooled by college friends who posed as "freaks" but immediately joined the ranks of Charles Reich's American Corporate State as depicted in his *The Greening of America* (1970). Or went into Daddy's business upon college graduation.

I don't labor under the illusion that my primary identity in life has ever been that of a writer. However, during the years of working on this manuscript, I came to understand the Polish writer Joseph Conrad's alarming admonition in *The Rescue* (1920): "There is no rest for the messenger until the message is delivered."

Some upstarts compose exhaustive schematic outlines and themes before arriving at their first episode of writer's block. I placed the cart before the horse, and only after the fact did I discover *Suspected*'s themes: reality versus perception, secular versus nonsecular, work versus play, individuality versus group speak, thinking versus feeling, idealism versus pragmatism, discipline versus pleasure. And, of course, East versus West.

To place these themes under one canopy, I am indebted to Herman Hesse's *Siddhartha* and *Narcissus and Goldman* in which intensely meaningful, self-disciplined lifestyles compete against shallow but worldly "wine, women, and song."

As my journey took on increased personal meaning, so too did my realization that control is mere *maya* illusion and cause for great difficulty when we try to make order out of chaos. My spiritual struggles with Eastern constructs paralleled my struggles with Judaism. And still do.

Single, and horny most of the time, I had unexpected but welcome one-hour and one-night stands that far exceeded my fantasies and realities at home. The residual "free love" of the 1960s, when combined with meeting spirited women, resulted in rather loose and casual attitudes toward passionate sexuality with multiple partners, though usually not with more than one at a time.

Regrets? Yes. They derive from what I haven't overtly shared in the pages to follow—my asinine, selfish, childish traits that have been, perhaps, intentionally if not thinly camouflaged within the rantings of this emotional exposé. And herein lies my ultimate discovery: After self-editing *Suspected*, I find my basic values and thinking from back in the day are not wholly different from those I hold today.

PART ONE

सचाई

TRUTH

There never was a time when I did not exist, nor you, nor any of these kings. Nor is there any future in which we shall cease to be.

—*Bhagavad Gita*

The Taiosts tell a story of a farmer whose horse ran away. Because the horse was a prize mare, the neighbors stopped by to express their condolences, to which the farmer said, "Perhaps."

The next week the horse returned, bringing with her five wild horses. When the neighbors stopped in to congratulate the farmer on his good luck, he answered, "Perhaps."

The next day, when the farmer's son was trying to ride one of the wild horses, he fell off and broke his leg. Again the neighbors gathered to express their sympathy for the farmer's misfortune. Again the farmer said, "Perhaps."

Three days later, army conscription officers rode into the village and seized all of the young men except the farmer's son who was rejected because of his broken leg. When the neighbors came by to say how fortunate it was that everything had worked out, the farmer said, "Perhaps."

—Bennett Goodspeed
The Tao Jones Averages:
A Guide to Whole-Brained Investing

Truth does not depart from human nature.
If what is regarded as truth departs from
    human nature,
it may not be regarded as truth.

The superior man loves his soul;
the inferior man loves his property.

The superior man understands what is right;
the inferior man understands what will sell.

The superior man blames himself;
the inferior man blames others.

                    —Confucius

The test of character and integrity is not
    fortune and fame,
but misfortune and isolation.

Those who know do not speak;
Those who speak do not know.

Do you have the patience to wait
till the mud settles and the water is clear?
Can you remain unmoving
till the right action arises by itself?

The difference between Right and Wrong
is the Sickness of the Mind.

                    —Lao Tzu

It is because we single out something and treat
it as distinct from other things that we get the
idea of its opposite. Beauty, for example, once
distinguished, suggests its opposite, ugliness.

In fact, all distinctions naturally appear as
opposites. And opposites get their meaning from
each other and find their completion only through
each other.

—Lao Tzu

You either got faith or you got unbelief
And there ain't no neutral ground.

They may call you doctor
They may call you chief
But you're gonna have to serve somebody.
—Bob Dylan

The truth will set you free.

—Jesus

That which is hateful to you,
you do not do unto your fellow.

—Hillel

I am a steadfast follower of the doctrine of non-violence
which was first preached by Lord Buddha, whose divine wisdom is
absolute and infallible, and was practiced in our own time by
the Indian saint and leader, Mahatma Gandhi. So from the very
beginning I was strongly opposed to any resort to arms as a
means of regaining our freedom.

—His Holiness the Fourteenth Dalai Lama

If you are bound to freedom, you desire freedom.
How do you become free of freedom?

The nature of nature is change.

Guru nature takes risks and sacrifices love.
Friends' nature takes no risks and enjoys love.
Friendship supports you.
Guru clarifies you, shakes you awake.

Objectivity is not bad,
but you must give up attachment.
Attachment is the problem.
Attachment is the source of pain and sorrow.
Enjoyment of pleasure is not bad.
Attachment to pleasure is bad.

       —Bal Yogi Prem Varni

Don't throw people out of your heart.
That does not mean you have to hang out with them.
—Neem Karoli Baba (Ram Dass's guru)

The mystic experience, the illumination, the great awakening, along with the charismatic seer who started the whole thing, are forgotten, lost, or transformed into their opposites.

Organized Religion, the churches, finally may become the major enemies of the religious experience and the religious experiencer.

—Abraham Maslow

From the records of religion and the surviving monuments of poetry and the plastic arts, it is very plain that, at most times and in most places, men have attached more importance to the inscape than to objective existents, have felt that what they saw with their eyes shut possessed a spiritually higher significance than what they saw with their eyes open.

The urge to escape, the longing to transcend . . . if only for a few moments, is and has always been one of the principle appetites of the soul.

—Aldous Huxley

For when a man no longer confuses
himself with the definition of himself
that others have given him, he is at
once universal and unique.

　　　　　　　　　—Alan W. Watts

Success means doing the best with what we have.
Success is the doing, not the getting;
in the trying, not the triumph.

—Zig Ziglar

Float like a butterfly, sting like a bee.
The hands can't hit what the eyes can't see.
—Cassius Marcellus Clay Jr.

I am the greatest.
—Muhammad Ali

Tourists don't know where they've been, I thought.
Travelers don't know where they are going.

—Paul Theroux

He who travels far will often see things
far removed from what he believed was Truth.
When he talks about it in the fields at home,
he is often accused of lying,
for the obdurate people will not believe.

—Herman Hesse

All journeys have secret destinations
of which the traveler is unaware.
                    —Martin Buber

A good traveler has no fixed plans
and is not intent on arriving.
                    —Lao Tsu

As you move through this life and this world
you change things slightly,
you leave marks behind, however small.
And in return, life—and travel—leaves marks on you.
Most of the time, those marks
—on your body or on your heart—
are beautiful.
Often though, they hurt.

—Anthony Bourdain

"Don't Let Me Be Misunderstood."
        —The Animals

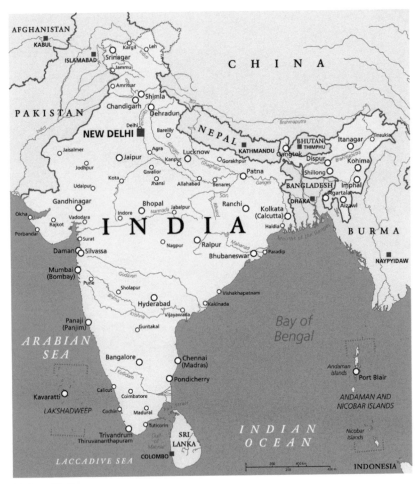

1. Map of India.

PART TWO

NAMASTE
1972

I realized that I had joined a pilgrimage to the East, seemingly a definite and single pilgrimage— but in reality, in its broadest sense, this expedition to the East was not only mine and now; this procession of believers and disciples had always and incessantly been moving towards the East, towards the Home of Light. Throughout the centuries it had been on the way, towards light and wonder, and each member, each group, indeed our whole host and its great pilgrimage, was only a wave in the eternal stream of human beings, of the eternal strivings of the human spirit towards the East, towards Home.

—Hermann Hesse, *The Journey to the East*

Benares, India
Wednesday, October 1, 1972

A myriad of ornate but inconspicuous temples of Hindu and Nepalese origins built on the banks of the River Ganges (Ganga) rise above *ghats* (steps) that lead flocks of the faithful into the spiritually cleansing waters. From the interior of a crumbling temple relic, which provided nothing more than porous shelter for a dozen barely clothed families scattered about the dusty earthen floor, I witnessed a corpse being laid upon a funeral pyre five yards from the flowing river.

An immediate male family member, clean-shaven and neatly groomed for the occasion, had built the sandalwood altar upon which the corpse had been placed with the help of an Untouchable. The relative donned a handsome white gown, the handspun *khadi kurta*, a flaming torch placed in his left hand. As he completed the seventh clockwise rotation of his arms over the deceased, he set fire to the pyre fueled by *ghee* (clarified butter).

Two and a half hours later, when the body had been virtually consumed—after the flesh, skin, and hair of the previously bludgeoned skull were no longer recognizable—family members uttered prayers and distributed the ashes upon the beckoning waters of Mother Ganges. During the exacting ritual, other corpses had been wrapped and placed on canvas stretchers by saffron-robed high priests in attendance.

This final sacrifice, to be set ablaze at one of the Ganga's ghats, is craved by all Hindus. Those without the inordinate sum of three hundred rupees ($30 US) are merely sent floating down the river. According to Hindu convention, women are prohibited from taking part in the rituals because they carry life in the womb. The draped body of a dead *Brahman* may be handled only by those the Brahman shunned in life, the Untouchables. Hindu hypocrisy transcends all.

Hoping their eternal spirit will be reincarnated into a higher caste and better life, thousands upon thousands of infirm but determined elderly purposely make their pilgrimages to Benares to die—to escape *samsara*, the interminable life-death cycle. I watched these living corpses arrive by train and later witnessed flames licking at the last remnants of their material presence. Was my soulful rendition of Neil Young's "Down by the River" sheer blasphemy, or was it representative of Carlos Castaneda's separate realities?

Some days ago, I had departed the decrepit, post–Civil War (1880) black steam engines of the Indian railway network after a perplexing series of berth-night trains from Lucknow, a twenty-two-hour uncomfortable but powerful fiasco. Midway between Lucknow and Muzaffarpur, the closest railhead to Nepal, lies Benares, the six-thousand-year-old spiritual capital of India.

Now called Varanasi, this sprawling, poverty-stricken district of urban decay is synonymous with Hinduism and India's poor, blind, and crippled seen *everywhere*, tapping their canes for balance, security, and their very survival. Sharing subsistence with the impoverished, the blind, and the crippled on the lowest rung of the Indian caste system are the *Harijans*, the Untouchables.

Affectionately named the "Children of God" by Mohandas K. (Mahatma) Gandhi, they too are shunned by all but themselves, the inhospitable streets on which they sleep, and the frenetic marketplaces they frequent. Like Moroccan *medinas* and Middle Eastern *souks*, these markets are intertwined by winding, narrow, catacomb-like paths that devour bicycle rickshaws and other indeterminable creatures of satanic lagoons.

The legendary source of the sacred Ganga, a world unto itself, can be traced to the mighty Himalayas, home of Mother Shiva. The Indian government brochure "Varanasi" proclaims:

THE GREAT WATERS OF HINDUISM AND ITS PILGRIM CITY
On the banks of the river that is almost a faith stands Hinduism's greatest city: Varanasi, built on the Ganga. For several thousand years, pilgrims have cleansed themselves of their sins here and sought release from the cycle of rebirth. In Varanasi, they believe all men can find identity with the spirit.

The Ganga starts where the Rishis [Hindu sages or saints] med-

2. The Benares ghats along the Ganges River.

3. Sacred cows roam at will.

itate in the high Himalayas; it meets the sea in Bengal, amid the realities of an industrial civilization. Somewhere there between the two lies India's turbulent present . . . and Varanasi, city of a thousand temples, called Kashi or "Light by the Devout."

Hinduism: deep and mystical everywhere. In a decorated doorway, in the glimpse of a glittering temple, in the sound of a sacred bell, in the chant of priests, and in the fragrance of sacrificial flowers.

Bulls and cows in Varanasi are branded in the name of the departed souls. They roam freely because it is believed each is invested with a human soul.

At the Kublai Khan hotel, I met two Indian teenagers who are not among India's starving. That their families are affluent and purport to be Christian is no coincidence. In fact, most upper-class Indians I have encountered are educated Christians who bitterly complain about the discrimination they suffer from the impoverished Hindu majority. Give me a break!

Into bucks and seducing Western "chicks," these spoiled brats believe that everyone and everything in India is corrupt. One of them felt compelled to offer five thousand rupees ($500 US) to join the all-India swim team. Unable to maneuver their Italian motor bikes in Benares, they grumble, "The streets are human zoos."

Although Indians are not physically branded into castes, each knows his or her place and that of others. Though I am ignorant of who belongs to which station, I realize the dung scrapers and street sweepers of Benares aren't Brahmans, and the well-to-do silk merchants couldn't possibly be Untouchables. There are five castes: Brahmans (priests), *Kashatrinjars* (warriors), *Varsas* (cultivators, traders), *Sudras* (farmers, serfs), and Harijans (depressed).

Federal regulations forbidding casteism have been as effective as integration laws in the American South. While progress has been grudgingly made, contemporary India has learned you can't successfully legislate against prejudice, especially when such attitudes and consequent discrimination have been the dominant features of Hindu religion, law, practice, and tradition for six millennia. *Intolerance City.*

Fundamental to an understanding of Hinduism and its resulting lifestyles are significant Vedas and Upanishads (Hindu scriptures) inscribed (in English) upon the white and red marble walls of the Benares Bishwanath Temple, found on the verdant campus of Benares Hindu University.

THE WHEEL OF COSMIC LIFE

For those who are wandering in the world, which is characterized by the evil of birth, death, old age, sickness, and suffering and are caught in the wheel of delusion (*maya*) characterized by three trends, light (*satva*), movement (*rahas*) and darkness (*tomas*), the only way to be saved is to take refuge in God with a pure heart.

God is one. He is omnipresent and the creator of the whole universe. The Wise call that one God by various names. He who is known as Vishnu (preserver) is verily Rudra (destroyer), and he who is Rudra is Brahma (creator), one entity functioning as three Gods, i.e., Rudra (Shiva), Vishnu and Brahma.

I gaze across the horizon upon scores of gentle green groves punctuated by no less than nine freestanding temples, their pink-and-orange towers jutting above the treetops. But wait just a minute. *Shock City!* Paradoxically, swastikas have also been engraved into the walls of these temples. Hitler twisted their ancient meanings: "Peace and Prosperity" and "Divinity and Spirituality."

In consideration of Indian traditions and my immediate reality, I am convinced that India is vast, India is rich, India is poor. India is an electricity-less muddied thatch village within the shadows of a behemoth steel mill. *Reality is perception.*

Too many Westerners ultimately condemn India as uncivilized and crude. Period. Yet untold ancient wisdom and thousands of refineries and factories litter its thriving metropolises. When you are physically within the boundaries of Afghanistan, a severely retarded and totally undeveloped tribal nation without any semblance of the industrial revolution save one matchstick factory, India and its government, in comparison, are perceived to be rich and powerful.

Hey, now. Listen up. Although considered impoverished when measured by Western standards, India is *not* undeveloped. Lack of meaningful and widespread birth control and efficiency, and unequal utilization and distribution of resources, technology and education are its problems. In essence, Indian resources cannot be equally distributed and consumed among *six hundred million people.*

For each middle-class retailer, government bureaucrat, and school-teacher, you can't avoid omnipresent throngs residing in earthen huts and on railway station platforms—so many suffering from disease and malnutrition. Witnessing the daily reality of the disadvantaged souls living near that steel mill brought tears to my eyes.

Government officials proclaim they are trying to help, pledging to equalize resources and opportunity by employing a democratic-socialist state. Perhaps what they envision may one day bear fruit. However, unless a great, tumultuous, and radical economic-political change of cataclysmic proportions takes place, most Indians—and their descendants—will be condemned to a karmic fate some feel is worse than death.

4. First employed in India during the 1700s, *chillums* were traditionally made of clay. Think smokestack.

Hare, who goes by only one name, expects to transcend his karmic fate. Born and bred in Kerala, the narrow communist-controlled tropical province hugging India's southwest coast, Hare has lived in Benares for a decade. A sculptor by trade, he supplements his income by carving stone and wooden *chillums* (pipes) while hanging with Western freaks. Turned on to Bhutanese and Laotian shit (dope, hashish) by my new friend, the only long-haired Indian hippie I have met, I believe it is time to get down and become one with Huxley, Cassady, Ginsberg, Kerouac, and Baudelaire.

ॐ

Benares, India
Tuesday, October 3, 1972

By 6:00 a.m., a godly number of human souls have already found sanctuary within the bodies of holy cows. I slept on the floor last night after donating my bent iron bed frame to the comfort and safety of belligerent roaches and lizards already occupying it. Even a filthy, razor-thin floor mat was better than the prospect of sleeping on baggage racks under rusting roofs of third-class Indian trains. In fact, all the rooms I have recently rented have been overrun by mosquitoes, bees, ants, and cockroaches. In Benares, vultures outnumber corpses.

Hare invited me, not for bed and breakfast, but for sunrise *ganja* (marijuana) and gondola. After paddling a bit more than a score of yards from the banks of the Ganga, I watched in astonishment as fiery pyres silently consumed themselves. Alongside the pyres, cloaked corpses were being dipped into the sacred river for their final journeys. Amid the calibrated resonance of priestly Hindu chants, white and orange marigolds, and the haunting inscape of tabla and sitar suggested by George Harrison's "Within You Without You," obeisant sons tapped the skulls of their dead fathers, symbolically releasing their bonded souls to seek rebirth.

5. *Sadhu* is Sanskrit for "the holy men" of India. Most live in *ashrams* (monastic communities/religious retreats) and temples—some in forests and caves. Some in towns and cities. Hindu culture inherently provides for their mortal sustenance and spiritual evolution.

After noshing on *puri* (fried wheat cakes) and *dhal* (a spicy lentil sauce), Hare and I withdrew to the Nepalese Temple and joined an ongoing vibrating sacrosanct dedication to Lord Shiva. Samsun, a loin-clothed *sadhu* (mendicant, friar, "forest" renunciates of the material world) with long hair and a flowing gray beard, then beckoned us into a small anteroom. We sat on a bedraggled bamboo mat. Ashen dots and circles adorned the holy man's shallow brown face. Multicolored chains and dull jewelry hung from his neck.

With staff in hand, Samsun began to pound ganja, tobacco, and saliva within the heels of his weathered hands. He then crumpled and set fire to a ball of dry, stringy bark. After the blessed mixture and smoldering bark were placed into a chillum, and between heavy fits of tokes and coughing, he embarked on vociferous chants to Mother Shiva. *Space City*!

Benares, India
Thursday, October 5, 1972

Sacred cows, roosters, children, walking corpses, and women in saris balancing baskets of clothing, vegetables, and fruit on their heads wait with me for the bus to Sarnath, located six miles from Benares. Sarnath was founded at the spot where Gautama, the Buddha, preached his first sermon to the world.

Upon earthly locations where Lord Buddha, the Blessed One, practiced yoga, large and small structures known as *stupas* have been erected. Each maintains four pairs of eyes "keeping watch for righteous behavior and human prosperity." About three hundred years ago, Ashoka, the great emperor, raised a stone stupa at this spot. The Dhamma Stupa now marks the location of a once-magnificent Buddhist monastery.

Local newspapers mark the locations and describe current events you don't read about in the good ole USA:

Bulandshahr News, September 21
Dusk to dawn curfew was imposed today in Dadri, about 34 kilometers from here [Bulandshahr], and armed police were patrolling the streets of the town following a riot over the alleged slaughter

of a cow. Nine people, including six policemen, were injured and about two dozen houses and shops set on fire. Nineteen people had been arrested until this evening.

India Express—September 28, 1972. Allahabad.
The railway police today rounded up 54 boys, all below 12 years, who were begging at the railway station.

Benares may possess more four legged rats than New York City. As for two legged rats, your call!

Raxaul, India
Sunday, October 8, 1972
Located on the Indian-Nepalese frontier, Raxaul was reached by a six-hour bus trip, flat tire and all. Daily life in the East is tolerable *if* you are not in need of emergency service. Apparently, the bus company does not feel the need for placing compulsory spare tires on its vehicles. And so, for two hours we waited in a crude outskirt while a candle melted chunks of rubber into a mangled patch.

Kathmandu, Nepal
Monday, October 16, 1972, Gadhimai Festival
I arrived in Nepal, a Himalayan kingdom, just before the Gadhimai, Dashain, and Diwali Festivals, great feast days celebrated by Hindus and Buddhists alike. Wide to narrow, the streets and alleys were packed with smiling Nepalese decked with bright flowers and carrying fresh baked flatbreads and other provisions in preparation for the festivals.

Street rumors foretold of a great spectacle, a ritualized mass murder of pigs, goats, yaks, and water buffalo. Deemed a "fortunate and honored" guest, I warily awaited this morning's slaughter. The rumors appeared to be true.

During the previous evening, the sounds of drums, bells, flutes, and whistles played by hundreds of faithful merrymakers dancing in long

6. Nepal encompasses more than 125 ethnic groups expressed by distinct and overlapping religion, language, geography, architecture, festivals, music, art, dance, verbal folklore, and potent firewater.

processions drew me outdoors. Colorful tribal garb and spears had re-placed the usual rags, hoes, picks, and begging bowls. The sight and smells of garlands of psychedelic-colored flowers, burning incense, offerings of rice, vegetables, fruit, and the sounds of Buddhist and Hindu chants and widespread wild abandon infiltrated Durbar Square's pagoda-like tem-ples. From the first light of dawn, congregants got loaded on rice-based firewater, visited friends and relatives, and sacrificed animals in their own homes.

Partying into the night, I soon joined melodious parades of increasing volume, intensity, and inebriation. *Thousands* of gifts and trailing floral bouquets had been placed about every temple I visited. The abundant square overflowed with *love*. Swaying alongside flower sellers and men carrying laughing grandchildren covered with beads and smothered by kisses were voluptuous Himalayan princesses elegantly dressed in flowing robes em-blazoned with kaleidoscopic designs. Among the celebrants were Jagat Raj Kumari, Lekha, and A. C. (Aishworya), all members of the ruling royal family. Balram Chetri, a sinewy young man, a commoner, seemed to have eyes for Princess Jagat.

At dawn, I approached a crowd assembling in front of the *Kot*, a thickly walled national defense arsenal and compound where Nepalese *Gurkhas* (soldiers) clad in T-shirts, khaki shorts, olive knee socks and polished black boots lounged in an interior drill field. Spry and confident, a German national assured me that the diplomatic community and members of the public would soon be allowed to enter.

Within moments, those standing about were escorted up a narrow stairwell and seated on metal folding chairs placed upon a concrete balcony overlooking the courtyard. Thus, there I sat, one of the "fortunate and honored" travelers in Kathmandu, mingling with many embassy and consulate types who obviously knew when and where to be this early morning.

Just below, to my left, is a small reviewing stand with a plush couch, two rows of thickly cushioned chairs, bright red carpeting, and officials literally dressed-to-kill in full military regalia. At various *maulis* (posts), each representing one of Nepal's army brigades, double-edged spears sporting vivid orange, maroon, and red scarves, flags, and flowers have been wedged into the ground alongside silver-and-gold bowls and trays of rice and burning incense. Above the reviewing stand and ringing the courtyard is a sea of humanity crammed onto every accessible veranda, windowsill, rooftop, and tree. Just behind me, an attractive *jeune fille*, an embassy secretary speaking thickly accented French, is discussing Ronald Reagan playing softball. Seems Reagan, the governor of California, broke a leg sliding into first base.

As more spectators continue to arrive, bloated herds of goats, pigs, and water buffalo are being led into the compound. Six thousand yaks have been brought from Tibet for the occasion, all to meet their Maker before sunset this evening. Processions, chanting, and music continue.

I had thought killing to be contrary to Hindu and Buddhist *Tao* (The Way). If it's any consolation, only male beasts will be decapitated this morning. A Swiss woman residing in Nepal for twenty years has printed a few pages explaining the events of this bloody massacre of innocents. "It is said that the mass sacrifices . . . symbolize the killing of animal pride and animal nature in a human being, leading to a state of peace."

My take? Fuck that shit!

Awaiting the spectacle to begin, I still have some moments to gracefully exit. Do I really want to view such butchery? The Barcelona bullfights eventually sickened me. Yet my adventurous, morbid curiosity craves what can be experienced, regardless of its (and my) nature. Anyway, I usually learn more from anguish than joy. Rationalization? Of course.

The first animals, provided by His Royal Majesty, are now being slaughtered—to the accompaniment of European waltzes. (Such was the scene at Dachau and Auschwitz when my people were being exterminated.) Men wearing bloodied T-shirts have just led a buffalo up to a wooden platform where the beast is being tied to a mauli and held stationary by four Gurkhas. At the burst of gunpowder, an armed soldier with a machete delivers one swift sure stroke, and the bull's head falls to the ground. At that very moment, you can see the bloody truncated neck before the headless animal plunges to earth. And the band continues to play!

7. The Kot.

As carcasses are dragged off, creating continuously wider pools of blood, each head is hand-carried to strategic locations in the courtyard where spears, flowers, and incense have been placed. Still waiting their fate, the creatures smell the blood of their own kind and shiver and retreat in terror. When each beast has fallen, the warm remains continue to spasm and grapple. As I look to my left, two headless carcasses are squirming, their feet moving as if to run.

The butchery is to be accomplished by one deft, immediate stroke. As you can imagine, things grow a bit messy when more than one attempt is needed. And needless to say, no one consulted Orthodox Rabbi Yacov (Jacob), my *zeyda* (grandfather), and a *shochet* (kosher butcher) on how to achieve painless ritual kosher slaughter.

Under an innocent and naive rising sun, the music continues, the rifle blasts continue, and bloody squirming continues while decapitated heads and bodies fall to the ground. The whole fucking bloody mess continues. I just don't get it. A *Mondo Cane* moment.

8. The "celebration" is not restricted to the Kot and the Kathmandu Valley.

Central Kathmandu's twisting, broken, poorly paved and earthen back streets host a multitude of *legal* hashish shops, hotels, and restaurants, many of which do not meet or satisfy most inhabitants' needs or desires. On the narrowest of alleys close to Durbar Square, wild emaciated dogs bark and fight with one another while young women wash clothing and babies in concrete subpools within the shadows of Hanuman Dhoka—a complex of palaces, courtyards, temples, and other architectural marvels of the East.

Heedless of the burned remains of the dead emerging from nearby funeral pyres, mothers suckle their newborns while stoned hippies, unperturbed by pigs ecstatically rolling in mud and eating shit next to passing anteaters, sip *chai* (milk-tea) with pie at the Pie and Chai Shop.

9–12. *Clockwise from upper left*: Within the Kathmandu Valley are three Durbar Squares (the "place of palaces"): Kathmandu (above), Patan, and Bhadgaon, aka Baktapur. Plazas fronting former royal palaces and residences contain Buddhist and Hindu temples "guarded" by divine statues, open courts, fountains, the faithful, roaming animals, nondescript informality—and *legal* hashish shops!

Kathmandu, Nepal
Friday, October 20, 1972

I had been told the best way to discover the wonders of the Kathmandu Valley was by bicycle imported from the People's Republic of China. Before starting out from Kathmandu's dairy on the morning of my expedition, I

13. Found in Kathmandu's Durbar Square is one of many manifestations of Lord Shiva, Mahakala (Bhairava) is a Hindu deity associated with annihilation. Buddhists consider him a *bodhisattva*, a compassionate soul who delays reaching nirvana so that he can tend to human suffering.

heard a familiar voice call out, "Marty?" I recognized Darlene Morocco of Milly and Darlene, whom I had first met on Terazoute Beach the previous April. She was shocked at the events that had transpired since we had last seen each other. Some hours later, I approached Pashupatinath Temple. And so it is written:

> This is the holiest of Shiva (Hindu) shrines in Nepal. Lord Pashupat-
> inath is the guardian spirit of Nepal. The temple of Pashupatinath is
> a double-roofed pagoda of gold-gilt brass. The gateways are plated
> with silver. It stands on the western bank of the Bagmati, about
> four kilometers northeast of Kathmandu. It contains the lingam
> [symbolic phallus] of Pashupatinath.

Atop surrounding steep hills perch dozens of spherical mini pagodas, all somehow deriving their strength from the Ganga of Nepal, the sacred Bagmati River. As in Benares, elderly Nepalese come here to die, their bodies burned at the ghats, their ashes distributed upon the surface of The River.

"Only Hindus can enter the main shrine," said a well-scrubbed Chinese boy who displayed extraordinary manners. Before long, we climbed a hill, walked past a congregation of chanting, orange-robed Buddhist monks, and found ourselves among multiple rows of small, spherical pagodas, temples, and ethereal stupas.

"Do you want to smoke with the holy man?"

"Who said that?"

My little friend seemed to know more than he let on. Within minutes, I was squatting inside one of the pagodas, having entered through a narrow crawl space. The straw and bamboo mats intended to cover most walls, ceilings and earthen floors could not conceal faded vestiges of green-and-blue, childlike scribblings and frescos.

Carefully chosen pieces of pungent sandalwood had been methodically arranged in a triangular fashion above a smoldering fire in front of a freestanding altar. Strategically positioned before both, wearing a barely perceptible loincloth, was an otherwise naked high priest sitting in the full lotus position. Layers of ash not only garnished his entire body, beard, and hair but also covered an assemblage of male disciples kneeling before their mentor.

This yogi, as the Chinese boy referred to him, was the leader of a cult exclusively dedicated to the spiritual consumption of hashish. For one hour, to the sounds and vibrations of nasal chants, the yogi prepared and smoked a nefarious collection of pipes and chillums. A middle-aged Tibetan gentleman, with the drawn ruddy facial features of the Native American Indian, soon entered through the crawl space and narrated a lengthy story. Bewildered, I continued to smoke until I was ushered out.

Kathmandu, Nepal
Saturday, October 21, 1972

Hapless Nepalese and Afghan buses have one thing in common in addition to rust, breakdowns, reckless drivers, and freeloaders. Most customers have four legs.

When I tell fellow travelers I must leave Nepal after two weeks, most look at me as if to say, "Only two weeks? What a waste." Truth is, I hate

14 and 15. *Above and below*: Unlike many singular Western houses of worship, Pashupati-nath reflects a *campus* of temples.

narrating the long depressive story of my predicament—of my friend, Mark Lewis, and his senseless murder by primitive tribesmen in lawless Baluchistan, a sprawling province in southern Pakistan.

I had concocted a series of fraudulent letters written while in Kabul and mailed to my parents by a trusted Afghan banker while I traveled in India and Nepal. My correspondence convinced ma and pa that violent Afghanistan was safe, and that "peaceful" Pakistan and India were dangerous. Too many angry roadsters are running away from home and family to relate to my love-and-consideration trip. I've promised myself to return one day and trek to Everest's base camp.

Mark's brutal and shocking murder also catalyzed another memory. On May 4, 1970, I kept an appointment I had made with a prominent New York City, Fifth Avenue psychiatrist, one Anita Stevens. Allegedly, Dr. Stevens was a friend of General Lewis B. Hershey, then director of the Selective Service System (SSS), otherwise known as the dreaded "draft."

During a previous "invitation" to Fort Hamilton in Brooklyn, which had recently been bombed by Vietnam antiwar protesters, I showed up with artificially placed needle "tracks" in my arm. My "reward"? A measly six-month, 1-Y military-service deferment from killing people in Vietnam. Why die for self-indulgent American insurance companies who invest in and profit from ruthless munitions factories making a literal "killing"? Fuck 'em.

Persistent rumors spoke of Stevens, an antiwar shrink who, for $250, would provide a psychological treatise guaranteed to generate a lengthy deferment. Apparently, the rumors were true. Entering the petite lobby of Dr. Stevens's practice across the street from Central Park and the Metropolitan Museum of Art, I joined several dozen longhairs from across the country, squeezed into every crack and cranny of the lobbyette. After nodding yes to all questions asked, Dr. Stevens produced a letter indicating I hated my mother and was intent on and capable of killing her. My diagnosis? "Paranoid schizophrenia with suicidal tendencies and a guarded prognosis."

"Like, far out, man." Holding the Holy Grail in my hands, I took the subway to elevated Queensboro Plaza station. And suddenly stopped right in my tracks. Platform kiosks were selling the afternoon tabloid edition of the *New York Post*. Stories splashed across the front page screamed,

"Murder at Kent State University," which was soon to be immortalized in Neil Young's "Ohio." Four unarmed student antiwar protestors had been shot dead by national guardsmen on the campus of Kent State University.

Within six months, without choice, I returned to Fort Hamilton armed with my letter and emotional angst—a virtual albatross hanging around my neck. No more track marks. Finally called into Dr. Freud's inner sanctum, I confidently, if not smugly, presented my letter.

Perhaps had I been summoned to a fort in Arizona or Montana, I might have succeeded. And why is that? According to my assigned military "interpreter of dreams," duplicates of my "personalized" letter had been submitted five times in the past twenty-four hours!

What to do? Become a Quaker? The American Friends Service Committee, a Quaker organization, was opposed to the Vietnam War. Their headquarters, located in an attractive red brick mansion at 15 Rutherford Place in Manhattan, offered a view of the East River and Queens during the frequent visits I made for *legal* draft counseling.

Per instructions to no longer rely on "tracts" and "letters," I consistently and legally made and broke physical exam appointments in New York City and later in Europe. Written submissions ("I was traveling") became good enough to require the SSS to reschedule each appointment, taking up to six months to do so.

One day, while in Marrakesh, Morocco, hanging with Crosby, Stills, Nash, Young, and Millie and Darlene, I received a post from the SSS. I had been newly assigned a 1-H deferment, essentially to remain effective until the advent of a thermonuclear world war!

Band-i-Amir, Afghanistan
Monday, October 30, 1972

I breathe within sight of one of the earth's sparkling jewels. At 12,000 feet, Band-i-Amir consists of five extremely dark, royal-blue mountain lakes that starkly contrast light-beige mountains and wide desert valleys. Prehistoric cliffs reach for the heavens, their rock walls throwing off vivid hues—reds, browns, oranges, and yellows. *Visual Ecstasy City.* All is found within the snowcapped mountain ranges of northern Afghanistan's Hindu Kush.

16. Without one track of railroad, Afghanistan has *never* been formally colonized. And probably never will. Fiercely proud and independent, tribal Pashtuns, Tajiks, Hazaras, and Uzbeks live in deserts, mountains, and towns under a range of conditions—from primitive to sophisticated.

17. One of the lakes in Band-i-Amir. Imagine camels and oases in the Mojave Desert!

Bamyan, Afghanistan
Tuesday, October 31, 1972

Café? Restaurant? Hotel? All of the above? Good luck. Try five afghanis (eighty to the US dollar) for a spot on a dusty floor.

18. The gatekeepers (*et moi*).

The jeep ride over the dirt road from Kabul to Band-i-Amir to Bamyan overcame the mysterious folds of the Hindu Kush. Directly behind my hotel and the neighboring cornfield are pierced rock cliffs into which stupendous statues of Lord Buddha have been deeply carved. Four score and seven Afghans inhabit caves adjacent to the Buddhas.

The Big Buddha, over 180 feet high, is physically overwhelming and dominates the mountain and town. If you stand directly in front of the statue of Lord Buddha, you gain a magnificent view of Central Asia: ranges of snowcapped mountains and the Bamyan Valley first described by Marco Polo many centuries ago.

19. One of the wonders of the ancient world, the Big Buddha was carved into the sides of sandstone cliffs during the sixth century.

I feel fortunate to have left Kabul. The nine-hour, ninety-three-mile route over white-knuckle roads gave me a good chance to see rural Afghan life.

People appeared poorer than I thought possible. Mountain and desert huts of mud and black tattered canvas abounded with children and women dressed in heavy red-embroidered material. Everyone waved hello.

My arrival coincided with a group of *jeune filles française chaude et sexy*. Bamyan, like much of Afghanistan, has been overrun by the French, many of whom are junkies *sans d'argent* (without money). I created an opportunity for one of the young ladies to meet my traveling Trojans. She refused.

Not so Carina. We eventually slept on an uncomfortable blanketed floor in a drafty, chilly open room featuring three bay windows looking out onto Bamyan's main and only street. In the middle of the night, I managed to kick open the back door to do my business under millions of brilliant stars and planets—and one behemoth Buddha.

Freezing my balls every time I had to squat and not wishing for an encore, I splurged fifteen Afghanis for a soiled, lumpy mattress in a dusty but private anteroom to share with Carina. But I still had to kick open the back door.

Our *chai-icana* (teahouse) is a converted hotel on the main street that once sheltered Attila the Hun. Today's special guest? A splayed cat lying dead in the "kitchen." Cat kabob, anyone? Mules, asses, horses, lorries, and jeeps threw up mud and fresh dung as they passed by. Sunrise in Afghanistan.

Strengthening morning rays caused me to soon wonder if the Big Buddha is male, female, or transgender? An ancient mystery. So outrageous. There are no words. Carina and I climbed through a maze of caves lead-

20. The Bala Hesar (fort), Ghazni (2008). Such villages and towns appear to define rural Afghan life.

21. A second mountain village located near extreme northern Afghanistan's Salang Pass and Tajikistan (1973).

ing to Buddha's head and smoked a bowl in Gautama's honor. Muslims removed Buddha's face centuries ago.

Who are these Buddhists who felt compelled to create such a physical manifestation of their God? Are they of the same mentality of those who built the cathedrals of Chartres, Ulm, Notre Dame, and Westminster Abbey? And the biblical Tower of Babel? Of course.

However, Buddhism, the religion, does not presuppose adherence to one almighty God that hangs out above. This ism seems to be more of an introspective, psychological self-awareness trip. Thus, do the mentalities overlap? Only to the extent that they both valued architectural wonders and deities as symbols, and devoted great amounts of money and effort to do so. I see Buddha's "great void" when I gaze at his faceless head. No eyes. No nose. No mouth. No ringlets. No hair.

Nancy Hatch Dupree, "the grandmother of Afghanistan," is a noted educator, historian, and archaeologist who has written several books for the Afghan Tourism Organization, including *The Road to Balkh*, its namesake located in extreme northern Afghanistan. Along with Samarkand, formerly considered Persian (Iranian) but now located within an Islamic region of the Soviet Union, and Bukhara, found in Uzbekistan, these renowned outposts had once been centers of Eurasian trade and cultural life found along the ancient Silk Road that stretched from Constantinople (Istanbul, Turkey) to Xi'an (eastern China). Back in their day, Zoroastrianism (worship of fire) was hot.

Professor Dupree, apparently, had also fallen in love, but not only with her husband. In *The Valley of Bamian*, she writes:

> Nestled within the folds of the awesome Hindu Kush is a beautiful narrow valley. Fortuitously placed, it gave haven to merchants, pilgrims, and servants of the ancient world, enabling them to amass wealth, fame, and power. Secluded in its mountain fortress, it was witness to, but rarely the victim of the constant upheavals of power, replacing power in the lowlands below. Serene, it inspired an effervescence of a profound religion which it radiated to the Eastern world. This was, and is, Bamian.

Depending upon your karma, Bamyan can become a bit too exciting. Considered the only accessible true tourist site in Afghanistan (hardship travel to Band-i-Amir is impossible for most), the Big Buddha also attracts older, straight, moneyed tourists, *federales*, and undercover Kabul narcos. Yet despite the narcos' obvious surveillance, they still managed to recently bust and detain four oblivious longhairs, locking them into their hotel room. A five-hundred Afghani *baksheesh* deal soon followed. (A word about baksheesh. Originally considered a voluntary payment or gift, it now spells bribery.)

Two more brother freaks got popped while Carina and I sat in one of a hundred caves, smoking Afghan Primo number one—until one of the narcos grew near but passed.

"Shit."

He soon returned, searched the cave, failed to find my stash, and split. We lit up again. Too soon?

The dude returned, again, this time with backup—*Dragnet*'s Jack Webb and Harry Morgan and *Gunsmoke*'s Marshal Matt Dillon and Chester, all of whom remained suspicious of us. They finally departed, stared at us from a distance, and soon busted another two security risks from Japan.

What to do? We quickly ran down Buddha's Middle Path with these

22. World-class smiles of Cat Kabob Man   23. Hanging with new friends.
and Son of Cat Kabob Man.

guys in hot pursuit. But never underestimate a hot lady and horny men. Carina stalled them by revealing mouthwatering shapely thighs while I ran straight for town and our private room. End of story? Nope!

Later, while hanging out in town, Carina and I again met our new friends, now assuming new identities: Eliot Ness and J. Edgar Hoover. They pointed at me and asked, "Smoke hashish?"

"Huh? *Moi?*"

The owners of our esteemed establishment, two of the finest Afghan gentlemen I have met, referred to the Bamyan and Kabul police as *"nakheil ikhoob"* ("no good.") At 2 a.m., they invited Carina and me for a smoke of their personal stash.

By 8 a.m. a bloody portion of a fresh carcass had replaced the splayed cat and was about to be butchered by the same dude who specialized in cat kabob. His nasal mantra? *"Kabob, kerai kabob, shish kabob, chips, kabob."*

An Afghan architectural engineer, somewhat more formally educated and sophisticated than the Butcher of Bamyan, is helping to fortify a smaller Buddha near the Big Buddha. (Preservation of the BB will begin next year.) He believes that Afghanistan is both rich and poor, containing large deposits of diamonds, silver, and other precious minerals, but lacking the technology and trained personnel to profitably mine them. Soviet, German, and American companies are staging men, machinery, and exploitative strings.

And who is to stop them? Did not the last war fought by the Afghan army on Afghan soil take place against the horsemen of Genghis Khan and the Mongols (or was it the Cossacks?) circa 1200 AD?

Features of modern society thankfully missing from my current lifestyle are mass media and technology. Volumes deplore their harmful effects upon our psyches and social behavior. *Victimization City* no more. So welcome. Such a blessing.

I hear of most major "current" events days or weeks after they take place; no barrage of television, newspapers and advertising to assault and waste my time. I'd rather use my days for meditative thought instead of judging the thoughts and behavior of others. Think of it as new unstructured time to experiment with.

I am learning how to entertain myself and enjoy my own company; traveling alone is a temporary and novel luxury because I do not have to make compromises. Reading and writing take up a bit of my time. When moving about, I translate a scene into single words and phrases, idioms of a sort, that literally shoot across my mind, wishing I could immediately jot down what I have just done or seen or heard or felt or thought. Is not all human endeavor functions of *Thinking, Feeling,* and *Doing?*

Depending on logistics and circumstances usually beyond my control, I scribble a note, a trigger for future prose. I have no idea if this phenomenon is natural for someone who wishes to compile a somewhat comprehensive journal, or just a vain exercise in compulsive, rigid neurotic behavior.

Lack of media can only result in a more creative Martin. Television corrupts our born abilities for imagination. Too much media and technology over too little time give rise to abnormal capacities for warp speed, stress, and distress—dark linings of the twentieth century. Human brains and minds lack the biological capacity and ability to measure and digest the chronic stream and rate and weight of instant change and immediate headlines. Result? Mental illness posing as sanity.

You might also investigate "America the Beautiful." Beautiful? Yes? No? Right? Wrong? Yes *and* no. Right *and* wrong. From my current whereabouts and perspective, Americans (and Europeans) worry about hairstyles, cars, fashion, pedicures, potholes, quality and price of food, college admission, politics, tee times, price of gas, television, vacations, cosmetics, pet food, pet rocks, and so on. And why not? It's all good. Right? Not so fast.

Why might I question predominantly white, middle- and upper-class American and European lifestyles derived from industrial and technological progress leading to enjoyment of the good life? Anything missing from this picture? You bet your ass there is. *No appreciation. Racism.*

"Don't fix it. Throw it out and get a new one. Buy a new 'toy,' tire of it in two weeks, and buy a newer 'toy.' He who has the most 'toys' wins." Wins what? Give me a break! When people strive for more, more, and more, without valuing what they already own, something ain't kosher in the silent American heartland.

Asphalt, basic hygiene, medical care, clean air and water, sanitation, education, and literacy (for men *and* women), employment and the like, long taken for granted in America and northern Europe, do not yet seem to permeate Afghan society. Simply put, too many do not appreciate what they already have while remaining blindly ignorant of most of the world's inadequate housing and substandard living conditions. Or simply do not care!

In a sense, America and northern Europe are solving fourth-wave computer problems while most of the world is still using fingers. We "civilized" folk are ignorant of foreign lands and peoples, fearful of those different from ourselves, especially their skin colors. Racism and fear of the unknown come to mind—including my own. Who to indict? To a large degree, the arrogant and condescending American educational system.

Surely, when I left home, I was more spoiled and less appreciative than I am today. To learn how spoiled I remain, I must first return home. No doubt, my expansion of perspective as a function of travel is the best teacher of all.

Kabul, Afghanistan
Sunday, November 5, 1972

James Brown tells us that "Papa's Got a Brand-New Bag." My bag? Maybe too earthy. To a masochistic degree, I did originally plan to lead an austere, ascetic lifestyle when on the road: sleeping on floors, taking long hot bus rides, eating inexpensive food only when ravenous. However, my intent has been, amazingly, if not temporarily, fulfilled and extinguished by one fourteen-hour return bus journey from Bamyan to Kabul. Is this what "capitalist pig" corporate types refer to as a "paradigm shift"?

By 8 a.m., forty-five Afghans were stuffed inside. Fifteen additional subjects of Mohammed Zahir Shah, the King of Afghanistan—and I—were relegated to the aged, thin metal roof that hemmed and hawed and nearly caved in. Thus began the fourteen-hour "express" bus journey to Kabul.

At first, the morning's cool air and mountain scenery allowed me to forget my contorted body, thirst, and physical weakness from dysentery. I squeezed myself into the right rear corner of the roof's baggage rack and curled into a ball on a blanket, balancing myself to avoid becoming roadkill.

My hands were constantly searching for bars and luggage to grasp, my churning stomach, liver, and ass aching under increasing layers of dust and dirt that covered my eyes, face, clothing, and backpack. Despite constant adjustments, I searched in vain for another few inches. Survival of the fittest!

However, the condition of the three American men with whom Carina and I had smoked in the Buddha caves really caused alarm. They were being personally escorted on the bus by three uniformed military police types, headed for the balls and chains of the Kabul Central Jail.

As we continued south, the scene grew more uncomfortable and hysterical. The Afghans hurled themselves, one another, and their goats and chickens into vacant crevices during incessant stops at tiny remote mountain huts and desert outposts. Each stop spelled more passengers, less room, and constant rearrangement.

No mercy was shown or expected. I bought an Afghan hat off an Afghan head but declined an offer to buy boots complete with muddy horseshoes nailed to the bottom of the heels. Less able to deny was a dull but throbbing back pain aggravated when I had to duck tree branches as the bus careened around blind curves.

Shit! Only six hours left. No doubt my contorted body was in peril of falling off the bus, aggravated by every endless bump and pothole. Changing position became futile. I began to lose my patience and tolerance after hours of exposure to the incessant noise, filth, vomit, snuff, saliva, and green mucus. (My mother usually blamed my irritability on hunger.)

24. The "express" from Bamyan to Kabul.

Amid this rolling carnival on wheels, jokes were made by the Afghans at the expense of the "prisoners." Blame them? No way! Whoever heard of someone getting busted for dope in Afghanistan? No different than being jailed for possession of a cup of coffee in an automated Horn & Hardart or a Howard Johnson's.

Although the kidnapped "prisoners" had already paid baksheesh in Bamyan, it proved "*nakheil ikhoob*" once in Kabul. Asinine *federales*, CIA operatives, and Interpol agents have been vainly trying to stop the totally corrupt hashish trade. Hashish trade? My God. What about the opium and heroin trade?

Thus far, my time in Central Asia confirms Afghanistan to be, in contrast to India, an eternal, independent, multi-tribal nation of desert sands, desolate mountains, rural villages, and ancient cities. Terribly crude and impoverished. Sand is sand. Rock is rock. Parts is parts. India is to Afghanistan as the United States is to India.

Previous desert-bound overland travel from Europe to India by means of Dorothy's yellow brick road undermined my belief in sheer, random coincidence. No such thing. Millie and Darlene agree. We have all repeatedly bumped into the same hippies already met somewhere between London, Istanbul, and Kathmandu. Bill had split Turkey with blue-eyed, soulful Valerie. She was dumped, not sold, in the holy city of Mashhad, in northeastern Iran. Tonight? I will again hang with Carina whom I first met on the boat from Istanbul to Trabzon in northeastern Turkey, a fifteen-hundred-mile "cruise" on the Black Sea costing but four American dollars. Dominic and Joelle wrote to me from Lahore, Pakistan. They are on their way to Kathmandu.

On my way to search for a gamma globulin shot to protect against prevalent hepatitis, a tourist organization referred me to the Ministry of Public Health, which referred me to a grimy clinic, which referred me to a United Nations compound. The immunity-boosting shot was finally injected by a nurse who explained that the GG shot is exclusively reserved for UN personnel. My compassionate savior had subtracted the dose from her personal allotment. (The UN, UNICEF, and Peace Corps are omnipresent.)

25. A glimpse of Kabul.

Over-the-counter tetracycline helped treat my liver, bouts of dysentery, and traces of lingering gonorrhea that I somehow picked up. Vitamins and malaria pills are, once again, part of my diet.

Upon completing *Sometimes a Great Notion* by Ken Kesey, author of *One Flew over the Cuckoo's Nest* and self-described link between the '50s Beats and the '60s hippies, I feel too sick to start *August 1914* by Aleksandr Solzhenitsyn. I seem unable to escape the cycle: food, weakness, diarrhea, dysentery, rice, antidiarrheal meds, watery brown stool, muddy squatter holes in the ground, and harsh toilet paper made in the People's Republic of China.

This morning I also managed to lose my traveler's checks, flipped out,

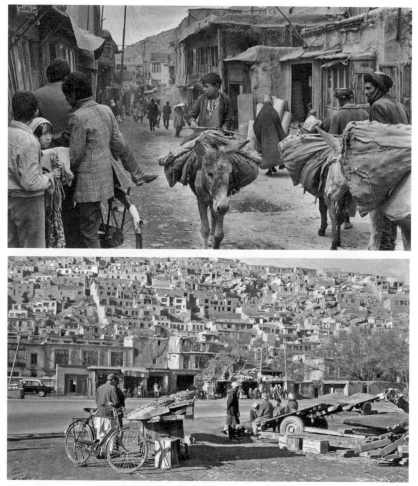

26 and 27. More glimpses of Kabul.

had an emergency meeting of my senses, and brought all under emotional control. In Europe, within forty-eight hours they would be replaced. American Express has no office in Kabul. Not so hidden meaning? I will never be reimbursed.

Same for an American chick I met who can't wait to get home so she can watch *All in the Family* on television. One Archie Bunker is the chief bigot.

And speaking of political blasphemy, all I can say is "Really?" Has Richard Nixon, court jester, been nominated for the Nobel Peace Prize? Can't be! And how long ago did this shit happen?

28. A caravan crosses the Lataband Pass on its way to Kabul, 1948, the year I was born.

29. Afghan families shop at a Kabul market. 1964.

30. Street scene, Kabul. 1951.

31. A modern traffic light contrasts Afghan men and *burqa*-clad women. Kabul, 1964.

32. A Kabul bazaar on New Year's Eve, 1969.

33. Men and trucks crowd a Kabul market, 1961.

Kandahar, Afghanistan
Thursday, November 9, 1972

To the west, between Kabul and Herat, lies Kandahar. Though dusty and seemingly primitive to my occidental eyes, it is Afghanistan's second largest city and once the haunt of Alexander the Great (356–323 BC). Founded around 1,000 BC, the town proudly houses the cloak of Muhammad, but much to my disappointment, it offers no evidence of Raquel Welch, with or without cloak, in *One Million Years BC*.

34 and 35. Glimpses of Kandahar.

Herat, Afghanistan
Saturday, November 11, 1972

The same can be said for greater and inner-city Herat, the product of many masters and servants over millennia. First arriving here from the West, from Iran, and now from the East, from India and Pakistan, I gain additional perspective: Afghans appear to be entrenched in the Middle Ages, centuries behind their neighbors who themselves are considered Third World.

One of many dysenteric episodes caused me to wake at 4:00 a.m. Dark lining? Sharing my sordid dormitory with a half-dozen, strung-out Austrian and French junkies. Dim candlelight illuminated a dusty floor strewn with a variety of melon peels, vomit, bloody toilet paper, and an assortment of vials, tubes, and ill-measured doses of heroin, opium, speed, barbiturates, and cocaine—all to be injected after being legally purchased from a Chicken Street pharmacy in Kabul.

Taints of dried blood, used syringes, and "works" of the trade competed for table space. Before sunrise, undeterred and light years from Cameo Parkway Studios in Philadelphia, somehow, someway, Dee Dee Sharp was serving "Mashed Potato Time."

Roosters heralded sunrise. Sunrise heralded sounds of an engine idling in a parched, trash-strewn alley, barely hidden under the makeshift, mangled hood of a dilapidated "magic bus," rumored to have once transferred lost European souls to Himalayan reincarnation in mere weeks. Most on the international hippie trail (IHT) wanted no part of such hasty insanity.

36. Drawing of the Herat Citadel (fort) circa mid-1800s.

37–39. Glimpses of Herat.

40–42. Glimpses of Herat.

43. Between bouts of dysentery and mad dashes to the designated hole in the ground *du jour*, I spent stoned hours watching Afghan life pass by. Save the main trunk road from Herat to Kabul via Kandahar and Ghazni, this may be the only paved road in Herat. The horses and buggies garlanded with flowers were mindful of those found in Macedonia's (Yugoslavia) Islamic towns and villages.

44. Another glimpse of Herat.

45. A weathered, rebuilt portion of the Ghazni Citadel, circa 1960s.

46. These homes are contained within the collapsed walls of the ancient Ghazni Citadel. Fort-like, such citadels protected Afghan towns and cities from foreign and domestic tribal invaders.

From one insanity to another. Compelling episodes of Afghan justice can be found in James A. Michener's *Caravans,* said to be firsthand accounts witnessed by Michener in 1946, in Ghazni, a town I visited located ninety-two miles southwest of Kabul.

These narrations convey a sense of the tribal mentality of "old" Afghanistan, which I suspect remain alive and well among some Afghans in 1972:

> In their beards and turbans they seemed like patriarchs of old, and I was assailed by the uneasy feeling that I had intruded upon some Biblical scene which should have terminated twenty-five centuries ago. The lean angry mullahs were from the Old Testament. The string of camels placidly grazing by the crumbling walls were of an ancient time, and the crowd of turbaned men, their faces brown from sun, their beards gray with desert dust, could have been waiting for some religious rite in Nineveh or Babylon.
>
> When the soldiers reached the stake, they inexpertly drove several nails into it and lashed their prisoner's hands to these nails, at the same time securing her ankles to the bottom of the stake. "This is the woman taken in adultery! This is the whore of Ghazni! This is the raging insult to all men who revere God!" . . . I stared at the shrouded figure, trying to anticipate what her punishment was to be.
>
> Now the men at my right . . . knelt to find stones, and the smaller rocks they discarded, but soon all were armed . . . they began throwing the rocks at the shrouded figure. From all sides stones whizzed toward the stake, and most struck, and it was obvious that punishment for adultery in Afghanistan was severe.
>
> Then I almost fainted. A large man with unerring aim pitched a jagged rock of some size and caught the woman in the breast. Blood spurted through the torn *chaderi* [or *burqa,* a garment worn by an Islamic woman to cover her entire body and face] and, at last, the woman uttered a piercing scream. I wanted to run away, but I was hemmed in by maniacs and I had been warned by many accounts that for a foreigner to make one mistake at such a scene might lead to his being killed. I prayed that the men had had enough, and then I saw why the soldiers had hammered the nails in the stake.

The blow was so terrible that it wrenched the prisoner's hands from the nails and allowed her to collapse in a heap about the stake. As she did so the crowd broke loose and rushed to the fallen body, smashing it with boulders which no man, however powerful, could have thrown from a distance. Again and again, they dropped the huge rocks on the fallen body until they crushed it completely, continuing the wild sport until they had built a small mound of stones over the scene, as a pauper family in the desert might have marked a burial.

And an account of a grieving father seeking vengeance upon the murderer of his son:

The young murderer was whisked to the stakes, stretched upon the ground face-up and lashed by ankles and wrists until he was spread-eagled . . . when the old man's address to the public ended and he knelt beside the young man's head, the prisoner at last saw the rusty bayonet and began to scream.

It was a horrifying, animal scream that came from far back in the history of human development. It was, I thought, exactly the right kind of scream for such a scene, for it put us all solidly in the animal category.

The old man steadied himself, twisted his left hand in the victim's hair, and pulled his neck taut. With the rusty bayonet in his right hand, he began sawing at his prisoner's throat, and with each awful passage of the bayonet, the boy's head twisted back and forth, while terrible screams emanated from the throat which had not yet been severed. I thought I would vomit.

With four powerful drags of the bayonet the old man slashed the victim's throat and silenced the horrible cries. Then he continued bearing down until the cartilage and bone were severed, whereupon with some awkwardness and fatigue from his exertion he rose, keeping his left hand twisted in the victim's hair, and marched triumphantly about the circle, showing each of us the death's head.

PART THREE

सच्चाई पर दोबारा गौर किया गया

TRUTH REVISITED
1975

FROM GOA TO THE GANGA

47. A royal court of Hindu hotties.

48. A New Delhi street poster.

New Delhi, India
Monday, October 13, 1975

As you might imagine, worn and tattered copies of Hermann Hesse's *The Journey to the East* can be found on earthen floors and dusty tables between Istanbul and Calcutta. As I begin my second journey, I cannot put Hesse and my first journey to the East out of my mind.

One of the characteristics of the Journey to the East was that . . . every single participant could have his own private goals . . . and . . . carried his own fond childhood dream within his heart as a source of inner strength and comfort . . . For example, one of them was a treasure-seeker and he thought of nothing else but of winning a great treasure which he called "Tao." Still another had conceived the idea of capturing a certain snake to which he attributed magical powers and which he called "Kundalini."

Is this to be the serious embarkation of extensive journal scratches and scribbles or a brief exercise in wordiness and self-indulgence? Mood, attitude, and motivation will dictate the outcome.

At the back of my really tremendous urge to relate our story, there remains a dreadful doubt . . . This doubt does not only ask the question, "Is your story capable of being told?" It also asks the question, "Was it possible to experience it?"

I was airborne one hour after boarding Pan American's round-the-world flight number two in New York City on October 10 at 6:30 p.m. It was much like the start of my first journey, having mentally begun some days before the physical departure. Like the rush you feel before the acid comes on.

But through what expedient is it possible to tell the story of the Journey to the East? I do not know. Already this first endeavor, this attempt, begun with the best intentions, leads me into the boundless and incomprehensible. . . .

I imagine that every historian is similarly affected when he begins to record the events of some period and wishes to portray them sincerely. Where is the center of events, the common standpoint around which they revolve, and which gives them cohesion?

Did I want to separate myself once again from all that was familiar? Such was the source of my panic attack as I kissed and hugged my friends and brother. Second feelings and thoughts consumed my heart and mind; the difference between *Thinking* and *Feeling* ceased to exist for what became my immediate future.

Once over the Atlantic Ocean, surely, it was my *emotional neediness* that prompted me to chat up a married couple. Retired to Taos, these octogenarians narrated their experiences with the Native Indians of New Mexico and Arizona. Placing appreciation of Western materialism in perspective, Mr. Alvarez concluded, "A hog sees no difference between the mud he wallows in and a string of white pearls."

In London and Teheran, aircraft personnel assumed variations of English accents. I had slept through Frankfurt "with a little help from my friends." Near Beirut, the pilot announced we would not touch down if political turmoil brewed at the airport. After we landed, competing Lebanese militias surrounded the plane. Rusting hulks and remnants of bombed and downed aircraft caught my gaze across the tarmac.

On the ground in Istanbul, I watched the Boeing 707 be fed and serviced by a gang bang of food and baggage vehicles. Two German *fräuleins*, a handlebar mustachioed Beirut businessman on his way to China from Zaire, and a lovely black stewardess from Liberia, now living in and enjoying London, occupied my time during the balance of the flights.

Heavy jet lag. So much for my biological clock. Slept on and off yesterday in the Ringo Guest House near Janpath Road and the Indian Tourist Office, two blocks off Connaught Place. The ten-cent-per-night youth hostel in Chanakyapuri I frequented in 1972 was closed.

Dawn. Sleeping next to me is Vicki, a recent arrival from mountainous Kashmir. Busted for fifteen kilos of *charas* (hashish), her previous lover spent three months in an inhospitable northern Indian jail. Vicki had been hospitalized in Dharamsala (temporary home of Tibet's Dalai Lama) for exhaustion and pleurisy.

Today will be spent with New Jersey Neil and rebellious Bal, a Punjabi Sikh who has defied tradition by cutting his long hair before leaving for Teheran. I doubt his boasts of "a wife in every port" despite his merchant marine card gained when living in Galveston.

49. Pan Am was founded in 1927, the year Babe Ruth hit sixty home runs—more than the entire American League combined!

As I write, sip tea, and finally relax in a shaded courtyard, I plan to breakfast in the Indian Coffee House, home of the "angry young men of India," or at the Milk Dairy on Mohan Singh.

As Neil and I headed for the dairy, I witnessed a frail, saffron-robed elderly priest accidentally trip and fall onto a broken glass bottle. Result? Pools of blood and a preventable death. Is it my Western arrogance or plain fear that notes a complete lack of emergency medical procedures? Then again, how many have died while frantically waiting for ambulances to navigate the traffic-snarled avenues of midtown Manhattan? Progress. At what price? *Reality is perception.*

Yes, that's true. My reality is my perception is my reality. The sun still rises in the East. Only now it rises more than seven thousand miles farther east—my new reality. When I reflect on the three years spent at home between travels, my perception of those years seems different now that I have returned to India. That I never left? Perhaps. In any event, I feel more confident of my internal strength that refused to permit New York City's relentless diversionary noise to inhibit my determination to seek more Truth.

My jet lag is waning. It took me fourteen months to reach Delhi during my first Asian trip, mostly overland, mostly desert, from London to Nepal via detours to North Africa and the Canary Islands. This time? Only twenty-four hours!

Here in Delhi, the monsoon ended in late June. Cruel, infernal, one-hundred-plus-degree temperatures of brutal summer have diminished to the nineties during midday. Early mornings are now cool.

Soon I shall again venture to Nepal, to trek and wonder and wander within the womb of Himalayan utopia. Now feeling vibrant and healthy, I envision a lifestyle a notch above that of 1972 when the romanticism of a starvation budget proved inviting—until it got real old. But comfort is relative, and so are the bedbugs of the Ringo Guest House.

As I contemplate my near-term travel options, I wonder what motivated Hermann Hesse to write *The Journey to the East*, a fictional character's expedition to India after World War I. Sex? Dope? Cheap thrills? Rock 'n' roll? Could it be that *my* preoccupations also served to kick-start Herman's ass eastward? Had he listened to Neil Young's "Everybody Knows This is Nowhere"? Highly unlikely. Surely, my impersonal edition of *Fodor's Guide to India, 1967*, didn't serve as a catalyst for his literary triumph. How about spiritual enlightenment?

My motivations to travel, certainly multidetermined, were born in the mid-to-late '50s when television in New York City consisted of seven channels: three major networks and four independents. During those years, I thought everybody lived as I did: in Queens, in Long Island City, in the low-income Ravenswood Project, in a six-story, redbrick apartment building.

Sitting in front of a twelve-inch, black-and-white RCA TV, my baby brother and I would choose among the available channels and offerings. One of them was *Andy's Gang*, starring Andy Devine ("Hiya, kids. Hiya, hiya.") who served as *maître d' et concierge* to cast members Froggy the Gremlin ("Plunk your magic twanger, Froggy!"), Midnight the Cat, Squeaky the Mouse, and a weekly serial titled *Ramar of the Jungle*. (My cousin, "little Cheryl," swears Ramar had his own show.)

Anyway, this young Indian dude, Ramar, wore a turban, rode an elephant, and pranced about India. And guess what? I wanted to be just like Ramar. Point of story? Here I am, once again, in the land of the sacred fuel pump! Funny. I had my parents buy me a Davy Crockett coonskin cap, but never a turban!

Despite the above, I would be remiss if I did not include a second motivation that led me to Hindustan, that being a trip I had made to Europe,

Greece, Turkey, and Israel during the summer of 1969. Round-trip airfare from New York to London was $200. With the friend of a friend, Julie Gem, aka Don Julio of Paul Simon and New York City schoolyard fame, I roamed about supposed "civilized" Europe until we mutually decided we didn't want to sleep near each other anymore.

I wound up in Israel, where I hung out in a Hebrew University trailer on Jerusalem's Mount Scopus with Bev Z., a Queens College chick dedicated to finding a doctor to marry. In a mountaintop amphitheater scraping against the Judean Desert, I "proposed." She "refused." Thank God. I woke up in a cold sweat. Must have been a dream! One of Dylan's?

50. After two to three hundred years of orthodox rabbinical life in central Russia, my *mishpuchah* (family) arrived in the promised land, circa 1800 AD.

Top draws in Jerusalem include the Old City labyrinth and the remaining Western or "Wailing" Wall of the Second Temple. Known as the *HaKotel* to Jews, and the *Al-Buraq* to Arabs, the wall offers comfort to visitors who offer prayers to God while placing messages between the cracks of immense limestone bricks.

51. The Wailing Wall in Jerusalem.

52. The Dome of the Rock Shrine.

Located on the Temple Mount in the Arab Quarter of the Old City, The Dome of the Rock (Islamic) Shrine (*Qubbat as-Sakhrah*) was built in the late seventh century CE. Impossible to overstate the shrine's significance to Arab and Jewish communities, it is believed to be the location where God created the world, where Abraham attempted to sacrifice Isaac (*Aqedah*, the binding of Isaac), where the Prophet Muhammad began his "Night Journey" to heaven, and where the feeling of divine presence of God on Earth is greatest.

(Oh, should you find yourself in Jerusalem, on Frumkin Street, please feel free to loiter.)

One more motivation to return to Bharat (India)? Something that Israel and India have in common, as expressed in "Rocky Mountain High." When John Denver, at age twenty-seven, visited Colorado for the first time in his life, he felt he had arrived home. Such was my feeling when I first visited Israel—and India!

What next? After I listened to Carly Simon's "You're So Vain" and whispered renditions of "You'll Lose a Good Thing" by Barbara Lynn and Mary Wells's "The One Who Really Loves You," my romantic efforts proved for naught. Bev sexually rejected me, again. (Guess I should have listened to

53. Am told that Jerusalem has no monopoly on Frumkin Street.

my mother and applied to medical school.) Ah, karma. I boarded Turkish Airlines to Istanbul, *never to be the same again.*

The Galata Bridge spans the Golden Horn, an estuary connecting the Bosporus Strait and the Sea of Marmara, linking the European and Asian districts of Istanbul. On the western side of the bridge, I was drawn to a slew of bohemian hotels and restaurants directly across the street from the Blue Mosque, the Hagia Sophia, and the Topkapi Palace Museum. My favorites? The Hotel Gungor and the Pudding Shop. Patrons included European hippie types and Turkish wannabes.

But my gaze at that moment was riveted on a smaller assemblage of vagabonds, drug addicts and spiritual seekers dressed in Asian robes, shawls, turbans, tunics, blankets and related accoutrements. Their sparkling eyes and measured tones told of opium den locations and personal overland accounts of eastern Turkey, Iran, Afghanistan, Pakistan, India, and the Himalayan kingdoms—Nepal, Bhutan, and Sikkim. Enraptured, I couldn't get enough, especially when hanging with these aspirants for Truth and smoking the shit they had smuggled into Turkey.

Both Istanbul and these rolling stones of questionable character provided me with a taste and feel of adventure—of more than adventure—of

54. Turkey, aka the Ottoman Empire. Istanbul, aka Constantinople, aka Byzantium.
Within Istanbul proper, you can ferry from Europe to Asia for ten cents.

something I just could not describe or verbalize but very much wanted
to experience. Something pulling and pushing at me at the same time.
Something alarming but pleasing. Torn between a desire to continue eastward or return home to complete college, hanging out in Istanbul crystal-
lized my commitment to return home before making my own journey to
the East.

I had also decided to take Eric Burdon's unsolicited advice, first heard
at the Monterey Pop Festival in June 1967. Want truth? Follow the music. In fact, Don Julio and I had sought musical truth earlier that summer
(1969). Location? Copenhagen.

Like magnets, Dylanesque cantorial tropes had lured us into a tiny, al-
ley-bound, bohemian head shop tended by laid-back longhairs and blonde,
blue-eyed Danish *kvinder* (women), strobe lights, and a black-light room
populated by psychedelic posters of Jimi Hendrix, Big Brother and the
Holding Company, and Quicksilver Messenger Service. Mutual stares and
smiles produced an invite through a curtain of Moroccan *goulimine* beads
to a darkened, dank, and cramped room where hashish was crumbled,
rolled into joints with harsh French *tabac*, and lit. Result? I got high and
nauseous at the same time.

No matter. These dudes also turned us on to a concert we soon attended.

Eric Clapton, Steve Winwood, Ginger Baker, and Ric Grech, members of Blind Faith, played that June in a neighborhood concert hall.

Later that summer, many weeks after bidding *güle iyi sanslar* (goodbye and good luck) to Istanbul, I joined one hundred thousand fellow freaks at a three-day, open-air music festival on England's Isle of Wight in Wootton on Woodside Bay. Bob Dylan and the Band, Ritchie Havens, the Who, the Moody Blues, Joe Cocker, and Free's mind-shattering "All Right Now" did not disappoint.

Also in attendance were Keith Richards of the Stones, and the Beatles' Harrison, Lennon, and Starkey. A planned super-session including members of Blind Faith was discussed in London's *The Melody Maker* but never materialized. Why Dylan did not perform at Woodstock earlier that summer remains a mystery to me; perhaps his scheduled public appearance at the Isle of Wight, his first after his bike accident in upstate New York in 1966, took precedence.

Soon thereafter, I met up with Don Julio in London, ready to grudgingly return to New York, New York. No doubt, during these three days on the Wight rock, there was "Something in the Air." Namely, Thunderclap Newman and revolution!

55. Festival of Music poster.

But not so fast. While enjoying the Kinks' brilliant "Sunny Afternoon" in what we thought to be a quaint green London park, little did we realize we had trespassed onto Saint James's Park, immediately adjacent to Buckingham Palace, the Queen's crib. When a group of fugitives from London's burbs boarded the Who's "Magic Bus," Mr. Gem and I decided to finish smoking the rest of my dwindling hashish stash.

The very moment we lit up, two bobbies approached and began to question us, knowing well the unfolding drama and my afternoon fate. Were we to become familiar with Charles Dickens and cronies? David Copperfield?

Ebenezer Scrooge? Jack the Ripper? Was my destiny to hang out behind bars beneath the Old Bailey, the central criminal court of England and Wales?

As representatives of Scotland Yard, the unarmed bobbies *respectfully* requested to inspect our passports and my stash. My bowels began to rumble. I contemplated wearing striped prison garb and ball and chain circa Paul Muni on a 1930s Georgia chain gang—until one of the smartly uniformed constables dropped and lost my small chunk of hashish in the grass. No shit! No grass? No tea? No dope? No jail?

You got it. I was sent on my "merry way" because the evidence was, evidently, unable to be found. No need for Don Julio to hire a solicitor. I would not have to grovel and appear before a judge wearing a *peruke* (wig), begging him to suspend jail time by presenting a paid airline ticket, and Don Julio would not have to dread returning home to face my mama without her son.

A not-so-petty detail. My first intention after leaving home during the fall of 1971 was to make a pilgrimage to India—until India and Pakistan went to war and bred Bangladesh. East Pakistan vanished from the world map. Plan B? Winter in Spain's Canary Islands and Morocco, quartered in a beat-up 1964 VW van I had purchased in Essen, West Germany.

Unknown to me at the time, plan B came to include karmic consequences beyond Western convention. Enter one Harry Bright, a fellow vagabond and Canadian nomad, and my introduction to a New Age biblical roadmap. *Be Here Now* had been penned and published in 1971 by Ram Dass (Dr. Richard Alpert) who had ridden shotgun and dropped acid and mescaline with Timothy Leary and Aldous Huxley at Harvard in the early 1960s. Need I say more? *Be Here Now* changed the nature of my trips to India. After having read it, I intended to explore Hinduism, Buddhism, Eastern mysticism—and how to achieve higher states of consciousness *sin* (without) hallucinogens.

A not-so-petty footnote. With newfound girlfriends and friends from home, including Ronnie Lewis, Mark's stunning, drop-dead gorgeous sister, I settled for a time in Agaete, a tiny enclave *sin electricidad* on the northwest coast of Spain's Grand Canary Island, thirteen hundred miles off the mainland. We soon met two local fishermen, Telo *y* Miguel, who became Don Quixote *y* Sanchez in our eyes. They approved. (None of us hung out with the *Guardia Civil*, Generalissimo Franco's not-so-secret fascist police.)

Wishing to hang tight with our girlfriends, *los Pescadores* occasionally visited and provided part of their daily catch for dinner along with full bottles of *ginebra* (gin). Eventually, our new amigos dubbed me "Don Martín."

My increasing emphases on awareness, Gestalt psychology, and existential influences are evolving, deepening my quest for a guide-mentor-therapist-teacher-guru. Western psychotherapies and the practices of Eastern spiritualism are, in many ways, one and the same. Both maintain techniques leading to liberation as described by Alan Watts in *Psychotherapy East and West*.

Consequence? I am seriously considering returning to the north Indian *ashram* (Hindu retreat) I once encountered near the Lakshman Jhula bridge at the confluence of the Himalayas, Rishikesh, the sacred Ganga, the Indo-Gangetic Plain, and Hermann Hesse.

My tale becomes even more difficult because we not only wandered through Space, but also through Time . . . For our goal was not only the East, or rather the East was not only a country and something geographical, but it was the home and youth of the soul, it was everywhere and nowhere, it was the union of all times.

Perhaps Hesse did not subscribe to *The Hindustan Times*, one of Delhi's English-language newspapers now censored by Prime Minister Indira Gandhi's recent arbitrary declaration of Emergency. Word on the street indicates Emergency not to be as repressive and fearful as you might think. At least not yet.

After visiting the chaotic subcontinent three years ago, I concluded that a dictatorial, severely disciplined central government that controls most every facet of political and economic life, for example, the one created by the Chinese Maoists, could offer India its only plausible solution toward reaching subsistence. Is Emergency the answer?

Fact is, it is impossible for someone who lives in the West, whose belly is full, to comprehend the dynamics involved here. Spoiled Americans and Europeans—surely that includes me—may never understand, may never "get" that democracy, liberty, and civil freedoms are useless if people cry out from hunger and disease. Perhaps that is why many Spaniards refused to complain about the depraved butchery of Generalissimo Franco; they remembered the multitudes who once died on the streets of Barcelona and Madrid from starvation.

(You can bet the farm that members of the only permitted political party in Franco's Spain—the Falange, a union of monarchists, fascists, and ultraright Catholics—never missed one meal.)

A needless delay of two or three generations for radical reform induced by Indian democracy imposes a life sentence of hard labor and misery on those innocents already born. Emergency has come about because of the utter failure of Indian democracy to improve the economies of its populations. To what extent it will harbor fascism, how long it will endure, and who shall benefit remain hostages of time.

That said, I do not want my outrage to be construed as a defense of what Mrs. Gandhi is perpetuating. (Some say "Mahatma" Gandhi would be jailed.) Western analysts have unanimously condemned the Emergency declaration. Perhaps I might reach a far more disparaging conclusion if I were assured this discussion would never be read by Indira's censors.

Despite the above, I find solace in the indisputable fact that the white sacred Brahman bulls and cows of India remain alive (and well?), that they continue to roam the streets of Delhi, and that they play no role in this unfortunate enterprise. If only they could speak, I wonder what the explicit voice of Lord Krishna would say.

New Delhi, India
Tuesday, October 14, 1975, Morning

Met two brothers, Indian freaks, who struck an invite to their farm in Gabhana village, fourteen kilometers from Aligarh. Then I'll hop a truck to Nepal. In 1972, the trains and buses from Delhi to Raxaul on the Indian-Nepalese border became an oppressive, four-day bummer I know too well and would like to avoid.

Why a bummer? Try reality and nomenclature. There are no more third-class trains in India. Third class is now second class. Before realizing the recent change, I had decided on second class because any class that is not the cheapest class avoids dealing with 99 percent of *six hundred million* sweating bodies at the same time, or so it seems. Having exclusively opted for third-class carriages in 1972—an integral part of a stringent budget that reeked of an intentional search for material abstinence—I've promised myself more comfort this time around. How so? The always accessible shower of the eight-rupee (ten to a dollar) Ringo Guest House is a far cry from the Chanakyapuri Youth Hostel's stingy allotment of *cold* water between 6:00 a.m. and 7:00 a.m.

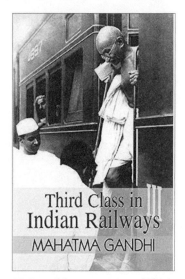

56. One of the many covers of *Third Class in Indian Railways, 1917.*

Two years after returning to India in 1915, having previously practiced law, prospered, and successfully gained rudimentary civil rights for East Indians living in South Africa, Mohandas K. "Mahatma" Gandhi had this to say in *Third Class in Indian Railways*:

> Having resorted to third class travelling, among other reasons, for the purpose of studying the condition of travel under which this class of passengers travel, I have naturally made as critical observation as I could. . . . There were no bunks in this carriage whereupon passengers could lie with any safety or comfort. . . . After reaching Raichur, the pressure became unbearable. . . . The guards or other railway servants came in only to push in more passengers. . . . Some lay on the floor in the midst of the dirt, and some had to keep standing. . . .

57. Typical crowded train platform in India.

On the way, passengers got tea tannin water with filthy sugar and a whitish looking liquid miscalled milk which gave this water a muddy appearance. . . .

Refreshments sold to the passengers were dirty-looking, handed by dirtier hands, coming out of dirty receptacles, and weighed in equally unattractive scales. They were previously sampled by millions of flies. . . . Every time you walked on the floor or rather cut your way through passengers on the floor, you waded through dirt.

The [water] closet was also not cleaned during the journey, and there was no water in the water tank.

What I have described is not exceptional but normal. . . . There is no order, no cleanliness, but utter confusion and horrible din and noise. Passengers. . . . squat on dirt floors and eat dirty food. They were permitted to throw the leavings [leftovers] of their food, and spit where they like. . . . But a third-class-traveler is dumb and helpless. He does not want to complain even though to go to these places may be to court death. . . .

Is it any wonder that the plague [the pandemic of 1917–1918] has become endemic in India?

58 and 59. At least one million people ride Indian trains at any one time. Feels like ten million to me!

At dusk, I dodged a motorized three-wheel rickshaw, careened off a sacred street cow, and jumped on a sawed-off Harley Davidson motorcycle-carriage in Old Delhi. No different than years ago; obscene poverty blanketing white-clad masses on Chandni Chowk Road. I had wondered how I would react to the misfortune and claustrophobic conditions. In 1972, when I came from Europe, my introduction was gradual. Today was a shock!

Have been hanging with soulful Neil, a fellow seeker and blues man, Canned Heat and "Going Up the Country." Without doubt, I must be "On the Road Again." Neil keeps telling me about the oozing sexuality of Thailand and Bangkok. Mercy, mercy, mercy!

60 and 61. The black and gold three-wheel rickshaws (*top*) and sawed-off Harley taxis (*bottom*) are not driven by Hells Angels. Most drivers, often bearded Sikhs wearing colorful turbans, have been bribed to make "courtesy" stops at black market currency exchanges and jewelry stalls—whether you like it or not.

Delhi, India
Wednesday, October 15, 1975, Dawn

Lonely on the occasion of October's full moon? Get down with the Dussehra Festival in Delhi, dedicated to the memory of ancestors. *People, people, people*: an unending stream of flesh, bones, dirt, chai, food, stench, taxis, Harleys, heat, beggars, cripples, crying and suckling babies, noise, and rickshaws. Didn't see gladiatorial combatants of the *Jetti* caste maim one another, as described below in one of the endless official Indian tourist brochures.

This feast is considered to be so obligatory that it has become a proverb that anybody who has not the means of celebrating it should sell one of his children in order to do so.

Entertainments resemble the gladiatorial combats of the ancient Romans, consisting as they do of contests between animals, or between animals and men, and above all between men. . . . Their profession is to injure one another in the presence of persons who are able to pay them for the satisfaction to be derived from this horrible sport, in which both princes and people take infinite delight. . . .

Champions put on gloves studded with sharp pieces of horn. They fight almost naked . . . and deal heavy blows on each other's heads with their murderous gloves . . . blood flows freely. . . . They tear at each other like wild beasts. . . . This disgusting spectacle sometimes lasts for hours together, to the great satisfaction of the spectators, who mark their enthusiasm by constant applause. . . . The wounds and dislocations of the injured are attended to by men of their own caste, the *Jettis* being generally very clever in surgery.

Delhi, India
Wednesday, October 15, 1975, Daybreak

Thank God for a half *tola* (three eighths of an ounce) of decent Afghan shit (dope). "*Aum. Shanti. Shanti* (Peace)."

The sky is growing lighter, the streets noisier. Birds are chirping. Signs in most shops support Mrs. Gandhi's recent declaration of Emergency (granting her authority to rule by decree, suspend elections, and curb civil liberties) and "20-Point Program" (reforms to alleviate poverty, unemployment, and most economic and social problems). Though lacking proof, I expect to buy a student card today. Counterfeiters can't be bothered with such details.

Am I getting used to living out of my rucksack? Ask local flies, mosquitoes, roaches, and bed bugs. Equally unavoidable is the degree to which the Indians have let things devolve to the point where layer upon layer of filth is accepted. But personal hygiene appears rigorous.

Delhi, India
Thursday, October 16, 1975

While reading detailed descriptions of his daily life and assassination, I experienced profound emotional upheaval during my visit to the Mahatma Gandhi Memorial Library and Museum in Delhi. His cremated remains are entombed within Raj Ghat, the official Indian government memorial. At Birla House, I witnessed history—the location where the Mahatma lived his final 144 days before meeting death at the hands of a maniacal Hindu from Poona who "pumped three bullets" into the chest of "the Father of India."

His spirit choked me with emotion. Gandhiji wore and ate nothing more than that of the poorest Indian. Nonviolence, spinning wheels, unquestioned humility and the establishment of a network of self-sufficient communes (Wardha in central India, 1935) continue to serve as monumental motivations for others, such as Lanza del Vasto, who founded similar communities of *Satyagraha* (Truth) in the south of France.

Today's politicians wear $500 suits, live like kings, are addicted to hypocrisy, and victimize those without. Gandhi could have lived like a *maharaja* (great ruler or king) yet chose self-imposed discipline and asceticism, catalysts that overthrew the British Raj.

From *The Assassination of Mahatma Gandhi* by the late Khalid Latif Gauba, a Hindu lawyer, writer and politician who converted to Islam.

In the far corner was the body of Gandhiji. At first, it appeared it was completely covered by a large blanket—but that was not so—his head was being held up by one of about a dozen women who were seated around him chanting prayers and sobbing in a plaintive union. Gandhi's face was at peace with the pale light. Also, they had taken away the steel rimmed glasses which had become almost an integral part of his features. The smell of the incense, the sound of the women's voices; the frail little body, the sleeping face, and silent witnesses—perhaps the most emotionally charged moment ever witnessed.

Gandhi: A Memoir is a superb and penetrating masterpiece written by William L. Shirer, author of the better-known *The Rise and Fall of the Third Reich*. Shirer discusses the bloody and devastating partition of British India into the independent states of (predominantly Hindu) India and (predominantly Muslim) East and West Pakistan, and of Gandhi's last days before the assassination.

The last act in the life of this great man now began. He arrived in Delhi from Calcutta on September 9, 1947, worn out by his efforts, which included another fast, to get the Hindus and the Moslems in Bengal to stop butchering one another. Worn out; and disheartened, saddened, and humiliated that all that he had lived and worked for—non-violence, tolerance, love—had obviously failed to take root among his own people. . . .

In Calcutta Gandhi had stayed with the Untouchables in the filthy slums. On his arrival in Delhi, he had been carried off, protesting, by Patel to the palatial home of G. D. Birla, one of India's wealthiest industrialists and a longtime and financial supporter of Gandhi. Patel explained to him that his life would be safer there. . . .

The Mahatma was devastated by what he found in Delhi, the streets clogged with decaying corpses, whole areas burned down, the frightened Mohammedans living in camps and old mosques in fear of instant death. . . .

January 30, 1948, was a Friday, the day of the week on which Christ, whom so many thought Gandhi resembled in life, was crucified. After his evening meal of fruit and goat's milk, Gandhi left his quarters for his daily prayer meeting. . . .

As Gandhi made his way to the prayer platform, the crowd of about five hundred parted to let him through. Many bowed and some fell at his feet. One who bowed as Gandhi approached was a heavyset thirty-nine-year-old Poona Brahman by the name of Nathuram Godse. As he lifted his head, he whipped out a black Beretta automatic pistol and fired three shots point-blank at Gandhi. All three bullets penetrated his chest. Crying out *"He Ram!"* ("O God!"), Gandhi collapsed to the ground, dead.

Edgar Snow, a friend of Shirer, and by 1948 a well-known correspondent for the *Saturday Evening Post,* witnessed the assassination. According to Shirer, "Snow's dispatch to the *Post* on the death of Gandhi (published on March 27, 1948) is one of the classics of American journalism."

What I remember about being at Birla House the night Gandhi was killed was how much more terrible a moment it was than anyone can describe in words. . . . Men and women did not really grieve . . . for Gandhi, who died almost instantly and who through the window over the low porch could be seen lying with a face serene and peaceful. But each man mourned for something in himself left without a friend, a personal sorrow, as if fate had seized an intimate treasure that one had always assumed would be there. . . .

Every Indian lost his father when Gandhi died. . . . This small man, so full of a large love of men, extended beyond India and beyond time. . . . There was a mirror in the Mahatma in which everyone could see the best in himself, and when the mirror broke, it seemed that the thing in oneself might be fled forever.

All-India radio then announced, "Mahatma Gandhi was assassinated in New Delhi at twenty minutes past five this afternoon. *His assassin was a Hindu.*" That Gandhi had been murdered by a Hindustani son, and not by a Muslim, ironically, had prevented even more bloodshed by and against both sides. Godse and his conspirators were hanged.

Gabhana village, India
Sunday, October 19, 1975

As I wake this early morning, am I still dreaming? I look up and see multiple archways of a palace. Really? A palace? Yes. I am a guest of Hare Raj Singh and his two brothers, Locki Raj and Ravi Raj.

Hare Raj Singh is one of few Indian freaks drawn to Ringo's Guest House. Metaphysics, yoga, history, Hells Angels, Solzhenitsyn and traveling to Kabul and Europe seem to be on his mind. Intelligent, street-savvy, British-educated and well-spoken, Hare Raj is all I am not. In fact, in comparison, my Brooklynese bastardization sounds like English as a second language. As for the meditative life, Hare believes it is for his later years. I agree. Why suppress wine, women, and song in our twenties?

Hare was brought up to believe his life would loosely fall into four historical and traditional phases: (1) childhood, (2) procreation and raising a young family, (3) work and meditation, and (4) final renunciation of the material world. He is, however, most skeptical of many traditional beliefs and practices, one based on an Indian folktale of a farmer who had two sons, one of whom killed three snakes during plowing operations.

The mother of the snakes took revenge by biting the farmer, his wife, and two children. They all died. Next day, the farmer's only surviving daughter, distraught and feeling grief due to the death of her parents and brothers, pleaded before the mother snake with an offering of a bowl of milk. She requested forgiveness and restoration of the lives of her parents and brothers. Pleased with this offering, the snake pardoned them and restored the farmer and his family to life.

Hare Raj had told me that his mother fed resident snakes with a cup of milk, and while she was away, Hare was instructed to leave a daily ration of milk in a darkened room where the snakes rattle. Of course, Hare Raj refused to believe his mother, and the milk went untouched. Upon his mother's return, the milk was consumed.

My time with the Raj Singh brothers prompted me to write a letter to Billy, my brother in New York.

Gabhana, India
Saturday, October 20, 1975
Dear Bro,

Yo. Peace and greetings from Hindustan. Bursting forth is a story and whereabouts difficult to properly convey in words. Allow me to try.

Landing in Delhi eight days ago, I met a Jersey dude who will contact you when he returns to the States. The following day, I hung out with three long-haired Indian brothers with whom I'm now staying. Hare Raj, Locki Raj, and Ravi Raj turn out to be princely sons of a formerly enormously wealthy family. Under the British Raj, their father was considered a maharaja.

But no thrones for these dudes. Rare for Indians, they are authentic freaks. While Hare Raj readies his leave for Afghanistan, his brothers will tour southern India in December. After Nepal, perhaps I'll join them.

Arriving in Gabhana village by bus, Hare Raj pointed to the schools, hospital, and cemetery his grandfather had generously donated to the tiny, off-the-grid village. As we walked past men and women working in the fields, Hare Raj summoned two boys who kissed our feet, insisted on carrying my pack, and addressed me as *sahib*. (Arabic for "owner." Usually reserved for a "white man" in India.)

Bill, this place is a total freak-out. Amazing and astounding. All three brothers and their extended family live in an authentic palace. Through exotic Arabic arches, "I can see for miles."

A delicious dinner was painstakingly prepared and graciously served on fine, etched silver flatware; *chapaties* (flatbreads), *dhal* (dried split lentils, beans, and peas), brown *bagmati chaava* (rice), *masaaledaar aaloo* (spicy potatoes) and *curd* (a cooling yoghurt-type food) followed rations of hot milk. Below three-story monolithic towers containing hundreds of detailed carvings, and above wide moats and deep wells, are thick, monstrous, twenty-foot-high doors sporting elongated shark spikes—to prevent elephants from knocking them down.

Honestly, the joint resembles a national historic site you would expect to be world renowned. Rather, it is located within the realm of Heartland Village India, far off the beaten path, in as rural a setting as can be found.

At dawn, as I photographed an awesome sunrise, the prototypic village below grew animated. Tending alongside white Brahman cows and black water buffalo were tenant farmer families return-

62 and 63. My royal welcome!

ing to "their" fields. Melodious rounds, chants, groaning wails, and the sounds of crows, parrots and vultures replaced my defunct alarm clock. We often sleep on the roof of the palace to escape the enduring heat.

The Raj Singh clan, once politically and militarily powerful in these parts, eighty miles east of Delhi, fourteen miles west of

64 and 65. The interiors.

Aligarh, had collected taxes for the British. Heavy steel safes, now open and empty, continue to litter barren courtyards. Although the British quit India in 1947, it wasn't until the mid-1960s that most royal titles and pensions were curtailed by the Indian government.

Most beautiful, these mellow men have completely rebelled from the party line bullshit pushed by their family. While not outcast, they are known as the "three strange princes" by village neighbors.

Not long ago, their extensive family owned and administered over one hundred regional villages. Still hanging on grand foyer walls are portraits of these ancestors whom the brothers refer to as "great bums" and "bum landlords," despising what they did for England. From the roof, I can see the freestanding estate their grandfather had constructed for the British viceroy, often invited to hunt wild partridge on their property.

When the brothers, ages twenty-two, twenty-three, and twenty-four, parody the Queen's upper-crust English accent, I crack up. Locki Raj, who vibes spirituality, has facilitated fine long talks on the nature of the Self and the Indian guru.

Now dig this. All three are well-acquainted and went to school with Guru Maharaji, whose father was a great and renowned Indian sage. However, to paraphrase Locki Raj, just as the Raj Singh brothers are not automatically considered powerful landlords as were their great grandfathers, neither should Guru Maharaji be revered as wise and holy (only) because he is of his father's seed.

After noting that their father, once an important landlord in his own right, owned Buicks (the great rajas only traveled in Cadillacs), Ravi Raj portrayed Maharaji to be a bumbling poor student who often got drunk in the seventh grade. Having attended the same "fine British schools," the brothers assured me that the "adolescent guru" had bribed his teachers to pass his studies.

Locki Raj believes genuine realized beings see no difference between India, the United States, and Mars, and believes those *yogis* (gurus, fakirs, swamis) who did not finish transcending their egos have been sadly seduced by the power of Western money. As I write, a young servant smoking a "gun"—a chillum filled with hashish—has just brewed and served cups of morning chai, that delicious mixture of boiled tea, milk, and honey.

Now antiquated and without great riches of the past, the Raj Singh stables no longer house black Nubian stallions. Long vanquished and vanished counts and viceroys are no longer greeted by lavishly feathered swordsmen and rich Persian carpets. From the discolored palace roof, you can detect the cast-iron partitions of Gabhana village where Untouchables are not permitted to visit their neighbors.

Consisting of baked mud and thatch, common to the majority of India's rural population, such primitive villages are the heart and soul of Lord Krishna's children. One of them, an Untouchable known as "the doctor," is a regional expert on the cultivation and consumption of ganja (marijuana, pot, grass, dope, weed, tea) and hashish. If mother knew her sons shared his chillum, she would faint.

These marked departures from the family jewels are far more extreme than our differences with mommy and daddy. To marry, they must do so by arrangement, and have thus far refused. If a woman casually lives with one of them, the local villagers would murder her.

66. Ravi Raj (*left*), Locki Raj, and the Raj Singh family jeep.

On Monday, we will share expenses for petrol and take the family jeep to Agra to experience the Taj Mahal under the full moon before I leave for the Nepalese Himalayas and Bal Yogi Prem Varni, the guru I first met in 1972. But who really knows? In India, Westerners must either shift with the currents and vicissitudes of karma—or else be broken by them.

I do feel more than a bit uncomfortable around the servants, though the brothers, long accustomed, treat them exceptionally well. Fact is, they lead better lives than they could on their own, a circumstance that must be placed within the context of values that exists within India, not America. With abundant affection, the two teenage boys prepare my meals and bath, help me wash, clean, and ready my bedding, and light and share my pipe. During all my previous travels, I have never been so exhilarated by such an experience, a karmic, once in a lifetime opportunity.

Please share my words with friends who care to listen and send a copy to mom and dad in Florida. Thanks. You can write to American Express, Yeti Travels PVT. LTD, Darbar Marg, Kathmandu. I should be there in a fortnight.

I love you very much.

Namaste,

Marty

(A brief note about international mail. Virtually every capital city in the world maintains a *poste restante* (general delivery) window that holds mail for any addressee for a specific time frame. Consequently, I must calculate where and when I next will be. Miscalculations mean no mail!)

Gabhana
Wednesday, October 22, 1975, 1:30 P.M.

The midday sun is high overhead—the extreme heat barely tolerable. On the veranda outside Ravi Raj's bedroom which overlooks once manicured and palatial grounds, Arlo Guthrie, *Alice's Restaurant*, and my Greek army bag were being detected, inspected, and infected by one of several monkeys in residence. Arrangements were made during last evening's chillum and chai for me to board a truck to Benares or Patna, take a second lorry or train up to Raxaul, and still another motorized buckboard to Kathmandu.

To overstate my exquisite welcome by the Raj Singh family is not possible. My clothing and rucksack have been laundered and mended. Even distant villagers express (feign?) interest in my welfare. Although most appear to be destitute, when considering real wages and purchasing parity, many are not, yet they live on a standard that would appall most Westerners. When visiting a grammar school this morning, I noticed well-behaved students assembled under shady banyan trees. Instruction in each class focused on a teacher and a small portable blackboard.

67. The Gabhana Unified School District #1.

Of the *Rajput* (military, warrior) caste, Raj Singh family heirlooms and weapons remain on display. Some eight generations ago, their ancestors were forced to flee Rajasthan, a desert-bound province in northwestern India. After arriving in Uttar Pradesh (state) and Gabhana, they evicted the local *raja* (ruler) from his palace. To this day, Ravi Raj and Locki Raj continue to fondly recall their grandfather sitting on a throne bedecked by feathers, jeweled clothing, robes, and swords. Many family photographs taken during joyous wedding parties display great opulence. Most of it has now been confiscated by the Indian government and sold as antiques.

Before starting a three-day jeep jaunt to Agra, Fatehpur Sikri, Mathura, and Vrindavan, Hare Raj pointed out a local sadhu heavily into voodoo. Surprisingly, a well-clad merchant was paternally talking with the renunciate. It seems this merchant had always refused to acknowledge the sadhu until the day he was stricken with lung cancer. Believing the sadhu to be the cause of the illness, he now takes acute interest in his welfare. The ascetic smoked his customary hashish chillum while the police looked on.

At one point in our journey, I was not at all surprised when the jeep became bogged down in ankle-deep muck. Post rescue, our legs sought relief from sticky clay and mud.

68. Cleansing water was drawn from a well worked by two bulky biblical oxen walking in the ancient circle they must.

Back inside the cavernous chateau, we rested, drank chai, smoked hashish, and listened to Cream and Credence on a record player over a simple dinner. As we relaxed, I reflected on the construction of most homes in the Indian villages through which we had passed. Like those in Gabhana, few consist of brick. Most are set on narrow earthen paths. Yet, beyond belief, many of the crudest wood and thatch huts contain sophisticated electrical machinery, gas-fed, four-cylinder engines, and black squeaky conveyor belts. And here, as in most of rural India, cows, water buffalo, goats, oxen, pigs, chickens, and stray dogs seem to roam about at will.

Absolutely nothing is wasted. (Sacred) cow dung becomes winter fuel. *The sacred fuel pump!* I now better realize that castes, originally based on occupation, are now hereditary; they remain strongly etched into the daily Hindustani psyche and are readily apparent in the lives and homes of Indian villagers.

The brothers proclaim most Brahman priests to be "rich bums" who have diluted original Hinduism as told by Lord Krishna to Arjuna in the holy of holy Hindu scriptures, *The Bhagavad Gita*. According to Locki Raj, Hinduism, as a cultural Tao, or way of life, has not existed in India for hundreds of years because of the influence of foreign invaders. He notes that the past twenty-seven years of Indian independence have been an experiment to restore Hinduism. Their conclusion? Purer forms of Hinduism have laid dormant for centuries; the modern version is nothing more than a farce, no longer what it was originally intended to be.

That Hinduism encompasses a far wider realm of belief and expression than most Western religions is also responsible for great confusion. That is, you can easily fall victim to concluding Hinduism to be polytheistic. Its mythology encompasses so many "gods," people find it easy to deny that Hinduism is monotheistic. Nevertheless, if truth be known, Hinduism is all about *a unity of one*. One God with virtually infinite manifestations, including those depicted in carvings, sculptures, paintings, and temples.

Although I doubt the brothers' capacity to confess, they crave the West "so bad" I can feel their frustration. Exclusively trained in private British schools, they possess broad horizons and normally speak to each other in English. I envy their wonderfully open, warm, authentic, and close sibling relationships. And though they have rebelled against the traditional, structured lifestyles their elders have set for them, they are constructive, *decent* people holding pervasive basic values their parents are proud of. Their sweet mother's greatest fear? If and when Hare Raj travels outside India, he might marry a foreigner. Sound familiar?

69. Brahma, the creator.

One full-moon evening, after Ravi Raj and I had plowed portions of his fields atop his tractor, we shared a chillum. And why not? Cannabis can be purchased at any licensed bong shop, as I did in Agra and Aligarh. Trouble is, without these guys, I could never find one. They

70. Vishnu, the preserver and protector of the order of all things.

71. Shiva, the destroyer of evil in the world, completes *Trimurti*, the Holy Trinity.

are indistinguishable from thousands of similar hole-in-the-wall shops and stalls. Ganja is sold legally. Charas is not.

Graffiti, lizards, flies, and my sorry ass now occupy the Raj Singh WC (water closet or lavatory) where you can "lounge" and write on a stone seat under which your "business" falls into a pan. Although I can sit on the throne, I prefer to stand and crouch, making for a wider and healthier movement. Employing the seat as intended no longer seems comfortable.

72. Nataraja, the "Lord of Dance" and an avatar of Lord Shiva, is rumored to reside in the Himalayas.

Hare Raj had more than once employed the entire palace for a different sort of "movement." Envisioned were Bengal Lancers, armies fighting to breach high walls, bejeweled and tunicked maharajas, shiny black stallions, and enormous elephants in front of ten thousand turbaned troops. Hare Raj had dropped acid.

My friend also maintains a fifteen-year court case against the Indian federal government. After independence, all royal princes had been allowed to retain or receive certain monies. Although Hare Raj had recently won his case, Indira Baby recently changed the law—and made it retroactive. Need I say more? Not when a critical comment regarding Indira's honorable person has been deemed illegal and grounds for incarceration.

Agra, India
Wednesday, October 22, 1975, On the Road

For most villagers, going to Delhi is as unimaginable as a trip to England or the moon. When Kerala, one of the "servants," joined our trip to Agra, it was a dream come true. He was absolutely freaked out. So was I.

On the road to Agra and the Taj, Nellie Bell, Pat Brady, Roy Rogers, and Dale Evans spelled backup for the brothers, Kerala, and Don Martín. We called on many nameless Indian towns until finally sleeping under radiant lunar rays in a park adjoining the Mahal; a breathing, vibrating architectural marvel.

How do you render an account of such incomprehensibility? Compare it to the national treasures built adjacent to it—mosques of exceptional taste and grandeur that appear drab and lifeless in contrast? Brilliant white marble, exacting symmetry and gold exterior encasements ensure the Taj

73. Kerala, his sister, and means of local transport. The teenage "servants" biologically belong to families of fifteen children each. Toughened street urchins before the princes took them in, they are now nurtured and schooled, have opportunities to meet foreigners, and lead lives far removed from those of simple peasants.

to be the most resplendent edifice in the world—and the only man-made attraction on Earth that fails to disappoint, regardless of expectation.

As we stood in front of it, I perused "Agra and the Taj Mahal":

The Taj Mahal—Crown of the Palace—is an abbreviation of Mumtaz Mahal, the regal title of Empress Arjumand Bano Begum, wife of Emperor Shah Jahan, who lived from 1592 to 1666 and ruled from 1628 to 1658. He was fourth in the illustrious line of the Mughal rulers of India. The empress died in 1636.

Mumtaz Mahal was first buried in Burhanpur. Six months later her coffin was disinterred, brought in a solemn procession to Agra, and once again given a temporary burial in a garden on the banks of the Yamuna (river). Shah Jahan issued orders for the building of the mausoleum.

How did Shah Jahan express his love and gratitude to Ustad Ahmad

Lahauri, its master architect? By cutting off his hands so another Taj could never be built—so insists local folklore.

Lucknow, Uttar Pradesh, India
Thursday, October 23, 1975

Next stop? An ancient enclave of phenomenal red sandstone palaces, forts, and mosques. Remote and semidesert-bound Fatehpur Sikri (1569) was built—and quickly abandoned—by Akbar the Great.

After chai and incessant maneuvers for children, animals, and more chai, and more children, and more animals, and more chai, we reached Vrindavan near Mathura. Although Vrindavan is considered a highly revered Hindu sanctuary of temples and sadhus, Ravi Raj chanted, "Saffron-robed priests are great bums fucking over the religion and people for money. They know they can make even more money if they wear saffron." Right on, Brother Ravi Raj. Had I not heard this from a native son, I would have placed these colorful dudes on an awesome pedestal.

Upon our arrival in equally revered Mathura, Hotel Plan A was closed. Plan B? Ravi Raj suggested the guest house of the Hare Krishna Temple. I

74. Failure of a dependable water supply doomed Fatehpur Sikri to silent oblivion.

silently expected a hassle—and was not disappointed. Two "official greet-
ers" laid their heavy trip on us, quickly realized we weren't into their version of Krishna and said, "Repairs are being made in the guest house and
therefore you cannot stay here." Another scam! We had been interviewed
for a hostel room!

Everywhere in Vrindavan and Mathura, sacred sites to which all Hindus aspire to make pilgrimage, we witnessed a stone menagerie of magnificent animal carvings and temples. *Everywhere.* When iron-clad tradition
precluded this pink-skinned, blond, and blue-eyed infidel from entering
their inner sanctums, I continued to be freaked by the onerous, plodding
parades surrounding them: breathing, groaning camels, cows, elephants,
oxen, water buffalo—and human—beasts of burden.

Quickies on the realities of time and travel in India:

- According to impeachable sources, a thirty-day construction
  project in 1876 now requires three hundred days.
- Traveling speeds up life: relationships, learning, everything. Distance from home magnifies angst. A cold becomes pneumonia.
- Time is not defined by rupees. Standardization is virtually non-
  existent. The scientific method is not evidence something exists.
  Interminable knowledge and wisdom cannot be measured.

These are but a few of the greatest differences between Eastern and
Western minds.

As I wait and wince and wait in Lucknow Charbagh Railway Station, I
painfully realize one obvious consistency in inconsistent India: the train
system still sucks. Confirmation of accurate and reliable information from
two different railway sources is impossible. "It's All Too Much," says George
Harrison. Schedules exclusively enrich lip service and their publishers.

Lack of dependable information is *the* great nemesis of the traveler.
What to do? Rely on one of the more useful provisions found on the IHT,
the exchange of information regarding hotels, eats, drugs, music, scenes,
trains, boats, black market dealers, scams, and the like.

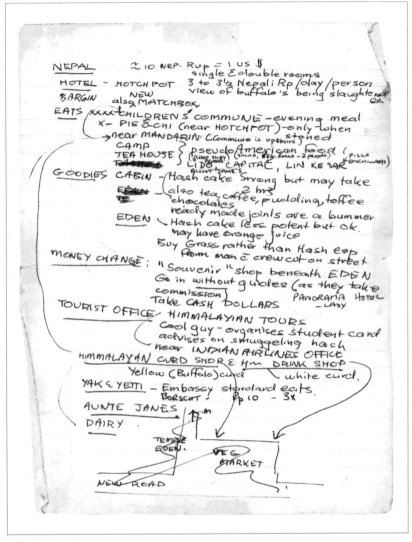

75. My longhand notes.

A parting thought on India. The British demonstrated genius in training the elite of India to not only rule the subcontinent for them, but also imitate British law, style, tradition, custom, and language. No surprise then, when in 1947, the year of Indian independence, many Indians (landlords, maharajas, bureaucrats, sadhus) did not wish the British Raj to come to an end.

Daman, Nepal
Saturday, October 24, 1975, Afternoon

As I stepped into Nepal, the sign read, "Leaving India. Thanks." For what? When it was followed by another declaring, "187.09 kilometers to Kathmandu," I wondered, didn't a wild child of Texas, Janis Joplin, warn that when we start moving about the world, we don't know where the road we take might end? Surely not in Detroit and definitely not in Kathmandu.

76. No one trying to sell me anything.

From a pamphlet simply named "Nepal":

It is bounded on the north by the Tibet Region of the People's Republic of China, on the east by Sikkim and West Bengal (India) and on the south and west by the Indian states of Bihar and Uttar Pradesh. The length of the kingdom is five hundred miles East to West and its breadth varies from ninety to one hundred and fifty miles North to South . . . Its lowest points lie in the jungle-like Terai land belt in the south which is about one hundred feet above sea level. [It extends upward to Mt. Everest.] Here, in the western part, lies Lumbini, the birthplace of Gautama, the Buddha.

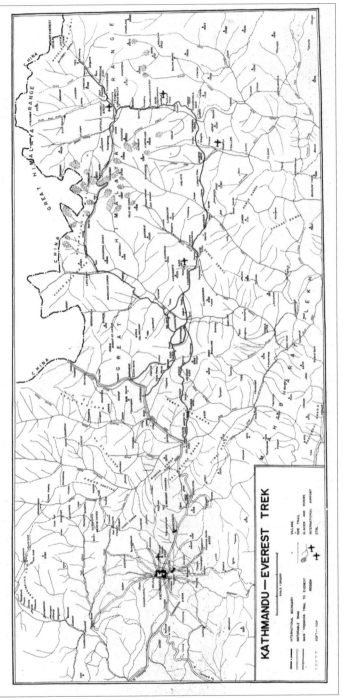

77. Known as "Shangri-La" in James Hilton's *Lost Horizon* (1933), Nepal and this map proved to be inspirational.

78. View from Daman in the early morning.

Far out! Paradise found! Daman, a reclusive road settlement, is located forty-eight miles from Kathmandu. Experience has its rewards. My previous visit to Nepal inadvertently indicated the exact point to view the classic span of the Himalayan horizon. Clouds normally conceal this view to most pilgrims who quickly pass by on late afternoon trucks. Making needless haste to Kathmandu, they become disappointed upon learning the view for which they long yearn is not to be found in Nepal's capital city.

I was soon aghast, shocked, exhilarated. As I climbed Zeppelin's "Stairway to Heaven," to the summit of a ten-thousand-foot "foothill" and passed over its northern face, I was met by that sight that astonishes and induces men to pause and become religious—the sight that gives rise to exclaim, "Nepal is truly God's gift to the world."

Before me stretched a vast valley beneath a steel gray-and-white blanket of clouds. Beyond and above the valley and clouds, and across the horizon, stood the heart of the Himalayan heavens basking under a life-sustaining morning sun. Not a ridge was inaccessible to the eye. Here lay the roof of the world where, at 8,849 meters (29,032 feet), Mother Everest poked her head above all else. Truly, there are no words. Another separate reality. Surely, this place is mankind's heaven on earth. Its cosmic scope resembles outer space, its massiveness beyond the realm of imagination.

The Great Spirit blessed the Earth with many jewels I have visited: the European Alps, North American Rockies, Afghanistan's Hindu Kush, and the

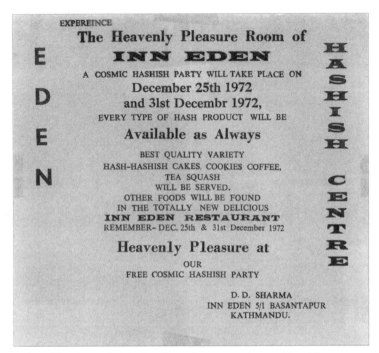

79. I could no longer find the Inn Eden. A very stoned scene. I loved it.

80. And some business cards.

South American Andes. Though all are uniquely precious gems, surely the star-studded diamond surpassing all others is the Nepalese Himalayas—causing a physical rush, an involuntary pumping of adrenalin to accentuate my body's excitement.

Situated above Daman, my rented shanty abuts a cosmic postcard; vivid orange, yellow, red, blue, and purple alpine flowers attend a foreground before the earth severely falls away to reveal peaks inhabited by Hindu, Buddhist, and Tibetan gods and goddesses.

As I continue to freak and rush in front of my cramped hovel—which opens its doors to one of the world's most dramatic vistas—and bake under deceptively warm alpine sunshine, the snow-clad peaks of Annapurna, Dhaulagiri, Manaslu, and Ama Dablam appear unimpeded. To my extreme right, in northeast Nepal, Everest poses for eternity, seemingly engulfed by wisps of ivory clouds, white caps, and ageless glaciers. Here lies a calming, peaceful Eden, a veritable utopia rising far above the heat and intensity of the Indian subcontinent. Oh, am I really witnessing these most fantastic sights?

What have I done to deserve and enjoy such physical and spiritual beauty? That paradise is overwhelming spurs an urgent need to relate all this to others, a natural obsession that strengthens when I am physically separated from those I love. My journal often serves as a confidant, a friend to whom I can immediately express and relate.

Sunrise, sunset. Sunrise, sunset. More spectacular and kaleidoscopic than words can describe; green, blue, red, crimson, orange, yellow, and white glacial peaks. *Daman is Nepal. Nepal is God Consciousness.*

Amid all this beauty, I've set aside feelings of having been "taken." When I attempted to rent my flimsy cottage, the Nepali caretaker requested Nepalese currency. I offered twenty rupees (about eighty-five cents). When he immediately said, *"Ah cha"* ("okay"), I immediately knew I had paid too much.

Kathmandu, Nepal
Monday, October 27, 1975

"Should I go to Thailand within two weeks or return to Pokhara [Nepal] for a month where I could sleep for free in chai shops and not spend more than ten quid? A sadhu would cook and lend spiritual instruction." The first words I heard this morning belonged to a young man from Sheffield, England. With a net worth of less than $400, he wants to see more than his rupees will allow. Work is the only solution. Yes, hippies are known to work as they travel the Trail.

Last evening, I once again "dined" in the Tea Room near the Delight Lodge. Predictably, the foreign/hippie scene of 1972 has moved from down-the-hill, unpaved, sleazy back alleys below Durbar Square to an area called "Freak (Jhochhen Tole) Street." Here, you find pie shops, hashish dealers, Western food and music, and black-market money changers—all within this pleasure city of the Himalayas. Some years ago, savvy Nepalis realized foreign hippies were unmitigated hedonists, and so Freak Street was born.

I had tried to ignore the rain and cold while hanging with Nepali farmers as we sat on the top of a grain-loaded truck during the five-hour excursion from Daman to Kathmandu. The vehicle bumped around and along the folds of forested foothills protecting quaint towns of simple one- and two-story brown structures resembling gingerbread. Sculptured terraces of green and gold wheat framed by sunken rice paddies covered gently rising valley floors and surrounding slopes.

Perspective and experience resulting from my previous exposure to Asia and the ensuing adjustments to home, work, and routine make me feel less shocked by it all. And that's the joint. That's the bomb. That's the key—*expectations*. I am now better able to focus on culture and individuals within rather than being seduced by alluring markets and back alleys that so assaulted and intrigued my five senses during 1971 and 1972.

Romantic notions have slightly dimmed under the light of harsh realities. Previously, after eighteen months of travel, I had lost the physical sensations of America and the West and had come to feel as though my home had never existed, as if I had been traveling all my life. It became the only lifestyle I knew. Today, I feel more relaxed and less anxious and obliged to experience it all.

Virtually all bohemians on the road have been influenced and conditioned by their family-bound, culture-bound, and religion-bound values and predicaments governed by rules and regulations that may or may not be self-evident or self-determined. In any event, when traveling far from

home, many of my nomadic colleagues come to adopt a different but con-
sensual set of values and vogues that, in a sense, replace those of home—
attitudes regarding dress, food, money, sex, shelter, religion, asceticism,
peace, love, brotherhood, and sisterhood. Perhaps counterintuitive, most
of these folks commit the same mistake they make at home. By substitut-
ing one value system for another, they remain out of touch with their own
Tao, be it in Pittsburgh, Santa Fe, or Kathmandu, be it unintentional, unrecognized, or unconscious.

If the development of individuality leading to higher states of consciousness is a function of separation from social convention, substitution of one
set of social conventions and values for another does not cut it, does not
achieve the freedom most young people are seeking. Rather, the majority
join the IHT culture, in which they earn emotional security by being like
everyone else (on the road). Again, they have renounced freedom for security, the exact same process that takes place at home—and from which
they are most probably trying to escape. *Reality is perception.*

Kathmandu, Nepal
Tuesday, October 28, 1975

Nepal's current economic insufficiencies dictate the acceptance of foreign
aid from any nation that offers it, generating fear that such policies will
Westernize and contaminate the country's unique flavor and tradition.
And although I have noticed many changes in Kathmandu—new shops,
hotels, restaurants, pie houses, and a fleet of shiny Japanese taxis—the
symbolic stone serpents, bulls, birds, lions and dragons, and the pagodas
and stupas they passionately guard, have retained their ancient, exotic
qualities.

From a pamphlet I found in the mud on Freak Street:

THE TEMPLES OF NEPAL

[They] may be broadly divided into two groups—pagoda and stupa.
It was through the development of places of worship that Nepalese architecture was developed. There are numerous pagoda-style
temples in and around Kathmandu Valley, which are from one to

five stories in height. They stand on a plinth consisting of one to five tiers. All these temples are made of brick and wood. They are profusely ornamented with carvings, paintings, and gildings.

In front of many of the temples are tall and imposing monoliths. Some display *vahanas* [animals on which the gods travel] and other figures of gods and goddesses that help to identify those within the temple.

My original exposure to and flirtation with Asian thought was provided by Alan W. Watts in *The Way of Zen*. By introducing Zen Buddhism as a "Way of liberation" without a concrete definition, Watts writes, "It has to be suggested by saying what it is not, somewhat as a sculptor reveals an image by the act of removing pieces of stone from a block."

I already sense this ain't gonna be easy.

Correctly postulating the Western mind to be ignorant of Chinese ways of thinking, he continues, "The problem here is not simply one of mastering different ideas, differing from our own as, say, the theories of Kant differ from those of Descartes, or those of Calvinists from those of Catholics. The problem is to appreciate differences in the *basic premises of thought* and in the *very methods of thinking.*"

I repeat. In the West, if something, anything, cannot be proven, communicated, or measured via logic, reason, and the scientific method, it simply does not exist. Not so in the East. Not so in China. Not so in Chinese philosophy. In fact, in addition to Confucianism (legal, conventional knowledge), there exists a second Chinese philosophical school, Taoism, "an inward liberation from the bounds of conventional patterns of thought and conduct."

Confucianism presides, then, over the socially necessary task of forcing the original spontaneity of life into the rigid rules of convention—a task which involves not only conflict and pain, but also the loss of that peculiar naturalness and un-self-consciousness for which little children are so much loved, and which is sometimes regained by saints and sages.

81–83. Durbar Square, Kathmandu.

Watts then suggests that Taoism's function is "to undo the inevitable damage of this discipline [Confucianism], and not only to restore but also to develop the original spontaneity." As I experiment with personal rebellion from the constructs, conventions and expectations of middle-class Western society, Watts reflects an ominous tone:

> In certain natures, the conflict between social convention and repressed spontaneity is so violent that it manifests itself in crime, insanity, and neurosis, which are the prices we pay for the otherwise undoubted benefits of order.

As I consider these conflicting Chinese schools, the resulting dilemma begs the question: Does a bridge exist between Western psychology and Chinese/Eastern theology? In *Psychotherapy East and West*, Professor Watts attempts to decipher the sources that bind them—change, consciousness, and liberation from one's problems.

In a purely Eastern sense, religion precludes belief in a God/Satan who resides above/below, yielding the power of eternal salvation/damnation. However, Hinduism and Buddhism, in common with the West's great religious movements, have also been historically, arrogantly, and profitably held hostage by cunning, self-righteous priesthoods that, perhaps necessarily, sugarcoated *The Word* for the presumed good of their illiterate, uneducated constituencies.

For such congregations, for whom spiritual abstractions of a "higher order" had little if any meaning or relevance, the condescending activities of their priesthoods resulted in the creation of a wide variety and mythology of gods and goddesses of all shapes, colors, sizes, and tastes. Arbitrary or not, designation of festivals, holy days, rituals, customs, and temples completed the sweetened concrete candy coating.

Despite this, Asian religions and mysticisms approximate abstract, self-introspective psychological examinations of consciousness and how to change it—partially explaining Buddhism's growing appeal to the logical, rational Western mind.

Although techniques differ, Eastern and Western doctrines can reach the same place. Gestalt psychology's emphases on awareness of the present moment and the immediate experience of *simply being* are integral to many Eastern doctrines, ending in an integration of both.

Nevertheless, you must focus on their conflicting goals. If Western psychotherapy is geared toward disturbed persons, Watts' notes that Buddhism and Taoism are "concerned with changing the consciousness of socially [well] adjusted people."

When viewing this struggle from a different angle, one and the same I inadvertently traced when describing the traveler who unintentionally and unconsciously substitutes new conventions of the road for the socially conditioned behaviors of home, Watts concludes, "For when a man no longer confuses himself with the definition of himself that others have given him, he is at once universal and unique."

One solution offered to resolve this struggle is insightful Western psychotherapy—to free the mind from social conditioning. Again, not so fast. Those experienced in Eastern ways have come to detect a related yet far greater enigmatic dilemma, which causes "private troubles" to pale in comparison:

> The psychotherapist must realize that his science, or art, is misnamed, for he is dealing with something far more extensive than a psyche and its private troubles. This is just what so many psychotherapists are recognizing and what, at the same time, makes the Eastern ways of liberation so pertinent to their work. For they are dealing with people whose distress arises from what may be termed maya, to use the Hindu-Buddhist word whose exact meaning is not merely "illusion" but the entire world-conception of a culture, considered as illusion. . . . The aim of a way of liberation is not the destruction of maya but seeing it for what it is or seeing through it.

Consequently, is it not more productive to assemble and investigate questions than to provide answers? Is not the struggle to find resolution more significant than the resolution itself? And is this not our life's work, where our strivings become more significant than their fruit?

Watts painstakingly examines the questions he has raised from a diversity of directions, including Zen's fundamental given; nature is not a problem.

The difficulty of Zen is the almost overwhelming problem of getting anyone to see that life-and-death is not a problem. The Zen master tackles this by asking the student to find out for whom the world is a problem, for *whom* is pleasure desirable and pain undesirable, thus turning consciousness back upon itself.

A *koan*, or riddle, is then given to a student by a Zen master.

The preliminary koan is in fact a concealed form of the question which the student has asked the master, "How can *I* attain liberation?" Though worded differently, the koan is actually asking "Who asks the question? "The oldest Zen poem states: The conflict between right and wrong is the sickness of the mind.

This mother of a mindfucker parallels the classic Zen koan: "What is the sound of one hand clapping?" Watts's hint? "The solution is not to be found in an intellectual answer."

Plagiarizing the wisdom and vocabulary of my former South Bronx, Junior High School students, I offer, "Mr. Funkyman, that's some very heavy shit."

And no less vexing are those paradoxes posed by genuine pilgrims seeking realization and enlightenment. Is it not egotistical to want to lose one's ego? Is it not living in the present when meditating for future benefits? You want answers? Better answer the koan. Seems all these paradoxes and "heavy shit" lead to fundamental questions that have no finite answers. Is religion an invention of psychology? Are Eastern religions posing as philosophies?

George Harrison is a serious student of Zen and Eastern mysticism. No choice, then, to blame Zen and Clapton's ax for motivating the exquisite genius of "Why My Guitar Gently Weeps." Blame of a different sort lies at the hands of this writer. How so? No doubt, the discussion above is guilty of weaving ill-understood strands of Eastern disciplines into the Temptations' "Ball of Confusion."

ॐ

The notebook in which I record my moments of confusion and clarity is my guru. Who is my notebook's guru? *Moi?* Can we bullshit each other? Of course. Writing is therapy, a record of what I said or did not say—of what is clear or confused—of what I recognize or deny. Writing is my therapist—Carl Rogers' non-directive mirror, *tabula rasa*, a blank slate, perhaps the best kind of therapist. The process provides greater transparency, allowing me to see areas of insecurity and confidence. Flashes of emotionally painful honesty and authenticity highlight reality as distinguished from fantasy. Sometimes!

My meager ability reflected in my written attempts at description frustrates me. Will my motivation to write continue? Record less in scope and reflection? Will I again reconceptualize the world and create new personal constructs? Who knows. I certainly don't. *Reality is perception.*

Kathmandu, Nepal
Wednesday, October 29, 1975

This morning, I didn't wake up and get myself a cold beer per Jim Morrison and "Roadhouse Blues." Surely, I must be a wimp.

Sulphur burps—courtesy of chocolate cake I had for breakfast at Aunt Jane's Restaurant—were extinguished with a chillum on the roof of the Delight Lodge, and panoramas of the Kathmandu Valley, terraced Himalayan foothills, glaciered peaks, and scores of pagodas sparkling under a strengthening early morning sun.

Last night, a Finnish freak freaked out when he discovered $500 in gems had been "stolen." After noticing an empty stash bag under his bed, he got crazy, suspected everyone, and asked to search my backpack. Having once had my valuables and travel documents stolen along a riverbank outside Marrakesh, I empathized with his plight—until Mr. Finn found the gems in a leather pouch he had placed in an old pair of jeans. The dude had even accused the harmless monk-like hotel manager and his son. Anyway, it makes you realize the bottom line. "Friends" on the IHP are merely acquaintances most will not trust—for good reason.

Feeling nostalgic, I bicycled to the Bagmati River and Pashupatinath, the mother of all sacred Hindu temple complexes in Nepal. The sadhus and hashish cult with whom I once shared many chillums were off to higher pastoral pagodas and could not be found.

Although Nepal was opened to foreigners in the early 1950s, "The City of Fine Arts," Patan, another remarkable community found within the Kathmandu Valley, was forbidden to foreign heathen until 1973. Supposedly, it resembles Nepal, circa 1951. Decaying brick and wooden buildings along unpaved muddy paths first built in the third century emptied into large courtyards where gossiping and the washing of clothes took place. As children played with cows and flew kites, they ran alongside my bicycle shouting, "Hello, goodbye. Hello, goodbye."

84. Durbar Square, Patan. (Oil on canvas.)

Before leaving, I bought two fine rugs from Tibetan refugees who, during amicable dickering, shared their warranted bitterness toward the Chinese who invaded their beloved monasterial homeland in 1951.

Bhadgaon, or Baktapur, completes the Kathmandu Valley "megalopolis." From the pamphlet "Nepal—Bhadgaon—A City of Devotees":

85. The deal was sealed when I also offered a pair of Levi's!

Bhadgaon is the home of medieval art and architecture . . . verily the storehouse of sculpture, woodcarving, and colossal pagodas connected to different gods and goddesses.

Bhadgaon is a city of devotees. . . . The towering temples, which hit you right on the eye, have a massive grandeur matching their delicate grace. . . . The way of the life of the people of Bhadgaon is so marvelously molded by two of the great religions of the world— Hinduism and Buddhism—that even a casual visitor cannot be but struck by the extreme tolerance that marks their very thought and deed.

Friends of friends. Bernie and Nancy work for the United Nations, live in a rambling home near Swayambhunath, the much loved and celebrated "Monkey Temple," and enjoy an otherwise unencumbered lifestyle. Invited to attend their friend's dinner party, I encountered an active community of foreign nationals, cutting-edge stereo equipment, and superficial cocktail jive. Apparently, Americans and Europeans stationed here cohabitate on a scale comparable to the wealthy of Scarsdale, Scottsdale, and Palo Alto. American-sized salaries, exempt from taxes, are spent at Nepalese rates.

86. Durbar Square, Baktapur.

87. A five-tier Hindu pagoda, Nyatapola anchors Bhatapur as a genuine and ancient medieval city from the fifteenth century.

I accompanied Bernie to the Dakshinkali Temple near Chobar Gorge, reached by driving over treacherous mountain passes that surround the Kathmandu Valley. Once there, Bernie met with a sadhu friend, a lama, who, during a previous visit, had given Bernie a ring to cure an illness that had continued to persist. The sadhu and I sensed that Bernie lacked faith in the power of the ring and of the power of the lovable, robust Tibetan-Buddhist lama. As they spoke, a dozen adults and children stared curiously at me, reciprocating my smiles and greetings.

The lama, sixty-five years old, had spent eighteen hermetic years in the jungle, lending credence to his young disciple's belief that his master is truly realized, no longer attached to the desires of his ego described by Ram Dass as "the ego-less feeling of enlightenment."

This freaked me out. Bernie and I, flesh and blood, were speaking with other flesh and blood—who is perceiving and appreciating the reality of life on another level of existence, on a higher plane of consciousness. I am so blown away. How many years of meditative and yogic practice is required to relate to the spiritual space in which this lama and others exist?

In addition to these flirtatious out-of-body fantasies, once back in Kathmandu, I indulged my appetite in the Swiss Restaurant, the Tea Room, and Aunt Jane's. Deception? Maya illusion? Perhaps. On the way to lunch one day, I observed dead mice, warm water buffalo carcasses, decapitated ducks, and the Swayambhunath Stupa.

Now serious to seriously trek, I purchased *A Guide to Trekking in Nepal* by Stephen Bezruchka. Preferring safety and companionship to isolation as I anticipate the next four weeks, I have yet to find a suitable companion, or any companion for that matter, of either gender.

Upon my first visit to Nepal, I undertook no major hiking during my brief stay, and so feel apprehensive about trekking alone. Though the grapevine provides encouragement and support, and reports too many sahibs and not enough *memsahibs*, it's impossible to know what to believe.

ॐ

88 and 89. The Swayambhunath Temple complex, revered by Buddhists and Hindus alike, and considered a sacred pilgrimage site, represents the journey from mortality to immortality, from Buddhist *dukkha* (suffering) and Hindu samsara (endless cycle of rebirth) to nirvana and bliss consciousness.

Kathmandu, Nepal
Sunday, November 2, 1975, 4:00 P.M.

As the late beat writer Neal Cassady (*The First Third*) wrote in a letter to Oregon-based hippie author and flower child Ken Kesey (*One Flew Over the Cuckoo's Nest*), "Oh, yes, the trip; like I say, one's image can be remade in twenty-one days."

After bribing officials to get a trekking permit at 6:00 a.m., I had succeeded by noon.

90. Trekking permit. Rumors declare the imminent designation of the Solu Khumbu District as a national park, leading to prohibitive permit and daily use fees.

Barabise, Nepal
Am scribbling aboard the Kathmandu–Barabise bus, bound for Lamosangu, the starting point of my trek to northeast Nepal's Solu-Khumbu District, Thangboche Monastery, and the base camp of Mount Everest. The scene is rural, primitive, and outrageous. I am the only sahib in the bus, in the bus station, in the neighborhood, in sight.

Average walking time to Namche Bazaar is ten to twelve days while one of the best times registered by a sahib, actually a blond mem-

91. My bible. Printed in Tripureshwar, Nepal. 1974. Two thousand copies.

sahib, was six days. . . . After all, a curvilinear distance of eighty miles is involved and what with switchbacks and diversions in the trail, it takes about 150 miles of walking from Lamosangu to Namche Bazaar. . . . After a day or two out on the trail from Lamosangu, shops, so common to the west of Kathmandu, disappear and the *bhattis* [inns and tea shops] become scarce. Usually, it is the tribal Thakalis and Newars that run these establishments. . . .

However, upon getting closer to Solu where the first Sherpa settlements occur, you begin to find tea houses and tea housekeepers who will often cook meals.

Filled with apprehension and challenge, I continue to question whether I can trek over these mountains with a loaded pack on my back. But others do and so will I, directly into the heart of Solu-Khumbu, into the pith of Nepalese-Sherpa dominion.

Lamosangu, Nepal
Sunday, November 2, 1975, 10:00 P.M.

I find myself part of a group of ten—five family members and four Nepali travelers—lounging in the great (and only) room of a Nepalese home after a rice, dhal, and disastrously hot, curried potato dinner. We will also sleep in this one room, protected by a straw roof and earthen floor. This morning's stiff neck has become a back cold. Is karma testing my resolve to trek Everest base camp? Can't be sheer random coincidence. Better put mind over matter!

I have rented a goose-down sleeping bag and jacket, and purchased woolen gloves, dextrose, Lasix (for prevention and treatment of high-altitude sickness), canned cheese, and iodine solution for water purification. Maps, protein and sugar wafers, canned sardines, honey, milk chocolate, bouillon cubes and other supplies were scavenged to supplement the lean staple diet of the high-country peoples: boiled white rice and *subje*, a potato and rice concoction with a few "greens" thrown in for appearance.

To lighten my load, powders and liquids have been transferred into plastic containers stashed among two pairs of tighty-whities, long johns, an olive-green woolen sweater, and threadbare corduroys. A compass, old canteen, half a towel and plenty of jam and peanut butter to spread on chapaties are intended to get me through the nights.

Balloons for the children I hope to meet, my Instamatic, six rolls of Kodak film, a flashlight, metal spoons, soap, toothpaste, toothbrush, medical supplies (Band-Aids, antibiotic ointment, tetracycline, gauze, adhesives, scissors, Lomotil, aspirin, and vitamins), two rolls of toilet paper, rubber bands, and small plastic bags for food storage complemented anxious trepidation in my bowels. I was scared shit. With all on my scrawny back, I walked to Kathmandu's Bag Bazaar, boarded the 4:30 p.m. bus to Lamosangu, and became the source of great curiosity during the rambling four-hour ride.

Three years earlier, I had taken day hikes along the Nepalese-Tibetan (Chinese) border and above Pokhara in central Nepal. Unaware of the Pharak and Solu-Khumbu regions of Nepal, I vaguely remembered hearing of an "Everest trek" and mistakenly thought all Nepalis were Sherpas.

Between trips to Asia, while in Florida praying for the convalescence of my father after colon cancer surgery, I had read a stunning article in *National Geographic* titled "Sherpaland." Nepalese, Sherpa and Himalayan anthropology, sociology and geography are diverse and fascinating. Geographically, the region's southern belt, the jungle-strewn Terai, stretches east to west, running parallel to Nepal's border with India. Inhabitants are of Caucasian stock and resemble their southern Indian neighbors in lifestyle and physical characteristics.

The protracted northern belt extends from 10,000 feet to 29,032 feet at the summit of Mt. Everest, known as Sagarmatha (Goddess of the Sky) by the Nepalese and Chomolungma (Goddess Mother of the World) by the Sherpas and Tibetans.

Extreme altitudes continue onto the northern plateau of the Himalayan ranges, forming land masses 14,000 to 20,000 feet high. Otherwise known as Tibet, this plateau is that dark brown blotch on the maps of the world I so vividly remember when going to grade school. China has occupied Tibet since its invasion in 1951. Of Mongoloid racial stock and considered "yellow," or Asian, the northern belt people are collectively known as *Bhotiya* (Tibetan meaning "from over the border") and can be subdivided into the Lhoba, Sherpa, Manapa, Niper and countless additional tribes and ethnic clans.

The central belt, consisting of midrange mountain valleys between 6,000 and 9,000 feet, is occupied by tribal Garungs, Tanangs, and Kirantes. Living in valleys below 6,000 feet, the Hindu castes add to the delicious complexity and uniqueness of the Nepalese people, well over thirty-five different groups, each with novel background, dress, and customs.

While Hinduism flourishes in the south, and the lamas of Tibetan Buddhism incarnate in the north, it is the exclusively unique and cohesive integration of Buddhism and Hinduism in the mid country that exemplifies the extraordinary peacefulness of the Nepalese people. That Hindu and Buddhist temples and congregants neighbor one another at Swayambhunath is but one concrete example. Ironically, religious constructs, responsible for the greatest joy, comfort, and fulfillment experienced by the peoples of the world, have also been cause for untold misery, death, and destruction. Yet, in Nepal, Buddhist and Hindu doctrines have been blended and continue to be observed on a dual basis—*in peace.* Incredibly refreshing!

Tomorrow morning, I will join a young Nepali for a ten-mile hike to his village. Feet, in this region and in most of Nepal, are *the* mode of transportation. In fact, they are the *only* mode of transportation. Motor roads simply do not exist. Having become quickly immersed in country-simple Nepali folk who radically contrast their Western-attired, big-city kin, I also sadly observe prevalent fits of coughing, tuberculosis, and terribly poor daily hygiene.

ॐ

Nepal
Monday, November 3, 1975

I woke at sunrise, settled my bill (twelve American cents for dinner, bed, and breakfast) and, after taking some slow steps up the very first steep ridge, realized that trekking with a pack is no fucking joke. Wanting no part of Don Sahib, my companion abandoned me before crossing over the first of many turquoise rivers via the first of many antique "bridges"—unreliable, dilapidated misconnections of rusting chains, frayed ropes, and cracked and warped wooden planks.

Initial panic derived from dizzying heights above virginal riverbeds and cascading waters provided little solace. Creaking and drooping under the slightest weight, these swaying catwalks never failed to astound me. The fact that they seemed to work and were the only alternative gave me no choice but to cross the next one, hoping it would still exist on my return.

92. This was the best of the lot.

Every step of the first long climb was a bitch. So was carrying my thirty-pound pack. Soaking wet with perspiration at Kaping, I took chai. My woolen sweater became moist, my head soaking wet. I had expected to start each morning fully clothed, perspire, peel off layer after layer, and reverse the process as the day grew late.

I was soon joined by a second Nepali companion, who too was no dummy, also wanted no part of my sorry plight, offered a quick *"namaste"*— and was *Gone with the Wind*. Had he seen the movie? (The literal translation of the Hindu greeting *namaste*, pronounced "nah-mah-stay," is "I bow to you." Common translation? "I salute the God within you," accompanied by a slight bow and hand gesture—*anjali mudra*—in which the palms are pressed together at the chest or head.)

However, moments later, José and a Sherpa guide appeared, the guide walking home to Solu-Khumbu, only *fifty* crow flies away! José joined me. As I learned to hike s-l-o-w-l-y, Sherpa dust became lunch. For ten miles I whined and napped, forcing myself up to Muldi at 8,200 feet, only to quickly descend into Surkeye—and depression.

For it was here that the dude who wrote the guidebook first pissed me off. By gearing my steps to his suggested times, I gained a rough estimate of hours between hamlets. Mileage meant zilch. And so did his estimates.

Soon, José and I began tiptoeing along a cliff at twilight. Mentally and physically wasted, hungry and cold, I felt growing desperation. Was sleeping outside safe? Rattlesnakes? Yeti, the Abominable Snowman? We could no longer see the trail—until a Nepalese "godfather" appeared carrying a flashlight. "Sleep, my house?"

Pleased to oblige, we followed Don Corleone for two miles and quickly learned the difference between Nepalese and sahib time. Nepalese "close" can mean one to five miles. "One hour?" Try two or three. Finally arriving at his home, we inhaled *tsampa*, a barley-based Tibetan cereal mixed with chai or milk, and were told to sleep on the porch, our packs secured inside.

Apparently, farmers in the lower valleys are glad to feed and put you up for the night for not more than a few rupees. In the warmer valleys at lower altitudes, you sleep on a porch. Higher up, trekkers attempt to escape biting cold and wind by bunking indoors.

The tribal Nepalese kitchen and house, often one and the same room, consists of straw, cardboard, tin, and traces of wood surrounding a fire built under a grill or brick "stove." Lacking chimneys, the smoke has nowhere to go, accumulates in the hut and lungs, and causes most trekkers to gag, cough, and quickly grow nauseous. With eyes burning and tearing, I regularly stepped outside to clear my head and throat. Between mouthfuls of subje and gasps of fresh air, I eventually grew accustomed to the purple haze, at least well enough to share balloons with the Godfather's beaming children and their young, sweet, appreciative mama. Without chalk and pavement, I was unable to teach how to play potsy (hopscotch).

93. No chimney. No porch. But lots of love and animals. And smoke.

When I try to determine my route, maps of identical terrain offer unique locations, pronunciations, and spellings. Several different towns bear the same name on the same map. *Consistent inconsistency.* Seeking directions from local tribesmen often proved more comical than helpful.

The grapevine had warned of becoming "Dr. Don." When the village chief noticed me attending to cuts on my arm after applying moleskin to burns on my feet, he pointed to a half-dozen cuts on each of his hands. Repeated explanations that I was not a medical doctor went unheeded.

According to rumor, an overwhelming majority of mountain village Nepalis believe all sahibs are doctors. And when placed in relative context, my meager knowledge of perfunctory hygiene and medical know-how appeared to surpass their experience. Many had not seen trained medical personnel for several years. Was my Nepalese *caporegime* (capo) going to make me an offer I couldn't refuse?

In Khumbu, the infant and toddler mortality rate approaches fifty percent! Easy to believe after seeing and hearing so many babies and children with respiratory infections, chronic coughs, insufficient clothing, and dismal nutrition. Their pants, often slit in the back, permit continual exposure to bitter cold and germs. Reliance on an exclusive diet of subje is barely sustainable for adult subsistence. Many of the growing children simply don't have a chance. As Cat Stevens asks, "Where Do the Children Play?"

I repeatedly emphasized the need for washing with water and soap, a practice not adhered to or seemingly known by most mountain tribes. *Hot* water? Forgetaboutit. Fact is, many do not appear to bathe or wear clean clothing. Sanitary conditions known in the West cannot be found.

As I continued to "mend" hands, feet, and infections, I discovered I had surrendered most of my bandages and antibiotic ointment. Enough. I stopped dispensing what I needed for myself but continued to instruct in simple hygiene.

Nepal
Tuesday, November 4, 1975

I woke at dawn after only two hours of sleep because devilish little ones constantly climbed onto the porch singing Nepalese folk songs. What were they doing up all night? Trying to please me? I had longed for a quiet, peaceful evening that was not to be. During this first night of yet another Nepalese festival, these caroling *baccaharu* (children), an assortment of preschool kids with precious smiles, wore flowers in their dark, dirty hair partly covering calligraphy printed on their foreheads.

Years of jogging had failed to prepare my mind and body for the trek. After fixing tsampa for breakfast, I was again faced with climbing an assortment of strenuous ridges.

Why was I subjecting myself to misery? "Maybe I'll just walk to Lukla (Airfield), eight more long, arduous days, and fuck the rest of the trek." But when I noticed shoeless tribal women transporting 110-pound (fifty-kilo) blocks of cheese on their backs—supported by straps worn across their foreheads—I had to temper my soliloquy. "Don Martín, get real. What is your fucking problem?"

A few words about the trails. They suck. I frequently cursed them. Instead of curling along the lower river valleys, the Everest trail climbs over peaks and ridges. Must be a podiatrist's wet dream—assorted loose rock, gravel, and dirt. When looking up and away from the trail, painful stumbles soon caused sore shoulders and hips. The trek was becoming nightmarish.

After hiking far above an expansive river valley, I briskly crossed a bubbling creek and sucked on rare fruit in Kirantichad before climbing 2,000 vertical feet to Namdu, the finale of the day. But not so fast. Fatigued, I lost my concentration and the trail, confirmed after two Nepalis far in the distance shouted out my mistake. At least *they* knew where I wanted to go. Sweaty, cold, and thirsty, I rediscovered the trail and rushed to Namdu before the sun died. At a creek, I refilled my canteen, added iodine, and soon learned that most of the water had leaked all over my clothes and pack.

Caught in darkness once again, and fearing I might fall off a cliff, I crawled to the top of a ridge, only to discover it was not the top. No longer able to notice even faint outlines of the trail, I continued to stumble until I noticed a flickering light about one mile ahead. I trudged on, my moist bandana barely keeping the sweat of my brow out of my burning eyes.

Out of breath that had grown thin, mean, and cold, I encountered a second savior who led me to another smoke-filled hut already occupied by two adults, one child, and one blind teen—all of whom were soon playing with balloons. Though I wasn't hungry, I ate the usual and proceeded to throw up before I fell asleep on the porch.

During these first days of the trek, though I didn't see more than two or three snowy peaks, I navigated through luxuriant green valleys, thick evergreen forests, and hilltop stations no higher than 10,000 feet. Terraced rice paddies, abundant water buffalo and marvelous tiny Nepalese women who defy gravity when carrying their loads become companions. José's whereabouts? No idea.

Constructs of life without cars, roads, and machines were deeply felt. Indigenous inhabitants think in terms of hours and days of walking, not minutes by car. A totally new way to *perceive* life. Emotional security, once again, became no more than a simple shelter and hot meal at the end of the day.

94. Map of my Everest trek. Not as easy as it looks.

Nepal
Wednesday, November 5, 1975

Woke at sunrise, hiked to Upper Namdu, and passed two sahibs who offered cheese and empathy. Continuing through a sloping valley, the first of countless ascents and descents, I approached Yarsa, confirming my view that Nepal's mountain towns and villages cannot be taken literally. The mental images held by Westerners simply do not apply to these settlements.

Beyond Yarsa appeared my next major hurdles—another mountain and *constipation*. Set upon by pain in my back, hips, and knees, I wondered whether paying fifteen or twenty-five rupees per day for a backpacking porter was not the bargain of a lifetime. But is it not more righteous to carry your own pack? Does such enterprise not smack of imperialistic servitude?

These ruminations became more than rhetorical when a young Hindu gentleman approached and offered his services for twenty rupees plus two cups of chai per day. And from that moment, the trek became transformative. The first three days had been far more demanding and strenuous than I possibly could have imagined. And now, here was the answer to my dreams: Min Bhodur of Yarsa.

Having divided my pack to carry half the load, I wondered why? Were compassion and empathy responsible. Fuck no. Western guilt? Jewish guilt? No matter, Min Bhodur was astonished.

Descending to the Sikri Khola (river), we met a New Zealand couple and two American women trailing their Sherpa porters and guides. We continued to climb until sunset, and bedded down with a family near Those, an established Newar community physically resembling twelfth-century Europe. No longer a simple hike in the mountains, I was being treated to a completely unexpected cultural extravaganza by the strenuous but welcoming lifestyles of tribal peoples. Dinner? Fixed by an elderly *hajurabu* (grandpa) with deeply ingrained Tibetan facial features who cooked in the wok he had carried on his back.

Sin Tzonke

Min Bhodur, thoroughly resourceful and possessing remarkable ability for improvisation and imaginative genius, swept the dust off our bedrolls with the branch and leaves of a *live* tree. Having noted the aboriginals' frequent use of live wood for fueling fires, I could now better understand initial discussions regarding the establishment of a Nepalese national park in Khumbu.

Determined to treat ill-equipped Min as an equal, I gave him my sweater, socks, and down jacket. Twenty-six, married with children, and wanting to go to Namche without proper clothing, Min's intent may prove questionable.

Of greater certainty was the joy expressed by two girl toddlers, the cutest I have seen, playing with balloons. I used pantomime to explain I had once been a schoolteacher before learning they do not attend school because the nearest one is in Jiri, two and one-half mountain hours east.

Now scarce, eggs and white rice had doubled in price.

Nepal

Thursday, November 6, 1975

I continued to develop rapport with Min as we spent most of the morning balancing ourselves over loose logs—yet another form of indigenous overpass—and was not surprised to learn that this was his first porter parade. We worked our way through periods of dizziness and nausea as we ascended to the 8,200-foot Thodung Cheese Factory.

A wall of *mani* stone carvings and mantras representing Sherpa prayers indicated the namesake summit. Mani stones inscribed with ancient Buddhist mantras—*Avalokiteshvara*, or *Padmapani* (the embodiment of the *bodhisattva* of compassion), and *Om manipadme hum* ("Praise for the Jewel in the Lotus")—are frequently found at the apex of mountain passes. Sherpas ritually pass them on the left as an omen and blessing for long life. The latter, perhaps the mother of all Buddhist (and Hindu) mantras, expresses the compassion of *all* Buddhas and of *all* Buddhist teachings and beliefs. To repeat, a bodhisattva is one who postpones the attainment of nirvana out of compassion to save those who are suffering.

95. The summit of a Nepalese mountain pass.

Some five hundred feet below the inscribed mantras, a Tibetan woman of noble stature offered me a cut of fresh meat, hide attached. Like most we now encountered, she appeared to be Tibetan, surely not Caucasian. After bargaining for the blood-soaked flesh in front of more stupas and *gompas* (Buddhist meditation stations), we descended toward Lukla and another host family. When Min failed to remove the fur before cooking the meat, I opted for rice and subje. Water buffalo became supper for Min and our hosts.

Who knows? Perhaps it was my generosity that prompted our host family's vixenish, sixteen-year-old daughter to seek me out later that night and point to her crotch and mine. She wanted a scene! Nepalese jailbait? Only my fears of machete-carrying Sherpa men chasing me in the morning caused me to refuse.

96. The Tibetan butcher, not the jailbait.

I was feeling travel-hardened at 10,000 feet; Kathmandu seemed but a distant memory. Psychological barriers had come to pose greater difficulty than physical prowess. Case in point is my current abstinence from hashish—and masturbation—wishing to harness my libidinous energy for the task at hand.

Nepal
Friday, November 7, 1975

Waking before 5:00 a.m. to boil water for tsampa, and feeling a stabbing pain in my left leg, I diagnosed myself as suffering from "sahib's knee," the cumulative effect of mountain hiking. During yesterday's rapid ascents and descents, the shock-absorbing cartilage in my knee became strained and stretched. Walking *uphill* is fine.

By 6:30 a.m., we had reached Kenja. Our first clear views of snowy peaks heralded a seven-hour climb to Sete and 11,700-foot Lamjura Pass, where all layers of clothing proved futile. Min Bhodur wore the down jacket. Sadly, we both recognized he could not continue to Namche.

According to Kathmandu-based mountaineers, "After five to six days of hiking, the climbs become easier." Beyond belief, after one, two and three hours of rigorous hiking, I did not tire. Had I finally beaten my body into shape? Had I reached a point of physical resilience?

Cresting a beautiful *gurans* (rhododendron) forest atop Lamjura, we retreated beneath tree line and were received by wind-bent trunks posing as old men and women ready to wither and die, their anemic branches and leaves submerged under patches of sullen, silent mist that roamed at will.

Although I was intent on reaching Jambesi, considered the first "major" Sherpa "town," my knee and the setting sun would not cooperate. Sleep? We stopped atop Lamjura, at the crudest, most isolated and remote outpost I have ever encountered: a sloping two-by-four bamboo lean-to hut and compound shared with cows, goats and yaks under a crescent moon.

Our ruddy-faced Mongolian-appearing hosts churned noodles past midnight while I vainly tried to dry my socks. After dining on lo mein and chow fun—stirring memories of schlock joints (Hong Hing, Sammy Wo, Wo Hop) located on Mott Street in Lower Manhattan's Chinatown—Min and I attempted to sleep. But doing so on absolutely freezing Lamjura's highest windswept slope was but a sign of things to come.

Without clean clothes, decent food, potable water, bed, and media, it was hard to believe that life existed beyond the Himalayan womb. I had ventured into yet another separate reality, a realm I could have never anticipated. Earlier, under the doting eyes of jubilant parents, I watched a conquering baby take its first steps. At that moment, baby and I were one. We shared a common accomplishment: exploration of the unknown!

Powerful Himalayan rivers are known for their roaring, dynamic turquoise and teal waterfalls forded by feudal stone crossings originally assembled by prehistoric cave dwellers. Recent New Zealand–Everest expeditions are planning to design and build well-constructed wooden spans.

The first white man to conquer Everest, Sir Edmund Hillary, admired and trusted by the Sherpas, was accompanied to Everest's peak by one of their own—Tenzing Norgay. To this day, no one else knows which man was first to set foot on Everest's summit.

97. Notice the support strap buttressed by mama's forehead, a common technique to transport foodstuffs, timbers—and babies!

Nepal
Saturday, November 8, 1975

"Good Shabbos." On this Jewish Sabbath morning, Min and I descended to Jambesi while pausing to taste gefilte fish caught in an icy lake before climbing the 10,500-foot, densely forested blue-green Salang Pass.

Gazing directly northeast under a cloudless sky, I caught my first glimpse of Everest's colossal majesty. During the next hour, as clouds quickly formed and reformed, rare audiences with an array of Himalayan gods and goddesses were granted, physical evidence I was moving toward Namche Bazaar and Kala Patthar, Everest base camp. We had reached Solu, the southern edge of Solu-Khumbu.

John Lennon. "Instant Karma"? At cold, cloudy, and windy Ringmo, Min Bhodur and I mutually decided it was best to change porters. Instant karma? Pasang Sherpa of Ringmo joined me while Min carried a merchant's load back to Yarsa.

98. Pasang Sherpa of Ringmo.

Pasang invited me to meet his immediate and extended family while visiting their extraordinary and spacious Sherpa-style homestead; rich, dark, wooden hallways and paneled walls, sturdy furniture, brick fireplaces, and open cupboards holding scores of shiny copper, brass, and silver plates and kettles. Pasang, age twenty-three, and I then climbed for one hour to Trasindo, a Tibetan-Buddhist monastery. Soft-spoken and mellow, Pasang, a friend of the chief abbot, won use of the main guest room in

99. Porters (oil on canvas).

the monastery. My heart content after inhaling noodles and chai, I listened to chimes and chanting monks as the world's highest mountains stood but four valleys away as the crow flies.

The terrain had dramatically changed from accessible "foothills" to massive, forested mountains of diminishing vegetation, farms, and terraces—from populated river valleys to steep and inhospitable ravines. The thinning atmosphere became increasingly colder and penetrating, making breathing harder to negotiate with each passing day.

Nepal
Sunday, November 9, 1975

We woke to a heavenly sunrise and tsampa, bid "namaste" to the abbot, and then plunged down deep, aggravating terrain, made a steeper ascent to Karikhola, and overcame a late afternoon ridge to Kharte in northern Solu. Trasingo remained visible many miles and two lengthy valleys behind us.

The weather grew colder. At 10,500 feet, Kharte was *frigid*. Feeling isolated and lonely, I made the acquaintance of three Californians and Jerry, a French Canadian from Quebec.

During the climb to Kharte, I incredulously witnessed Nepali men lugging twenty to thirty thick bamboo poles they had tied together—work normally reserved for elephants or pack mules. The hauling of fifty-kilo foodstuffs continued to be the domain of lady Sherpa porters, still walking barefoot. My guilt and ambivalent feelings about hiring a porter continued.

100. Layers on, layers off, layers on . . .

Nepal
Monday, November 10, 1975

After ambling over a 15,000-foot pass to reach Phuiyan, we steeply descended to Surkya and the roaring, deep green Dudh Kosi ("milk river"), so-called because of its frothy, icy whitecapped waters. Skipping lunch, we approached Lukla's Short Takeoff and Landing (STOL) Airfield signaling arrival into Pharak state where dense ravines leapfrogged Phakding, Chaumriharka, and Churtrawa.

In most parts of the world, the 15,000-foot mountains we climbed today would be final destinations. Not so when dwarfed by K-2, the world's second highest mountain (28,250 feet), Ama Dablam, Lhotse, Nuptse, and Everest.

Highlighting the changing local population, not yet exclusively Sherpa, were handsome women of Tibetan-Chinese facial features, long braided hair, colorful lengthy dresses, beads, scarves, and shawls.

Namche Bazaar, Nepal
Tuesday, November 11, 1975

Rising above the Dudh Kosi, the highest of the high rivers of the Nepalese Himalayas, and Thubug, the last settlement found in Pharak, Pasang and I, gleaning motivation from early morning views of the South Col between Everest and Lhotse, easily cruised the rather difficult two-and-a-half-hour climb to Namche Bazaar. Need it be said that Mt. Everest and its colossal colleagues serve as headwaters for many of the great rivers of Asia: the Indus, Brahmaputra, and Ganges.

We had finally reached *the* Sherpa village, a community of winding, narrow, intersecting stone trails. Homes, hotels, cafes, and poorly stocked pantries portray little structural resemblance to those in the West. Namche, situated between and below two enormous glaciers at 11,500 feet, occupies an immediate and spectacular locale that is but a tiny portion of a most inconceivable panorama.

Although I had longed to rest my body and mind this day, I had not anticipated the additional cost of a porter. Solution? Walk one hour north, to Syangboche, to the modern and exorbitant Japanese-built Everest View Hotel, to buy more Nepalese rupees and risk exposure to deadly altitude sickness.

Now well above and beyond Lukla, I could no longer deny the increasing influence of Western culture and money on local Sherpa lifestyles. Trekkers in the lower valleys had been of limited means. Consequently, most farmers were far less affected, friendlier, and exhibited purer, kinder, and more generous and natural behaviors among one another that were extended toward us. In Namche Bazaar, the price of eggs and chai had tripled.

For sure, I conclude this trek can be partitioned into two distinct experiences. The trip through the lower valley regions from Lamosangu to Lukla is predominantly an indigenous cultural experience, relatively untouched by Western influence. In contrast, the portion of the trek between Namche Bazaar (11,500 feet) and Kala Patthar (18,500 feet) is essentially one of nature as you pass among pinnacle giants and celestial gods, and discarded supplies from well-heeled Japanese, American and European climbing expeditions.

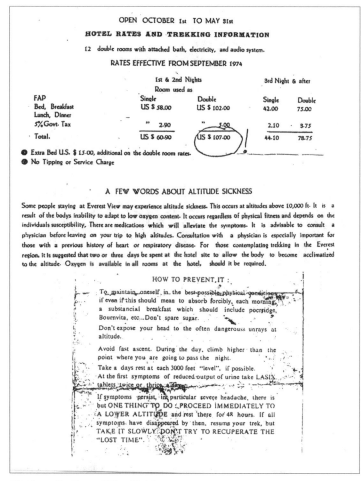

101. From the Everest View Hotel.

In the rarified air of Khumbu, too many Nepalis and Sherpas have grown accustomed to the free-spending, well-equipped expeditions facilitated by Lukla Airfield. Rumors abound of two doctors, German and Japanese, available for consultation at Pheriche, a 14,000-foot outpost. Lobuche and Gorak Shep exist only to serve the needs of trekkers. Sherpas manning these remote outposts will retreat to the lower valleys in the latter part of December when few trekkers challenge the biting cold and snow.

Despite wearing long johns, shirt, sweater, down jacket, and socks to bed, I spend most of my nights tossing and turning. With great trouble, I must keep one set of underwear clean and dry. No one sleeps on porches anymore. In Namche, I resupplied my staples and purchased another pair of woolen socks for insurance. They proved useless. After buying fifteen chapaties for the next few days, Pasang and I approached the Tibetan Buddhist Monastery of Tengboche (also spelled Thyangboche, Thangboche and Tangboche.).

102 Tengboche Monastery.

Pangboche, Nepal
Wednesday, November 12, 1975

Clear, crisp, and cold early morning air allowed fantastic, unobstructed views of the mountainscapes surrounding Tengboche. Finally, within the folds of the highest Himalayas, I felt emotionally overtaken by our immediate proximity to glaciers and snowy peaks. At dawn, we hiked along majestic brown and green forested mountain trails while skirting icy cold, rushing, turquoise streams, tributaries, and rivers.

Tengboche is situated in a meadow harboring Nuptse, Lhotse, and Everest, a triumvirate some consider to be one. Mesmerized by 22,349 feet

Ama Dablam ("Mother's Necklace"), a naturally chiseled wonder, I almost slipped on patches of ice now covering the trails.

While lunching on fried potatoes and chapaties dripping with jam and honey, I waited for my washed clothes to dry under a surprisingly warm midmorning sun. A brief tour of the hallowed retreat allowed inspection of murals, sanctuaries, balconies and golden Buddhist statues and figurines. Ignoring our presence, several lamas in dark purple robes danced to the sounds of chimes emanating from a sunken courtyard. Others contemplated Everest's dynamic essence from the full lotus position.

Resisting the relative comfort afforded by Tengboche, Pasang and I continued to gently hike, gradually climbing to Pangboche, a partially ice-bound rock village at 13,000 feet. We had risen above the Earth's ultimate tree line. Fences and structures consisted only of stone to withstand nonstop howling winds.

Many inhabitants of the Solu-Khumbu District and neighboring Sikkim and Bhutan, known collectively as *Bhotiya* or *Bhotia*, are related by ethno-linguistics. Most reside in what is known as the Trans Himalayan region that divides Tibet from India.

103. Ama Dablam. Reminiscent of Switzerland's Matterhorn, this mountain became a constant companion while walking between Namche and Everest.

104–106. Ama Dablam.

ॐ

Two women caretakers are smoking hand-rolled cigars in the house where we will sleep for the night. Plummeting temperatures and rising prices have become constant companions. Despite adding disinfecting iodine to my water, my urine, usually yellowish at lower altitudes, is now crystal clear.

Yak dung—more available and cheaper than wood—feeds a measly life-sustaining fire. Sleep and altitude don't mix. Lacking anything soft, I woefully drowse on bony hips, realize I've lost weight, and recognize my body craves nutrition to sustain a stable metabolism and relative warmth.

The hikes, though now gradual, have become more strenuous because the thinning air contains less oxygen. Absence of sleep, food, and warmth pose greater challenges than altitude and topography. Frequent interior drafts fanning intermittent flames produce more smoke than warmth. Insulation? Try corrugated cardboard and pictures from glossy Western magazines stuffed into cracked, thin, porous walls. I dare say, the frigid weather is growing comparable to January nights in central Asia and up-state New York.

107. Pangboche. This community school was built by Sir Edmund Hilliary's Himalayan Trust in 1963.

108. Standing by the community school in the frigid cold.

During these bone-chilling days, clarity is not obscured by clouds un-til 3:30 p.m. Completely absent after sunset, they are replaced by a pro-nounced half-moon that illuminates breathtaking surrealistic views—too often seen in the middle of the night when I shiver outside while pissing and shitting and missing the cocoon of my sleeping bag. Warmth? Mere maya illusion. Unable to find critical-mass nutrition in white rice and subje, I turn to milk chocolate bars, pure glucose, protein wafers, sugar candies, and a variety of pungent flatus.

Pheriche, Nepal
Thursday, November 13, 1975

By midmorning, Pasang and I had completed a three-hour walk along an icy river through barren landscape to Pheriche (14,340 feet). Enveloped by snowy pinnacles and naked glaciers, Pheriche has more in common with the moon than Earth. Originally established as a migratory yak-herding settlement, Pheriche's "urban sprawl" includes a half-dozen stone shelters, three of which are disguised as open-air "hotels."

109. The Pheriche Valley.

Along with seven to ten trekkers from distinct and distant lands, I reside in the only habitable no-star accommodation: The Sherpa. Inches above its earthen floor is a series of warped wooden shelves on which hikers find the unexpected: canned fruits, vegetables, fish, and meats that have been donated by government-sanctioned international mountain expeditions— and are prohibitively expensive. Food, warmth, shelter, rest, Everest—and each other—have become our only companions. Although short jaunts during sunlit hours are revitalizing, the nights are endless.

All are required to sleep here for at least two nights to allow nitrogen levels to adjust, reducing the possibility of altitude sickness. Recently, several mountain climbers died, including one member of the successful 1975 British expedition. While backpackers may descend rather rapidly, apparently, during ascents above 14,000 feet, oxygen-carrying red blood corpuscles require time to multiply.

My current mode of travel is timeless. Stopping at dusk for rest and nourishment in a stranger's home has been taking place for thousands of years. Most will not turn away a stranger in need. In this sense, having never really traveled before, I am genuinely grateful for the experience afforded me by the hospitality of these most compassionate Nepalese, Sherpa, and tribal peoples. Dr. Dolphi and his Japanese cohort mercifully offered two sleeping pills. The rumors proved true.

Pheriche, Khumbu, Nepal
Friday, November 14, 1975

> *Waiting for the Sun*
> —The Doors

Courtesy of a contaminated something, I shit all night, my stained underwear left outside, frozen to death. Though dehydrated, I fasted for the remainder of the day. I am no longer burdened with or interested in brushing my teeth, washing my hands and face, or combing my hair. Haven't seen a mirror for more than two weeks. My beard feels like a steel brush. Am happy just to keep warm, eat, belch, piss, fart, shit, and sleep three hours a night.

Lobuche, Nepal
Saturday, November 15, 1975
At 16,200 feet, Lobuche refers to both a seasonal settlement and a mountain (20,100 feet) directly adjacent to Nuptse (25,800 feet). Those of us here, the same seven to ten pathetic souls I have been with since Namche, remain continually cold, tired, and lumped together in a drafty room where we sleep on the floor. And now I know why Tibetan lamas are into bladder control.

Eating is no less a farce. Everyone is more than happy with the house "special"—boiled white rice, subje and hot chai. Tomorrow heralds my personal assault on Everest Base Camp. No dung, firewood, or maintained outpost can be found above Lobuche.

Managed by a legendary personage, his wife, and their ten-year-old son dubbed by all "the monster," our hosts perform a rather entertaining two-hour ceremony while cooking their limited menu. A Russian dude compared the immediate scene to descriptions of the Soviet Gulag (prison system) as described by Aleksandr Solzhenitsyn in *One Day in the Life of Ivan Denisovich*.

Lobuche, Nepal
Sunday, November 16, 1975

I am a steadfast follower of the doctrine of nonviolence, which was
first preached by Lord Buddha, whose divine wisdom is absolute
and infallible, and was practiced in our own time by the Indian
saint and leader Mahatma Gandhi. So, from the very beginning, I
was strongly opposed to any resort to arms as a means of regaining our freedom.

—His Holiness, the Fourteenth Dalai Lama

Sleep last night? Good luck. Too fucking cold!

Gorak Shep, a miniscule transient outpost, sits on the edge of a frozen
lakebed covered with white, silky sand. At 17,100 feet above sea level, it is
defended by a series of stone cairns and icy, treacherously sharp, rocky mo-
raines. Slowly moving along the Khumbu Glacier, I reached the memorial
plaque dedicated to those who died climbing in this area. Beyond it and
the white stretch of beach, I began the ninety-minute ascent to the top of

110. Mao Tse-tung, the "Red Bandit," and the Chinese Communist People's Liberation Army invaded Tibet in October 1950, after which a seven-
teen-point "agreement" was ratified by The National Assembly of Tibet. In
1959, the sitting Fourteenth Dalai Lama repudiated the "agreement" and
affirmed his government to be the only legitimate sovereignty of Tibet. A
government in exile was established in Dharmsala, northern India.

111 and 112. Mount Everest. Sagarmatha (Nepalese).
Chomolungma (Tibetan). Zhumulangma (Chinese).
And one wannabe Sherpa.

Kala Patthar, the toughest and steepest climb since Lamosangu when considering the extreme degree of difficulty and altitude—18,500 feet.

With the cloudless sun still low on the horizon, I was overtaken by Everest's glacial magnitude when finally facing the planet's most dominant landscape—and the fact that I had walked all the way there. However, when frightening and relentless gusts fought to tear my camera and jacket from my body, I decided to retrench and retreat across the white sandy beach. Weakened but adrenalized, jubilant, and triumphant, I felt euphorically embalmed and comforted by a peaceful and deep contentment within. Although my complicated interdependent systems had been taxed and depleted, only after descending and returning to Lobuche did I feel extreme fatigue.

Pasang, who accompanied me to GorakShep, did not climb to Kala Patthar. Headaches. Two and three years earlier, he had climbed above the renowned base camp. That night, we rested at Lobuche and braved *chang*, a fermented, barley-based, alcoholic devil's brew.

Tengboche Monastery, Nepal
Monday, November 17, 1975

Numb but joyfully skipping down the graduating hills to keep warm, I could finally feel my toes and fingers thaw when sunshine reached the valley floor. At Pheriche, I retrieved my copy of Lao Tzu's *Tao Te Ching* from Dr. Dolphi.

Some hours later, at the Lotse View Hotel, Pasang and I settled-up and parted ways. In retrospect, I feel extremely fortunate I made the decision to hire a porter. Especially Pasang. Far more than a guide, Pasang became an honorable friend who revealed a loving, tolerant, peaceful vibration rarely found among men. It was my distinct honor and good karma to have spent time in his presence.

Christoph von Furer-Haimendorf's *The Sherpas of Nepal*, found among sardine tins at Pheriche, intimately describes Sherpa culture: family life, religious beliefs, economic life. Apparently, single women are, comparatively, quite free to engage in casual sex before marriage. And although not encouraged, such erotic behavior is commonplace without stigma. (Now they tell me.) The role women play in Nepalese society and within the family appears far greater—and on a more equal footing with men—than in most Hindu and Buddhist societies.

The arrival of the potato crop in 1860 and the accompanying barter system revamped Himalayan commerce. Based on personal relationships and mutual respect among traders, the trafficking of potatoes, salt, and other commodities became an extensive feature of survival in Khumbu and Tibet. The annexation of Tibet by China put an end to most of this commerce which, in turn, had disastrous economic consequences for the Sherpas.

Perhaps I have overlooked their most pervading feature because it is so obvious.

The Sherpas are a tribe of Tibetan origin who occupy the high valleys around the base of Mount Everest in northeastern Nepal. All Sherpas belong to the Sherpa ethnic group. And the Sherpas of the Himalayas are more than mere carriers. They are exceptional guides, great mountaineers without whom no expedition would be possible. They adapt exceptionally to this low-oxygen environment because they are children of the mountain, born and raised at more than 4,000 meters altitude.

I had been told of an 18,000-foot mountain pass leading to Tibet from the Nepalese village of Thami. Really? Would it not be intense to walk to Lhasa (capital of Tibet) as Heinrich Harrer captivatingly described in *Seven Years in Tibet*? As a German national in British-controlled India during World War II, Harrer, an accomplished world-class mountain climber, recorded his escape and subsequent residence in Lhasa, where he became a respected counsel to the then-sitting Dalai Lama.

A second compelling but tragically sad account of Tibet is found in *My Land and My People: The Memoirs of His Holiness the Dalai Lama of Tibet*. Countless sources have documented the attempted annihilation of Tibet and its people by the Chinese Communists. That said, my current intrigue lies elsewhere: the miraculous, metaphysical discovery and declaration of the Fourteenth Dalai Lama.

With the passing of the Thirteenth Dalai Lama, the search began at once for his reincarnation, for each Dalai Lama is a reincarnation of his predecessor. . . .

First, a regent had to be appointed by the National Assembly to govern the country until the new reincarnation could be found and grow to maturity. Then, in accordance with the time-honored customs and traditions, the state oracles and learned lamas were consulted . . .

In 1935, the Tibetan Wood Hog Year, the Regent went to the sacred lake of Lhamoi Latso at Chokhorgyel, about ninety-nine miles southeast of Lhasa. The people of Tibet believe that visions of the future can be seen in the waters of this lake . . . A detailed description of these visions was written down and kept a strict secret.

In the following year, high lamas and dignitaries, carrying the secrets of the visions, were sent out to all parts of Tibet to search for the place which the Regent had seen in the waters.

The wise men who went to the east arrived in our region of Dokham during the winter, and they observed the green and golden roofs of the monastery of Kumbum. . . . Their leader asked if the family living in the house had any children and was told that they had a boy who was nearly two years old. . . .

Two members of the party went to the house in disguise, together with a servant and two local monastic officials who were acting as their guides. . . .

The lama spent the whole day in watching the little boy with increasing interest until it was time for the boy to be put to bed.

The narration continues with a description of confirming "tests" the growing entourage of high officials conducted with the young boy. His selection of "correct" symbolic objects—among them black versus yellow rosaries, an ornate drum, and a walking stick—convinced the entourage that they had found the Fourteenth Dalai Lama.

They reported all the details to Lhasa by telegram. There was only one telegraph line in Tibet, from Lhasa to India, and so the message had to be sent in code from Sining through China and India; and by the same route an order came back to take me at once to the Holy City.

Having satisfied my curiosity concerning the supernatural metaphysical Tao by which the Fourteenth Dalai Lama was found, I turned my sensory instincts to *Mani Rimdu*, a festival of great merriment, food, drink, dance and song that was about to take place.

From all of Khumbu, monks, lamas and Sherpas ritually travel to Tengboche Monastery during November. (The exact dates for the festival are fixed according to the Tibetan lunar calendar.) Nineteen days in all, the holiday celebrates the founding of Buddhism in Tibet by Guru Rinpoche in the seventeenth century.

113 and 114. Tibetan-Buddhist sand mandalas are geometric representations of the universe. They promote spiritual guidance and meditation while portraying the cosmos beyond that of human understanding.

To commemorate the belief that Buddhism is recreated during Mani Rimdu, incredibly ornate, colorful, and inspiring sand *mandalas* (Sanskrit for "world in harmony") are constructed while Hindu/Buddhist *puja* (prayer rituals) are performed by the monks and lamas to bless the mandalas. The dances convey Buddhist teachings on many levels, but their main purpose is to conquer satanic demons.

Monday was devoted to rehearsals for the event. After convalescing for some hours at the "suburban" Lotse View Hotel, I ventured up to Tengboche to find many familiar trekkers huddled inside a room of absolute frenzy. The entire hall was filled with screaming Sherpa parents and children filmed by delicate cameras atop tripods. No less mania was taking place in the large kitchen. Not to be denied an opportunity to make a profit, local merchants scalped food to the highest bidders at fantastically inflated prices. Superbowl in Sherpaland!

During midafternoons, monks robed in dark purple danced under charcoal skies. (Storm clouds, without fail, follow brilliant sunny mornings, and may be the only element of Sherpa life that even hints at a semblance of scheduled predictability.)

Tengboche Monastery, Nepal
Thursday, November 20, 1975

Moving up to the madness at Tengboche and hoping the chaotic frantic partying and body heat would spell more sleep, I also wanted to catch dancing Sherpas stoned on chang. Merriment continued till dawn.

One late morning, a ceremonial parade led by the presiding Chief Lama and his processional entourage of trumpeters, flag carriers, musicians and, of course, the faithful, took place. A colorful and dramatic cavalcade of participants, most of whom wore deep-purple robes and hats, proceeded from the main entrance of the monastery, down its grand stairway, and past throngs of devout believers. With the mountains and cast of thousands as a backdrop, the ghost of Cecil B. DeMille had been successfully placated.

Finally halting at an astrologically prescribed arena, all participants paid mutual homage to one another employing chai, rice, white scarves, rupees, and other venerated objects.

115. Each Dalai Lama is descended from Guru Rinpoche, the founder of Tibetan Buddhism (717 AD). Here, a presiding Chief Lama blessed the faithful. Verbal tradition proclaims that the guru was born at eight years old, found floating on a lotus flower on sacred Lake Dhanakosha.

As the afternoon crept on, I reacquainted myself with many of the Sherpas I had met on the way to Kala Patthar including the "hoteliers" and "maître d's" from Lobuche and Pheriche—and the Dennis the Menace of Khumbu, "the monster.

Like clockwork, clouds and miserly mist soon shrouded and saturated the hallowed congregants, creating an eerie, spiritually convergent ether. The spontaneous vapors, seemingly self-sufficient, intermittently "opened" and "closed," permitting partially obscured glimpses of awesome Lhotse, Nuptse, and Everest. (Everest is also known as the "Triple Crown" and "Everest Trilogy." Some consider Lhotse, at 27,940 feet, to be the fourth-highest mountain in the world. For some technical reason, Nuptse, at 25,791 feet, is not thought to be a separate entity. Many consider all three to be one mountain. I'm flexible.)

116–120. *Above and opposite:* Is this not Shangri-La?

A phenomenon of a different sort took place when "real" tourists, invading for just one or two days of the festival, revealed an outrageous assortment of Japanese Nikons, German Leicas, and multiangle and zoom lenses set on tripods. As I photographed the scene with my American Kodak Instamatic, I was glad not to be toting a camera worth more than the worldly possessions of most Nepalese.

That morning a helicopter had landed, leased for $300 an hour by a German couple who chose to tour Nepal in one day. Good luck. When they took off for environmentally conscious Tiger Tops, an exclusive resort charging body parts, the chopper first dove straight down into the valley below. I wondered what the immediate population thought of this inexplicable flying machine.

During my past and current travels, one specific day or group of days infrequently stands out as unique. If any adventure falls into that category, it is the Mani Rimdu Festival, an unequaled "days of days," a series of unparalleled Himalayan spectacles and fanfare—of which I knew nothing until it smacked me in the face!

This point in my narrative is also as good as any to briefly footnote the perseverant if not insane trekkers with whom I've spent the past several weeks. Jerry, a French butcher, lives in Montreal. Jean Pierre and Noel make love and war in Paris. They plan to live in southern Morocco for two years while Jean completes alternative community service rather than serve in the French Foreign Legion with Stan Laurel and Oliver Hardy.

Complementing this band of enlightened gypsies are a refined and soft-spoken Swiss couple from Bern, along with Luigi and Maria from Bologna. Radical, warm. and personable Italians, they share my political views and lifestyle. A gay Spanish couple from Barcelona will shortly return to their homeland to participate in the historic transitional events now taking place: the imminent demise of fascist Generalissimo Francisco Franco and the changing of the Iberian guard. The husband, Raoul, did not reach Kala Patthar. A victim of altitude sickness, he had to prematurely descend.

And wandering about is a narcissistic American freelance photographer trying to break into the business from Paris, several American Peace Corps worker-students from Evergreen State College on a cleanup project for credit, and an Australian couple heading to Srinagar, the capital of

Kashmir, India. Upon my suggestion, the Aussies now plan to visit Ladakh in India.

Churtrawa, Nepal
November 19 (?), 1975

I screwed up my days, dates, and datelines. Is today only Wednesday? (And if so, what day of the month is it?)

Slept soundly after taking too many sleeping pills supplied by a Kiwi (New Zealand) nurse. Woke with a hangover and severe laryngitis, ensuring I was silent and disciplined all day. Not a wholly bad experience.

121. Under resplendent sunshine, all was aglitter!

For ten rupees, I was permitted to sit upon a veranda overlooking Tengboche's monasterial courtyard, the Everest trio, and Ama Dablam. Despite the presence of television dudes, clicking shutters, and the Sherpa and sahib characters I have mentioned, the morning belonged to the lamas—spirited, robed dancers wearing intricate and striking hats, pants, shawls, gloves, and masks.

All things must pass. And so, after some time, I finally tired of the dancing, of the cold, of the rice and subje, and of "the monster." With great ambivalence, I packed, bid my farewells, departed to Namche, splurged on an egg-and-rice omelet, and continued down the mountain into Pharak, immediately south of Solu-Khumbu and Everest. Relative warmth and privacy were found at 9,000 feet—no sahibs, no Sherpas, no porters. Fatigued but spiritually euphoric, I was once again able to sleep below 12,000 feet.

Lukla (Airfield), Nepal
Thursday (?), November 20 (?), 1975

I breakfasted with Luigi and Maria. Upon the arrival of what appeared to be a toy-like remote-control plane, I foolishly entertained thoughts of returning to Kathmandu that very morning. When an agent of the Sherpa Coop informed me that there would be "no trouble" getting out tomorrow, I grew suspicious and dried out under the sun most of the day until I got the shits again.

Lukla, Nepal
Friday, November 21, 1975

Woke at 5:00 a.m. By 9:00 a.m., I wondered, "Had mellow Don Martín been fucked over?" Apparently, there are several charter companies that fly in and out of Lukla from Kathmandu. Because I had purchased my ticket in Kathmandu from the Sherpa Coop, I was not allowed to board today's flight managed by a competing company. *Chaos City.* Having completed Lao Tzu's *Tao Te Ching* and its focus on acceptance of reality as it is, and finding no evidence to the contrary, I must conclude the Master had avoided Lukla airfield.

But wait. Had karma prevailed? A third plane this morning? Nope. Canceled. Why? To plan for the newly proposed Sherpa-Himalayan National Park (SHNP), the king's brother had reserved nearly all the planes in Nepal to ferry government officials to a meeting in Syangboche.

After collecting data, the government is ready to enact legislation establishing its first protected reserve. But not so fast. How will the SHNP interface with local culture and its needs? And if such a concept is foreign to the Nepalese government, imagine its acceptance by the Sherpas.

Without my knowledge, but without complaint, a Sherpa Coop agent had switched my original reservation forward three days, meaning I was now assured a seat on Saturday's plane and refunded sixty rupees. *Refund?* Absolutely unheard of in Asia. Translation? Ultimate confusion.

As I waited and grew nauseous—and feared it might be an initial symptom of prevalent hepatitis—I continued to read *Hinduism*. According to professor R. C. Zaehner, Hindustani *boychiks* and *girlchiks* are raised in the same vein as their Jewish peers, having in common that both religions are considered "ways of life." I suspect that Islam is no different. Maybe a little. Maybe a lot. I know so little of Arab/Muslim theology and culture.

Lukla, Nepal
Saturday, November 22, 1975, 8:00 A.M.

Flying in and out of Lukla is not for the squeamish. Landing leaves no room for error. Pilots throw their propellers into hard reverse before they touch down and must gun their engines as they race down the steeply graded (12 percent) grass and earthen runway for takeoff—without access to instruments and radio transmission.

Considering the extreme landscape, the strip was constructed at an elevation of 2,800 meters (9,200 feet) with an abrupt drop-off to a river valley below. The approach is through a maze of spectacular mountain peaks often shrouded in clouds.

More cast members from Mani Rimdu have arrived with all sorts of baggage. Many carry bloated egos, trying to impress one another with tales of the important Sherpas they "know."

Further indication of Lukla chaos? Poor communication with Kathmandu. When the two-way radio is in denial, no one on the ground has any idea which company's plane is landing. On those occasions when the pilot has no idea who hired him, the passengers are asked!

Resembling black-and-white grainy photographs of 1906 Kitty Hawk, Lukla also features a warped wooden outhouse that professes to be a terminal. This morning? No radio transmission because the radio operator failed to show. And maybe no planes and pilots. Many believe Lukla to be the most dangerous airport in the world.

122. Lukla (STOL) Airfield, 1976.

123. Tenzing-Hillary Airport, 2018.

Hinduism's final pages are nudging me ever closer to Sri Bal Yogi Prem Varni's Yoganta Ashram in Rishikesh. An additional memory this morning? Today is the twelfth anniversary of the assassination of John Fitzgerald Kennedy, thirty-fifth president of the United States.

Kathmandu, Nepal
Sunday, November 23, 1975

By 10:00 a.m., I was seated within a narrow STOL aircraft behind a crew of one. Mercilessly whirled about as though a single grain of sand in a storm, the plane eventually landed at Kathmandu's Tribhuvan International Airport, or TIA, named for a former Nepalese king.

Within thirty-five minutes? More euphoria! The trek had taken me to a higher plane of consciousness on which the pettiest details of life were deeply experienced and vividly appreciated. A warm shower felt like pellets of heavenly nectar.

Kathmandu, Nepal
Thursday, November 27, 1975, Thanksgiving Day

My dear friend Joel,

Picked up mail and want to immediately respond to your gracious letter and questions. During the day, any day, depending on location, I normally wake early and think about breakfast, where I will sleep that night, whether to change money on the black market, whom I may meet, and how great I feel to be part of a foreign scene often described as exotic, tantalizing, chaotic, and fucked up. Will I receive mail today? Where is my next destination? How long before I arrive there? How will I do so? What costs are involved for transportation, food, and shelter?

Today I'm staying at the Delight Lodge, sharing a double room with a Bostonian for sixty-five American cents. Unlike most of India and Nepal, Kathmandu is a "hippie mecca" of Western food, restaurants, good hashish, and much-sought-after decadent debauchery. Most of the Nepalese homegrown is worthless, but every now and then I run into some killer "Mustang," "Buddha Weed," and (Thai) "Stick"—all for pennies.

I will soon return to India, to a palace owned by an Indian family that befriended me. Next stop is Sri Lanka (Ceylon) via Madras, to warm flesh and bone marrow thoroughly chilled after completing a captivating trek to Everest Base Camp. But plans are plans are plans. And the problem with making plans around here? Logic and reason have yet to arrive in these parts. Less popular is cause and effect.

In reference to your unusually disciplined law school study habits, best not to forget that panacea (instant solution and gratification), not perseverance (paying one's dues), has become the American "Way," or Tao.

How easy it is for me to conclude that losing your teaching job is a bitch, a loss you must accept. Practicing what I preach is another matter. Consequently, I have been concentrating on accepting—rather than judging—that which is beyond my control. Especially people. Though I often fail, I feel better when not engaged in absurd ego comparisons.

Yin complements *yang*. You found a new lady friend. Does she have any friends? Surprisingly, I find I am not oriented toward women right now, possibly because I meet very few and chances of remaining with one are slim. Bangkok, the international "city of sin," may offer temporary relief.

My vanity craves your flattering description of our raps at home. However, my *Atman* (true, natural Self) realizes they only strengthen rather than weaken the illusions of my ego.

Meditation practice? Whim suffices. Philosophy? The *Tao Te Ching* calms me. Yet, when things don't go "right," it's difficult to think as Lao Tzu. Had he lived in Nepal, he might have become a corrupt, drug-dealing government official. To undertake his "Way of Life," his Tao—total acceptance, to simply *be*—ain't easy. Allegedly, *acceptance* is what is meant by the Tao, "the Way." "Let It Be." But is acceptance not tantamount to resignation?

My lifestyle has become fleeting; my behavior simply affects only myself. Transient relationships are expected and accepted. Committed friendships rarely occur among the scores of people I meet each day. Some have been toughened by constantly being on the road, and fear that their identities, souls, and worldly belongings may be ripped off—more so by Westerners than Asians.

Countless are downright hostile, either wrapped in bizarre personal head trips or iconoclastic inner spaces. Unable to handle the wide assortment of disenchanted egos seeking to impress each other—all types traveling for all sorts of conscious and unconscious reasons—many become overwhelmingly dogmatic, denying the need to question their entrenched Tao. (Notice how nonjudgmental I have become? Ha!)

You asked about this period of travel as compared to last. To paraphrase previous notes, I now entertain that perspective of having once adjusted to Western materialism after completing a lengthy journey and would like to think I am more centered in the now. Although I feel tension while living between two worlds—the social conventions of life in the United States and those of life in foreign countries—ironically, I am bound by the rules and expectations of neither. As a white man hanging in lesser-known locales, I am often viewed as "special," a "celebrity" of sorts, ignorant of the society I have invaded.

But there exists a third society to consider, the unwritten, unconscious codes of the international hippie trail, a veritable culture and elastic community of wandering souls, hippies, and bohemians who parallel process people and behavior at home. That is, most emulate each other, establishing normative values, mores, styles, and fads. Tight budgets, masochism, travel stories, Eastern clothing, idealism, and diverse uniformity describe their nomadic search for novel individual and group identities.

During my previous journey, I learned it, lived it, and began to see through a lot of it. Today, I can be more myself, less in tune with the masochism of a starvation budget, no longer wanting to live a totally "romantic," impoverished lifestyle. And while it no longer makes sense to walk five miles under a broiling sun to save ten *paisa* (cents), my integrity and sense of morality remain compromised and outraged when ripped off. You must discriminate and learn when to argue, when to give in, and which battles to ignore.

My good friend Alan Watts discusses consciousness-raising as a function of one's departure from and nonacceptance of social convention. If he is correct, when on the road, I enjoy a great, if not transitory advantage. And though I would surely frown on travel as an enduring lifestyle, did not Janis (Joplin) urge, "Get it while you can"?

Watts presents another argument you might find interesting: the English language's incomplete and fraudulent representation of natural behavior. Western language artificially fractures an event into the subject, the action, the object of the action, and its consequences. In truth, the event has transpired simultaneously. Denying this reality, linear symbolic language mistakenly implies that the impetus for each action is exclusively the subject, a notion diametrically contrary to the Eastern concept of the universe as ONE. Watts prefers Chinese, where characters are pictographs.

Today being Thanksgiving, I have been invited for turkey dinner by an acquaintance who works for the United Nations.

Namaste,

Martin

My references to Alan Watts in my letter to Joel recall Dolphi, the twenty-eight-year-old German psychologist who befriended me at Pheriche. Well-versed in Watts's beliefs that Chinese and Japanese characters better serve and represent communication because they symbolize (picture) nature, he concludes that Western delusional thinking separates our Selves from reality.

We flirt with higher consciousness as a function of nonconformity, as a separation from social convention leading to greater awareness of one's individuality. However, if this be so, can Western psychotherapists be effective agents of change if they are unwilling to look outside themselves or unable to transcend their Western postures? In other words, in therapy, clients cannot be dealt with effectively unless both the client *and* therapist are willing to investigate their behavior in terms of the social and cultural conventions of their mutual environment. Obviously, complications emerge if client and therapist are of different cultures.

While the good doctor and I solved little by our discussions, are they serving as one more omen guiding me toward the ashram at Lakshman

Jhula? Most Eastern-oriented schools adhere to the beneficial necessity of a teacher to guide the neophyte aspirant of yoga and meditation. *Physical Presence City.*

A related take on this is made by William James in *The Varieties of Religious Experience: A Study in Human Nature.* Just when I believe I have gained enough worldly knowledge, wisdom and experience to intelligently wrestle with "higher" notions of religion and philosophy, I read something that puts me in my place, leaving me couched in chaos, confusion and misunderstanding. In that sense, I am duly humbled by James, a meta-physicist, philosopher, and psychologist who taught at Harvard University from 1872 to 1907, and who "cultivated deeper levels of subconscious experience linked to God" to make sense of the world.

I should have known when scanning the title of Lecture One: Religion and Neurology. Better to bring attention to the front page of the paperback edition. "Pragmatism's leading exponent defends his belief that the evidence for God lies primarily in inner personal experience rather than in abstract philosophical systems." Makes sense so far. However, from that point on, James employs "abstract philosophical systems" to make his experiential argument. To have ventured beyond his treatise's glossy synopsis was sheer folly.

George Ivanovitch Gurdjieff, the mystic philosopher, and his contemporary esoteric cohort, Peter D. Ouspensky, first met in Moscow in 1915. I know nothing of Ouspensky. The little I know of Gurdjieff's metaphysical school increases my intrigue. Gurdjieff, who died in 1949, is credited with writing the absorbing *Meetings with Remarkable Men.*

Meetings with Remarkable Men presents us with the key itself to the life of the Great Master as it describes Gurdjieff's search for answers to the fundamental questions of life throughout remote areas of the world.

From the foreword:

He calls us to open our eyes. He asks us why we are here, what we wish for, what forces we obey. He asks us, above all, if we understand what we are. He wants us to bring everything back into question. For Gurdjieff was not, and could not be, only a writer. His task was a different one. Gurdjieff was a master.

Letting sleeping dogs lie is not one of my habits. However, after also being introduced to G. I. Gurdjieff's three-volume *Beelzebub's Tales to His Grandson: An Objectively Impartial Criticism of the Life of Man*, I am again humbled by my vast ignorance.

Patna, India
Friday, November 28, 1975, About 8:00 P.M.
Railway Station Dining Room

Is life a piss? Should I give it a try while waiting for my train to Aligarh? That the Stones' "Ride On, Baby" is blaring overhead is beyond me.

I arrived this morning from Kathmandu on Royal Nepal Airlines. Unlike the unreliable propellers of Colombia's Aerocondor (Flying Fish) airplanes, all four of the Royal Nepalese aircraft labored above the foothills and valleys of southern Nepal. Once more, I was able to stalk the majestic, whitewashed ranges of Nepal's northern tier and nostalgically relive the trials and conquests of the trek.

Looking to buy duty-free Johnny Walker Red and One-Horned Cigarettes purchased at TIA? A discreet Patna rickshaw driver who screamed, "Buy whiskey," certainly did. I doubled my money.

Yes, I have returned to phenomenal but disparate India. *"Vive la différence."* Since its recent emergence from the Middle Ages, Nepal appears virtually virginal and innocent when compared to the British-bastardized Hindu homeland. Delivered from ethereal mountain peace, I have been harshly thrust upon the Indo-Gangetic plain of disarray, disharmony, and discord.

Now this is what I'm talking about: the logistical nightmare I negotiated when purchasing my railway ticket and berth. The inquiry desk informed me I must first change trains in Varanasi (Benares) to reach Aligarh from Patna. Without alternative, I found the second-class ticket office, waited in a queue, and purchased a seat to Aligarh via Varanasi for ten rupees.

As I retrieved my backpack, I met the Swiss couple from the trek who had purchased tickets to Delhi via Aligarh leaving later this evening.

Ravi Raj and Locki Raj had told me that trains from Patna, to and from Delhi, stop in Aligarh. Puzzled and pissed, I returned to the inquiry desk and asked the same clerk if the Delhi train stops in Aligarh. His reply? "Yes!" Why he didn't first tell me there is a direct train to Aligarh is evidence of Indian mysticism found in every railway station—collectively, a veritable world unto itself. At any one moment, I have been told, more than *ten million people* travel on the railway network, not including millions more who make the railway stations, platforms and tracks their home.

So I returned to the second-class ticket office to buy an open ticket and overnight berth to Aligarh. Ticket yes. Berth no. Directed to a reservation window, I found a swirling mob of sweating, would-be travelers frantically pushing and shoving one another. Finally reaching the clerk, I was given a slip to fill out in triplicate and had to queue-up once again. One hour later, when the clerk asked, "Which train to Delhi do you want?" I had to return to the inquiry desk to find out the available times.

Now back at the berth reservation line, I patiently waited until finally being told there were no more sleazy berths available. Though hot and dirty, the berths are desirable, if only for relative comfort and safety. On most trains, a few are reserved for foreigners. If Indians do not offer bribes for what remains, they are automatically told, "All full."

Returning to the fucking inquiry desk, I learned that a second train to Delhi departs at 10:24 p.m. Still swearing to myself, I wasted another hour on another line before booking a berth for this train. Hours later, once calm, I had to laugh despite breathing in coal-fueled black smoke spouting from steam engines first used by the Union Pacific and Central Pacific when they first met in Utah in 1869.

Another reason to hassle for a private berth? During my first trip to Hindustan, I endured long nights in overcrowded cattle cars called third class and slept on luggage racks six inches from the ceiling, but above the fray below. *Never again.*

ॐ

Patna, India

Friday, November 28, 1975, 9:40 P.M.
Railway Station

Impatience compelled me to return to the inquiry desk to learn if the 10:24 p.m. Delhi train was on time. As I did, the scene before me resembled this afternoon's shouting and shoving match. In addition, four large, heavy black telephones set on a wooden slab of a desk in front of the inquiry officer kept ringing incessantly—more rapidly than could be answered. His comedic job became impossibly hilarious as eight to ten demanding Indians shouted in his face.

As the masses began to bed down for the night on platforms, in the main lobby, on the adjacent streets, and even on the floors and tables of the first-class waiting room, I bid all a pleasant *shubh ratri* (good night).

Gabhana Palace

Saturday, November 30, 1975, Evening

After twenty hours of rocking and rolling within northern India's railway labyrinth, I joined a frantic mob in Aligarh's bus station while Carlos Santana's "Black Magic Woman" blared on a transistor radio, a recent introduction to this part of India. Within moments of my arrival at Fort Gabhana Palace, the Raj Singhs and I were reminiscing, sipping chai, and stoning with the Nepalese Mustang (hashish) I had smuggled across the border.

A *s-t-o-n-e-d* rap. When I receive letters asking how this trip compares to my first, I tell my inquirers I prefer mescaline—actually, its second cousin, psilocybin. Psilocybin is much more physical and erotic.

A litany of personal weaknesses including laziness, insecurity and my surrender to subtle social pressures inevitably imposed their will upon my return home. My spiritual intensity subsided. I had required local reinforcement and support to practice my *Vedic* devotions. Perhaps I didn't look hard enough; perhaps I became too frail to continue yoga and meditation in diversionary, materialistic New York City. Perhaps I simply lost interest.

Vividly remembering how my perceptions of life at home changed over intervals of time—one month, six months, one year, two years—I no longer question the homecoming experience, a debated topic of heated conversation among those on the open-ended road. I want to think I had (and have) become more of an individual and less of a follower. Sometimes.

So why did I fly direct from New York to Delhi this time? To bypass the arduous, blistering, desert-bound overland journey from Istanbul to Teheran to Kabul to Rawalpindi to Calcutta. Now having reached India healthy and energized, I hope to eventually explore the Orient, frowned upon by most treading on the IHT.

My dissenting expression regarding the destructive, dehumanizing influences of groups, societies and like institutions upon human individuality? "Fuck 'em." Invariably, their leaders' hidden agendas promote self-serving indulgences at the expense of their members.

Is it essential that the policies and goals these institutions espouse be examined and appreciated separately from those who materially benefit from them? Duh! Great ideas live thousands of years longer than their advocates, who are too often needy and greedy souls who pathologically attach themselves to them. Those who compose the leadership of such groups selfishly abuse and alter their central themes and original reason to be. *Hypocrisy reigns.*

Examples? Look no further than one of the world's great religious movements. Catholicism has become a diluted, dispirited representation of the pure teachings of Jesus. How many gay Roman Catholic cardinals, bishops and priests preach the purity of heterosexual marriage while sexually abusing choir boys? To speak even indirectly with God, good Catholics no can do. They need a confessional broker.

Locki Raj's complaint? Fundamental, unadulterated Hinduism has long been whitewashed by a Brahman priesthood that profitably interpreted *The Bhagavad Gita*, the Hindu *Torah*. Without doubt, Hinduism is widely diverse and tolerant, and so is the Indian clergy. You can bank on it. The priests do. Buddhism? Judaism? Islam? Christianity? Why does each accommodate a rigid fundamentalist sect? To reveal the transgressions of "faithful believers" whom they deem to have become infidels gone astray. Hence, the evolution of Truth Squads.

I am of the persuasion that all the great mystical personages—Buddha, Krishna, Mohammed, Jesus, Moses, and others—were spiritually enlightened ("realized") beings who practiced stringent forms of internal and external discipline. My fellow theorists profess that they were all one and the same spirit taking on different forms, speaking different languages, eating different foods, and living at different times, but preaching the same message—*love*. Some even include Mahatma Gandhi in this group, perhaps the only Christ-like "realized" figure of the twentieth century. Advocates of this theory hold that existing divergent forces and karmic dynamics found on the face of the earth during each epoch to be responsible for the appearance of these great, divinely inspired theosophists.

Abraham Maslow, the Big Bad Daddy of humanistic psychology, in *Toward a Psychology of Being* and *Religions, Values, and Peak-Experiences,* theorizes that the original mystical visions vibrationally imparted to these spiritually supersensitive Enlightened Ones were deleteriously translated into structured religions, each specifying rules, regulations and brokers (priesthoods, ministries, rabbinates) by the worldly *organization man*— who must be cautiously viewed with great suspicion—for he is the former of groups and abuser of ideas, usually to his own advantage.

Aided by continuous invasions of India by the Muslims and their Mughal cousins, organization men have decimated Hinduism. I was a romantic fool to expect to find a peaceful meditative society and philosophy mirrored by contemporary Indians. The study of the nature and aim of humankind—its source, being, and consciousness—is no longer a pursuit of the masses, but rather a practice found among exceedingly few genuine sadhus, priests, and gurus, most of whom have renounced the physical-material world for hermetic life in the jungles and northern mountains. Those few who venture out to teach do so for karmic reasons. Shri Bal Yogi Prem Varni is one of these men.

Wide spectra of political and meditative societies have also managed to couch themselves, cleverly and profitably, in altruism. Check out the United Nations. Find any peace in Southeast Asia? In Africa? In the Middle East? In South America? In Central America?

Some years ago, while practicing Transcendental Meditation (TM), I consciously chose not to associate myself with their self-absorbed leaders and members tied to the money and power trips of the International Meditation Society (IMS). However, I did not condemn their meditative techniques. Although the IMS removed meditation from its Vedic (Indian, Hindu) context, and wrapped its peaceful and relaxing benefits into a commercial and "scientific" package marketed to neurotic, spiritually bankrupt Western societies that crave panacea, why did they throw out the baby with the bathwater?

Does anyone buy a refrigerator because it looks attractive, is the right color, but not plug it in? Not once did the IMS mention Indian meditative philosophy, spiritual liberation, and higher consciousness. Hey, *the truth doesn't sell.* Instead, TM is primarily marketed to increase financial profits while paying lip service to eliminating neurosis. Advertisements remind members to watch Maharishi Mahesh Yogi on television. The IMS missed its karmic calling—selling used Gitas. Gives Steppenwolf's "The Pusher" new meaning!

Am I to be considered a purist for the stance I have adopted toward TM? Perhaps. Do I give a shit? Fuck no! Although most Westerners would run from it were it not veiled in tantalizing terms promising instant solution, is not introducing it with half-truths both deceptive and ambiguous? And responsible for the high dropout rate?

As for governments, do they maintain the will and allocate enough resources and tools to improve society, their questionably stated goal? Come on. Conversely, when one citizen or small group of individuals helps one another, positive energy is created. Work on this micro level, as opposed to the macro, is the only work that can realistically be considered an agent of positive change.

Gabhana, India
Sunday, December 1, 1975

Under a toasty sun after a delightful soaking of hot water from a communal bucket on a tiled veranda, the Raj Singhs and I were serenaded by *Another Side of Bob Dylan*. Seems Bob just wants to be friends with us.

Familiar with his genius, Ravi Raj defines Dylan as a "twentieth-century messenger, a prophet of the gospel."

Late Sunday Night

Sholay, India's hottest motion picture, features an outrageous band of outlaws, in-laws, heroines, and super cops, all of whom sing, dance, hold hands, and seem effeminate. I am told such musicals attract millions of illiterate rickshaw drivers and peasants. Locki Raj feels the plot is realistic: Indian gangs utilize Land Rovers and machine guns to ambush trains—including the one I took to the Indian-Nepalese frontier in 1972.

Madras, South India
Thursday, December 4, 1975

After rising at 5:00 a.m., Locki Raj, Ravi Raj, and Gunda and Kerala put me on a bus to Delhi via Aligarh while extending an open invitation for me to return.

In Delhi, I obtained a student concession and reservation from the *same* office for the 16UPGTE Express to Madras. Distance? Fourteen hundred miles. Duration? Forty hours. Cost? $4. Saved thirty-five rupees ($3.50) with the concession. Somehow, my reservation miraculously materialized from an HO quota (headquarters or emergency), intentionally set aside for the privileged of Indian society. The British Raj lives!

Stall number sixty-four of Delhi's Shankar Market, home of the Piccadilly Circus Bookstore, advertised *Cutting Through Spiritual Materialism* and the *Upanishads*. Excitedly waiting to board my train, I recalled Locki Raj's counsel: "South India is radically different, held together by similar but purer strains of Hinduism. Most foreign invaders ignored the South."

Often confused, the *Upanishads* are encompassed within the *Vedas*. Both are revered fundamental ancient Sanskrit texts revealing Hindu theology. The Cliff Notes version? Primarily and ultimately formless, Godhead (the originator of all things) and our internal souls are one and the same.

Juan Mascaro, a Spanish academic best known for his English translation of *The Bhagavad Gita*, tells us about the *Upanishads*:

Revelations of the *Upanishads* is quite definite: Atman, the mystery of our life, the light of our soul, the love which is the source of infinite joy, the vision of the good and the beautiful which is the source of everything beautiful or good that man can create upon the earth, is something which is above reason and therefore can never be attained by reason alone.

More Indian mystique. Finding change of a one-rupee note (nine cents). How do vendors in railway stations, on trains, and on the streets expect to do business without making change? No problem. The majority merely place the onus on the customer while chanting "no change." However, upon closer scrutiny, I solved another layer of the Indian enigma. Most customers allow the shopkeepers to keep the change. If I refuse to buy the product because they won't make change, a concealed stash suddenly appears. Why bother over nine measly cents? The more money I save, the longer I can travel.

Payoffs. Don't want to wait months for the installation of electricity? Tired of standing in second-class on Indian trains? Try offering baksheesh (a tip or bribe).

Law and order. Fear of reprisals have created a dearth of witnesses for prosecution of most crimes. Due to the declared Emergency, they are no longer necessary. Four days ago, five notorious *dacoits* (mobsters) were gunned down by the GPD (Gabhana Police Department).

Madras, India
December 5, 1975, 12:00 Noon
Concession Office of the Southern Railway Train Station

In Agra, during our first stop, a wealthy, Western-suited Indian gentleman boarded. Upon learning he had spent six years studying petroleum engineering in Tulsa, I offered my ignorance of Oklahoma. When I learned he was on his way to Los Angeles and New York City, I offered my knife.

Surely supervised by camouflaged Italian *madres* shouting "*mange, mange*," dining car waiters wearing spotless, summery white sport coats—kidnapped from the Italian Riviera while serving Cinzano—served three vegetarian meals a day: omelets, rice, puri, dhal (lentils), and fried hors d'oeuvres including vegetable croquettes with cocktail sauce. Supposedly herbivorous, an awful lot of Hindus ate an awful lot of meat they had stashed in tins brought from home.

Also equipped with two first-class carriages sporting air-conditioned WCs and shiny white porcelain squatter urinals—permitting comfortable smokes prior to crimson sunsets—the train also accommodated those "passengers" who chose not to buy a ticket and occupy its roof.

Madras, India
December 6, 1975, 7:30 A.M.
Malaysia Lodge, Armenian Street

Due south, we passed Nagjui, Jansi and Wardha, the last being the home of Gandhiji's nonviolent community. ("Ji" is a Hindi honorific conveying respect.) In Itarsi's petite railway station housing the hungry and infirm, I noticed a sign in English: "Ticketless Travel is a Social Evil." They must be kidding!

In *Return to the Source*, Lanza del Vasto, the Italian philosopher and poet, recounts his personal search and pilgrimage for spiritual purity. Led to central India in 1936, to Wardha, he lived for three months with Gandhi at the Mahatma's commune where he was renamed Shantidas, Servant of Peace. He recounts their meeting:

> In the doorway under the slope of the thatched roof, a little half-naked old man is seated on the ground. It's he!
>
> He waves to me—yes to me!—makes me sit down beside him and smiles to me. He speaks—and speaks of nothing else but me—asking me who I am, what I do and what I want. . . .
>
> He walks with a very lively step along the sandy path, carrying a long bamboo stick. His bare head is shaven, he is naked to the waist and wears no holy cordon, his legs are bare and his loincloth is tucked up between them.
>
> That was more or less how he was dressed when he entered Buckingham Palace to shake hands with the late King of England. . . .

124. Not an uncommon sight throughout India.

His skin is the colour of old ivory. To tell the truth, he is far from handsome. His shaven skull has great wings of ears, his nose dips over his toothless mouth and sometimes, when he ponders, his lower lip hangs down over his short chin; but there is something touching in his ugliness, rather like that of the newly born child when it opens its mouth wider than its whole face. . . .

Every statement he makes is illuminated by different approaches to the same point, so that the humblest intelligence has access to it and the keenest is riveted. Not even the most trifling detail is beneath his dignity, just as in his eyes every man has his worth and nothing is without its importance. . . .

He refuses to touch any food that the Indian peasant—the poorest and worst-fed on earth—could not afford, nor will he give any such food to his guests. But by a careful combination of the same ingredients and quantities, he composes healthy, nourishing meals which he tries out on his own household before introducing them first in his schools then in the thousands of villages run by his disciples. This ascetic who is known the world over for his fasts shows, of all men I have known, the most concern for the health and well-being of others. . . .

The hot hours go by. People keep entering or leaving his room through the doorless doorway. He goes through his papers, dictates letters, and gives advice to those who have come to seek it. . . .

When work is done and care put away, the Mahatma makes a sign, and his flat, fiddle-like spinning-wheel is brought to him. And until night falls, he draws from it an even, strong thread, while the sound of the wheel nurses thought.

Observations from the train. The countryside had radically changed. Via tunnels and bridges, we passed through forests and over the Central Ghats (mountains). Nearing Madras, the monsoonal rains of November and early December had flooded semitropical terrain. Partially submerged under still waters were moist and muddied stems of graceful palmyra palms, thousands of acres of rice paddies, and the lower portions of telephone and electrical poles.

Telugu, Tamil, Malayalam, and Hindi are spoken by most inhabitants of Tamil Nadu (state) and Madras, population 2.5 million. Not infrequently heard, English often provides their only common language.

When viewed as a vast conglomeration of races, languages, religions, foods, dress, customs, cultures and conflicting loyalties, the Indian nation epitomizes everything the homogenous northern European nations are not. Maintaining *fourteen* official languages, including English, and more than five hundred dialects, even differentiated America seems somewhat uniform in comparison.

Particularly noteworthy are changes in skin color, clothing, and fashion. Southern Indian women wear a great deal of nasal jewelry and bright-yellow, orange, and red saris commonly wrapped around the waist, with the loose ends worn over the shoulder revealing washboard abs, extremely dark-skinned shoulders, and Caucasian (rather than Negroid) facial features.

Fried puri, usually served with hot vegetables and chutney on a dried palm leaf and found predominantly in the North and always in railway stations, is rarely consumed in the South. Still tired of Nepalese rice and subje, I've yet to try the traditional rice-curry meal sold in all restaurants.

Most hotels and cafés employ a peculiar variety of English signs: "Rama Krishna Lunch Home," "Lodging and Meals Hotel," "Meals Section," "Meals

Ready." Because I prefer to frequent the plentiful sidewalk snack stalls and wagons rather than sit down for restaurant meals, I have had to tighten my belt to keep up my pants.

At the start of any extended trip, weight loss can be somewhat drastic. Increased activity and unfamiliar diet quickly lead to shedding unnecessary pounds. After two to three months, most body fat disappears. New edibles are either assimilated or rejected by means of explosive elimination.

In an unnamed village near Madras, I was overcome by the poverty around me. Toddler boys and girls begged as though playing a game. They weren't. In fact, every night in Madras, like Calcutta, the streets are littered with the homeless. So many bedraggled beggars. Tens of thousands sleep on public pavement—with and without families—with and without possessions. Emaciated women and children barely subsist on United Nations' donated rice, resting on rags and cardboard, often joined by rickshaw drivers who literally eat, sleep, live, and die on and under their beasts of burden.

Call me callous. Call me insensitive. It took only four days in Madras to become disgusted by obnoxious rickshaw men who lend no mercy when ringing their ice cream bells on every corner. Bothersome and impetuous, irritating, and parasitic, they view travelers, as do many Indians in the tourist industry, as rupee machines, perhaps the only machines to which these simple folks can relate.

Jolted out of my berth while still two hours north of Madras, I viewed Gudur covered by a refreshingly cool sheet of steel-gray clouds. The temperature had radically changed; now ranging from midday 80s to low 70s during evenings.

No doubt, New York City offers infinite diversions from the discovery of Self. Madras offers the Kalaiarangam Theater featuring Laurel and Hardy in *Block-Heads*. Throughout the city, beyond the silks and saris, is a prevalent motion picture industry complete with outrageously colorful billboards equivalent to those adorning Sunset Strip in Los Angeles. Below one of them, on Madras Street, Chidambaram Nataraja Temple is dedicated to Nataraja—the Divine Dancer, the twirling goddess of multiple limbs.

A tangential thought: All about India, people view statues that have come to be treated as Gods. Although Hinduism adheres to one all-pervading spirit, this unity of one physically manifests itself in infinite ways.

Thus, Hindu mythology includes "gods" of land, sea, sun, moon, sky, fire, cosmetics, perfume, hairspray, and so on. Not idols, the statues represent spiritual oneness. But the story is not that simple. What I have portrayed thus far is the way it is supposed to be.

Considered the father of contemporary humanistic psychology, our good friend, Big Bad Daddy Abraham Maslow, is back, still depicting his "organization man" as the guilty party who operationalized original, divine, mystical/religious vibrations and visions. How? By inventing rules, regulations, holidays, ceremonies, figurines, and other concrete representations that historically appealed to simple, uneducated people—to those who did not easily abstract. Centuries of abuse have led these statues and symbols to become godlike—and are worshiped as such—a total departure from original monotheistic Hinduism.

After tolerating excruciating bus breakdowns for sixty kilometers from Madras, I visited Mahabalipuram, home to exquisite stone temple architecture of the Pallava kings of the sixth to eighth centuries. The Five Rathas and Shore Temple, set upon the beach, bless the Indian Ocean. Such beaches are part of a palm tree paradise that extends far north and south of Madras.

125. Divine floods submerged most of Mahabilipuram when the Gods grew jealous of its elegant monuments and temples, according to local mythology. Undaunted, the masses are drawn to this site each winter to attend a monthlong dance festival.

Before leaving Madras earlier that morning, I began to feel congested. Big Indian cities suck. And so I am scheduled to leave later this evening for Tiruchirappalli (India). Will fly to Jaffna, Sri Lanka, if tomorrow morning's train is not more than three hours late. During November and December, monsoonal turbulence prohibits maritime travel.

The Indian visa stamped into my passport reads:

00588

Tourist Visa

Date of issue: July 17, 1975

Date of expiry: January 16, 1976

Good for three (3) journeys if passport remains valid.

Period of stay in India.

Three (3) months from the date of entry into India.

If I have interpreted correctly, I have three months from the date I entered India. Since I entered India on October 12, I must leave by January 12. Right? Wrong.

Explaining to Indian Immigration that in one month, when my visa expired, I would not be near said office, I politely requested my visa be extended. A young woman examined my passport, added up the days I had thus far spent in India (eighteen), and asked me why I wanted a visa extension when I still had seventy-two days left. Disagreeing with my reasoning, she told me I had three months to spend *in* India, suggested I ignore the wording of my visa, and refused my request for a written statement to this effect. "This is standard policy for the entire country," she growled. Knowing India, I suspect that when I really do need to extend my visa, the likelihood is that it will be interpreted in a *different* way. Time will tell.

Praise Mother Shiva. I am physically alone, sequestered in an eight-rupee hotel room with attached shower and toilet that doesn't flush. I know no one in Madras. The hotel and city are not conducive to meeting people. Silver lining? Not having to compromise myself—a freedom of sorts.

More travel Tao. "Familiar" with procedures for travel by night berth on second-class trains, I walked to Madras' Egmore Railway Station, entered the Office of the Chief Commercial Officer of the Southern Railways to receive a student concession, and completed the business at hand while allowing ample time to reach the airport for my flight to Jaffna.

Night school. Queens College, 1966. Peer pressure to see Sergio Leone's Italian spaghetti Western starring Clint Eastwood, Eli Wallach, and Lee Van Cleef—*The Good, the Bad, and the Ugly*.

> Would Jim Morrison go to class?
> Would Jimi Hendrix go to class?
> —Fast Ed

Now playing at the Casino Theatre on Malaysia Road and Mount Street is Jeff Bridges in *The Last American Hero*. Idling chains of buses billowing blue exhaust did not move until ticket takers ensured that every member of the faithful had paid their due. Though I reached the movie in time, I had to rush my smoke in the WC. So did two other guys. No peer pressure.

Progress? The buses in Madras lack windows. Canvas flaps protect against rain and sun. Despite them, I can see prolific ads for television programs. In 1972, I saw none.

126. Madras street life.

More India mystique. Most I meet would rather give misguided information than admit they do not know, and repeatedly teach me that there is no free lunch. If someone directs me to a mosque, hotel, temple, or urinal, or provides any inconsequential service, whether solicited or not, baksheesh, usually a few rupees, is demanded.

One of the finest chai stalls in all of India serves its specialty piping hot and foaming, aerated when poured between two metal cups held two to three feet apart. A talent to behold. The friendly owners cook and clean all day and night. A single rupee nets two cups of steaming chai and hot buttered rolls. Residual result? If lucky, the shits. Unlucky? Dysentery.

127. A Madras greasy spoon.

Blown-up headlines seen in *The Hindu* remind me of London's tabloids. A legacy of the British occupation, such flavor can also be tasted in local architecture, traffic patterns, accents, bookstores—and greasy *samosa* (deep fried pastry filled with potato and peas) and chai stalls.

Less tasty are incessant advertisements smacking of class distinction that accentuate India's tendency toward the straight and narrow. Perhaps they could be taken seriously if economic conditions permitted most to have a real need for banks, cars, perfumes, vacations, cleaning detergents, and televisions.

Time to get down with street posters reflecting Emergency. On black marketers:

VOLUNTARY DISCLOSURE SCHEME FOR
UNDISCLOSED INCOME AND WEALTH
NO PENALTY
NO PROSECUTION
REASONABLE RATES
EXPIRES DEC. 31, 1975

How about:

ECONOMIC OFFENSES BRING STERN PUNISHMENT
HELP CONSOLIDATE THE 100 NEW GAINS OF EMERGENCY
SUPPORT THE 20 POINT ECONOMIC PROGRAM

And one found in most railway stations:

ADDRESS ALL GRIEVANCES TO THE STATIONMASTER

Really? When my path is partially obstructed by malnourished, blind, and disfigured souls, many using canes for ambulation or sleeping on station platforms, need I continue?

As I begin to crash from the heights of my blissful Himalayan afterglow, writing is becoming a greater part of my natural flow. Not so for my Kodak Instamatic. I do not want to play the role of the affluent, arrogant, condescending sahib, a role that does not appear to bother most Nikon-toting Westerners. Perhaps I am too sensitive. Perhaps I am not sensitive enough. Not a question of right or wrong; it's just the way I feel.

Hikkaduwa, Sri Lanka
Thursday, December 11, 1975

At 6:50 a.m., the Indian airport at Tiruchirappalli provided quiet isolation and nap time. Jolted awake by the janitor, I passed through customs, met Madonna, noted two propellers of questionable character, and boarded Air Ceylon.

What are people most generous giving to others? Advice. Want some

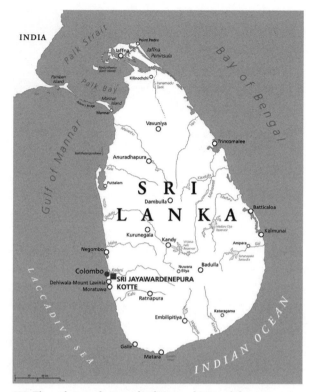

128. Three thousand years of indigenous history did not prevent European (Portuguese, Dutch, and British) scoundrels from exploiting what was once called "Ceylon," known today as the Democratic Socialist Republic of Sri Lanka or "Resplendent Island" in Sanskrit. More "white man's burden" bullshit.

unsolicited advice? Avoid Jaffna Town, down and out, decrepit, and empty with little to offer. Couldn't even find a burnt, greasy puri. Beyond it were views of bountiful palm and fruit trees—and luscious Madonna—as seen from the confines of our "retiring room" (hotel) above Jaffna's railway station. Sri Lanka, formerly Ceylon, thus far, appears poor and simple in relation to India.

When told the next morning's 6:30 a.m. train would be crowded, railway officials assured us we could reserve and purchase third-class tickets for forty rupees each (twelve Sri Lankan rupees to the US dollar). At 5:00 a.m., I was duly informed that there were no third-class reserved seats! As for Madonna, think Doris Troy's "Just One Look." Oh, my fucking loins!

129. Handwritten notes.

For the first two hours on the train, we perched our bags and butts on the floor before squeezing onto equally uncomfortable wooden benches. Though humid, hot, and sticky during the eight-hour journey, we took opportunities to view a rather large chunk of the northern part of the island, including several sparsely settled towns and villages, including Anuradhapura and its tall, monumental Buddhist stupa of whitewashed stone.

Breakfast? Try moist shelled peanuts and cold, rock-hard ears of corn on the cob. No hot nutritional food, but no hordes of beggars. Where was the pleasant, relatively affluent society I had expected to find?

No matter, Sri Lanka became a striking tropical paradise of palm trees, lagoons, tea and rubber plantations, and jeweled beaches meeting jade-green mountains—not exactly Jones Beach State Park on the south shore of Long Island. We soon pulled into Colombo's railroad station, collected our belongings, and headed to the Horton Street Youth Hostel where we were welcomed by booming rhythm and blues, "96 Tears" (Question Mark and the Mysterians), and too many Australians.

The Fort, Colombo's central business district, is a surprisingly clean and modern commercial center boasting elegant hotels and movie theatres featuring *Patton* and *Jesus Christ Superstar.* Enormous shops, restaurants, and wide avenues and boulevards starkly contrast Pettah Bazaar, the hectic souk just down from the railway station.

A wide variety of cafés and whiskey bars—and women for forty rupees—cannot be avoided. Needing little encouragement, I spent the evening in a tavern making friends with a merry group of well-dressed Sinhalese who sang, banged on tables, and generally carried on as most happily drunk people do. Ragged snake charmers dancing and their writhing serpents etched a different impression. But having had my fill of the big city, I hopped on a bus transport to Hikkaduwa, the paradisical beach community in which I am now living.

Bus stop Tao. At every stop, passengers are set upon by a provincial host of maniacal street hawkers selling coconuts, shrimp, and sweets while nasally chanting *"eladay"* (ice cream) and *"pelaki"* (fish). When our bursting bus approached one of many Buddhist monasteries, no one was permitted to board. Unheard of in India!

We passed a good number of old Christian churches and Catholic schools. Though predominantly Buddhist, reflecting the southern school of Buddhism as opposed to Tibet's northern school (don't ask), many Ceylonese were converted from heathenism to Christianity by the colonial Dutch and Portuguese. Nevertheless, men who walk to church on Sunday mornings are known to appreciate the healthy, well-tanned legs and thighs of the fairer sex wearing popular miniskirts.

Less stimulating are the bright, orange-robed Buddhist monks, many in their late teens. Though Buddhism is constitutionally sanctioned in Jaffna and the north where Hinduism is prevalent and South Indian Tamil is spoken, recent rumblings of racial and religious discontent have been heard.

Before Ceylon became Sri Lanka in 1972, the island was considered economically prosperous. No longer. Mrs. Sirimavo Bandaranaike, the current prime minister, has imposed a somewhat integrated socialist system that lacks the hard currency on which her bankrupt guarantees are based.

Tea remains Sri Lanka's chief export, satisfying approximately one-third of the world's demand. Primo grades are grown above 4,000 feet. When tea is served in local, once-numerous milk bars, you are given chutney to chew—in place of impossibly expensive sugar. Why so expensive? The importation of most raw materials and all manufactured goods has been banned by the current dictatorship.

Case in point: A pound of sugar that cost three-quarters of one rupee five years ago now costs seven rupees. Mrs. Bandaranaike, ignoring pragmatism, believes that only Sinhalese sugar, among other indigenous commodities and wares, must be consumed regardless of harm to growing children. Most milk bars in Sri Lanka were shuttered many years ago. Seems no can do without milk, which is now more dear than sugar. So is petrol. *Cold-hearted bitch.*

Pink House, my highly touted abode in Hikkaduwa, owned and operated by the devoutly Christian Martin family, is meeting all my needs. Son Benedict is about to leave for work in Oman.

Madonna, with whom I have spent most of the three previous days and nights, and who has traveled about Asia for some years, did not accompany me to Hikkaduwa. A travel-hardened and well-defended siren, she prefers to impress with stories of rich engineers she seduced in Delhi, and of the family who saved her life. The fabulous Miss M stereotypes homebound Americans as being of one mind and looks down on many of the young travelers she meets. Do I see in her my reflection? Although glad she didn't accompany me to Hikkaduwa, I sure miss that wanton walk, racy rack, and those luscious lips.

Before dusk, I showered, smoked, watched the sun set into the sea, and inhaled one of the finest meals I have enjoyed since arriving in Asia: wok-fried noodles and vegetables, steamed rice, green beans and carrots, French fried potatoes, *roti* (flat bread), sliced eggplant, stewed potatoes, tea, and a freshly picked fruit-salad dessert, all for sixty-five cents US. Little did I know my meal was prelude to a hot, sticky, itchy, sleepless, and torturous night spent under a worthless mosquito net. By midnight, I wanted to cry. Socks, long-sleeved pajamas, and wrapped hands proved useless. I woke to multi-sized punctures and sweaty, bloody scratch marks all over my body.

In Hikkaduwa, the ratio of Australians to others approaches nine to one. Most are of the macho, beer-drinking variety—apathetic souls with an unrecognized penchant for "isms"—fascism, racism, and sexism A dissenting sensitive few believe the disposition and behavior of the majority parallel the Australian government's racist "preventive apartheid" immigration policy. Having arrived via Thailand, Indonesia, and Malaysia, many "mates" carry surfboards and literally follow the sun. So do many healthy, gorgeous, young, blonde, and athletic "Sheilas" (women), whose politics would never be my concern. Think Neil Young's "Cowgirl in the Sand."

In reality, "idyllic Hikkaduwa" is becoming less so. Although Sri Lanka is considered an untouched paradise by swarms of jet-setters, I have come too far to hang with snobbish Germans, French and Scandinavians. And so, at dawn, with my pack on my back, I sauntered down a palm-shaded beach to an eight-rupee room located within Mica Villa, a large old mansion that houses freaks and vegetarians.

On this flawless day, trees are casting shadows upon the foaming surf. Blue-and-white waves crest and break against magnificent coral forming majestic ten-footers on which mostly naked "mates" and "Sheilas" surf. Snorkeling is fantastic. For twenty miles to the south there is nothing but deserted beach.

All about my primitive, open-air shower stall are palm trees, coconuts, verdant lusciousness and those magnificent cresting waves. Behind me? A well into which I lowered a bucket attached to a rope. Adam seeks Eve!

Rays of sun are dying. Dinner is simmering. I retire to my room for a smoke and walk along Hikkaduwa's orange sunset-lit beach. Ocean breezes caress my batik sarong.

130. Hikkaduwa sunset.

Hikkaduwa, Sri Lanka
Friday, December 12, 1975, 7:30 P.M.

"Oh, what a beautiful day" has preceded yet another immaculate seaside sunset. Magenta and pink hues are faintly interrupted by the black bodies of Sinhalese women and children, their perspiration glistening under the reflection of the dimming sun.

While hanging out on the quaint colonial porch with Eric, the "boss man," I learned he opened his home to young people only two years ago. Realizing that Hikkaduwa is no more a simple village of few houses and trawlers, my landlord bellowed: "Tourist money is the compromising culprit." Yet he is about to invest eight thousand dollars to install a modern shower. *Paradise lost.*

Nostalgic reflections on the Hindustani railway network: Imagine a slippery serpent slithering into a befouled, pandemoniac station, each feeding each other, a metaphoric codependency. Peddlers, beggars, passengers, and porters *everywhere*. A genuinely outrageous, unique, and intense phenomenon. A universe unto itself. The most surprising part of all is that the chaos, queues, and bureaucracy actually do work, the trains being the cheapest and best form of Indian transportation—despite my aggravation and whining.

When you step into any Indian railway station, you enter a vast realm; another separate reality consisting of kaleidoscopic passengers, first- and second-class waiting rooms, reservation halls, puri kiosks, restaurants, retiring rooms, suggestion boxes, nasal chants ("chaiiiii"), bookstores, beggars, and red-coated porters. And contrary to collective criticism, including my own, most trains actually do run according to schedule. Quite frankly, I have come to love this singular Indian experience, one that starkly contrasts the undeniable discomfort of third-class Ceylonese box cars.

Although the Hindustani link of the IHT encompasses northern India—Amritsar, Bombay, Delhi, Dharamshala, Agra, Benares, Gaya, Sarnath, and Calcutta—it does not substantially venture south. The same is also true in Iran, where pilgrims who wish to unravel the mysticism of the East and make great haste to reach Kabul and Afghan hashish, Delhi, and Kathmandu, quickly exit Teheran and neglect to visit the southern palace and mosque-laden treasure cities of Isfahan and Shiraz. Consequently, it is mostly those who return to India who come to experience Madras, Cape Comorin, Kerala, and Sri Lanka, and escape the IHT's "Desolation Row."

Hikkaduwa, Sri Lanka
Saturday, December 13, 1975, Morning

Laid back Saturday morning musings. Sir Edmund Hillary describes the first successful climb of Mount Everest (1953) in *High Adventure*. An ironic coincidence found in the Hikkaduwa Public Library? Fuck no!

Sri Lanka calls forth images of island life in the 1930s: old black cars with running boards and silver grills, laid-back lifestyles on large haciendas without electricity, and fishermen in old, creaky catamarans. Homes erected on stilts along the shore give no hint of 1975.

Friendly and innocent, men, women, and children vibrate an indescribable but elegant approachability. Not too shy—but not too bold. Whether on the beach or in the jungle, exuberant Sri Lankans want to peer at this strange sahib. Private moments are not to be found. But unlike the Indians, the Sinhalese are not trying to rip the skin, forget about the shirt, off my back.

Only one mosquito caused last night's havoc. Exposed parts of my body reveal trench warfare. A variation thereof also takes place on the floor of my room. Without exception, each morning I find hundreds of swarming ants determined to overcome Goliath, a bee-like insect. "Soldiers" slowly surround it, climb over it, engulf it, and eat it. The bee crawls about one inch per hour until there is no more left of it.

Flies, perhaps imported from the deserts of North Africa and the Middle East, are everywhere, quick as lightning, very bothersome, and often worse than the malaria-laden mosquitoes. Resident milk cows appear helpless.

Ocean waves—incredibly beautiful, loud, strong, and numerous. Four simultaneous series of breakers eternally scrub virgin sands while carrying scores of surfers. Each become shattering, thunderous crescendos. Blue, green, turquoise, and teal motifs morph into white foam and mist. After initially cresting, each wave continues toward the shore, crashing twice more before making its final approach. With great anticipation, the waves lift their collective heads, patiently wait to the last possible moment, and finally explode against the beach. The repeating process allows you to witness all stages at once.

The beauty of the rich, oxygenated ocean also supports spectacular fishing, harvested by nets found on wooden catamarans. Four rupees buys a succulent fried tuna dinner. No middleman.

Several hundred meters inland, overgrown by the jungle and infested by snakes, an abandoned railroad track runs parallel with the beach. Its tunnels and trestles duplicate images from *The Bridge on the River Kwai* (1957), starring William Holden and Alec Guinness. I highly doubt they attended a nearby Buddhist stupa, one of many punctuating the island.

Too many tourist shops in Hikkaduwa cater to too many nauseating tour groups on two-and three-week package deals from Norway, Sweden, Germany, France, and England. Batiks, gems, and painted wooden masks help them kill time.

131. One of the many stupas on Sri Lanka.

Each morning I nurse milk-chai without sugar at a small seaside café that offers roasted roti served with occasional solitude. But breaking roti with me this day was the owner of one of these tourist traps. We soon put business aside and made plans to visit Galle on the country's southwest coast.

Leaving his car and dear petrol at work, Mr. N. Weerashingghe and I took a bus to the Galle Fort, first built by the Portuguese in 1588, and fortified by the Dutch after driving off the Portuguese in 1649. At the Galle Board of Education, while my mellow mentor was meeting with an old friend for tea, I acknowledged similarities to 65 Court Street in Brooklyn, home of the New York City Board of Education, where most administrators do absolutely fucking nothing.

Most noticeable in Galle's terribly vile and busy fruit, vegetable, meat, and fish markets were advertisements for *Olga and the Sex Revolution*. My new Ceylonese *nanpar* (friend) believes the film has been showing for the past six months.

132. Where do I buy tickets?

133. Galle municipal parking.

134 and 135. Mr. N. Weerashingghe and the Galle markets.

While complaining about the increasing worthlessness of the inflated currency, Mr. N. W. purchased a bunch of *valaippalam* (bananas) he had plucked from a pile of delightful, fresh-cut fruit located next to a pile of delightful and fragrant freshly deposited dung. They were quickly washed under a rare street-side tap. Moments later, when I tried to buy bananas from the very same vendor, prices jumped 500 percent!

136. The Weerashingghe family.

Hungry and hot, we caught a local bus inland where, at his home, I met Mr. N. W.'s three-year-old son, twenty-eight-year-old wife, and a host of in-laws, aunts, uncles, and cousins. Heaped on a well-dressed table were generous mounds of roti, dhal, rice, carrots, and tropical fruits which the women served—but they did not eat until the men were finished.

During dessert picked from their garden grove, valued photo albums were proudly presented, each containing faded, brownish wedding pictures that appeared remarkably similar to the vogue in place at the time my parents were married (1947). Offered upon our departure were spontaneous choruses of "*ayubowan*" (pronounced "I you bo won"), a lovely valediction conveying "May you live a long life."

On the way to Mr. N. W.'s factories, we stopped in the modern home of his older brother, an abode equipped with electricity, lights, ceiling fans, and a refrigerator from which we selected and enjoyed bottles of carbonated passion juice manufactured by Elephant House.

Finally, in thick jungle, we entered a crude shed where crusty old black men were molding ivory into animalistic shapes based on nothing more than their imagination. A second primitive shed contained machinery for the extraction of gold. Deep within the bowels of unchartered Ceylonese caves are veins of topaz and like gems, all given professional presentation in the Hikkaduwa Jewel Garden.

Returning to town after a warm and wonderful day, I passed a new Buddhist monastery where, in its courtyard, twenty robed monks sat on floor cushions. An array of attendants were about to serve dinner.

Kandy, Sri Lanka
Wednesday, December 17, 1975

The sun is on strike. Blue sky is rarely seen this time of year above Kandy, when the all-consuming monsoon makes its presence known to all.

The charming Grande Dame of Kandy and wife of Kandy's chief of police, Mrs. Herath, owns and operates the Traveler's Nest, one of many bed-and-breakfasts found within the warm and inviting homes of engaging local families. If desired, Western food is served.

Moist rain forests and a half-dozen fleeting tropical downpours introduced me to Kandy's cool climate, lush upland jungles, imposing white-and-gray layers of monsoonal clouds, and medicinal mist that soothed my weather-beaten skin. And praise Lord Buddha. Last night, no mosquitoes.

As I recline on the comfy veranda of this sprawling ranch, I survey sloping rice terraces below palm and banana trees. Save the sounds of bathing elephants and the courting singsongs of blackbirds, only the mantras of insects disturb these precious moments of unadulterated Sinhalese serenity.

Three white-robed men banged out a Moorish drumbeat while a fourth played a whiny Arabic-sounding flute. Intricate tiles and ornate gold statues of the Buddha, Siddhartha Gautama, filled Sri Dalada Maligawa, the Temple of the Tooth. I was ushered into the inner sanctum where the Buddha's tooth lies. The chamber was guarded by four monks who make sure the toothless faithful do not abscond with the holy molar.

An older, thick-walled monastery houses a statue of the Buddha sitting in the full-lotus position. Reclining postures symbolize Gautama's need to rest. Escorted by a young monk whose prominent family decided his reclusive fate thirteen years ago, I learned my new friend has not yet transcended his ego or visited nirvana. However, perhaps he has shoplifted at Cargills, a popular department store chain in which displays of Santa Claus and Christmas cards might contaminate his Buddhist purity.

I have completed *Cutting Through Spiritual Materialism* by Chogyam Trungpa, a Tibetan Buddhist meditation Master and renowned scholar, teacher, poet, and artist. "Trungpa" means "attendant," and refers to a venerable line of Tibetan lamas.

> Walking the spiritual path properly is a very subtle process; it is not something to jump into naively. There are numerous sidetracks which lead to a distorted, ego-centered version of spirituality; we can deceive ourselves into thinking we are developing spirituality when instead we are strengthening our egocentricity through spiritual techniques. This fundamental distortion may be referred to as "spiritual materialism."

Bandarawela, Sri Lanka
Friday, December 19, 1975

Local literature declares, "When the upland areas near Kandy and Nuwara Eliya are wet, the Ella-Bandarawela region is almost certain to be dry." Bullshit! At the Nandana Tea Factory, colorfully dressed teenage girls provided contrast to surrounding deep green hills while picking a variety of tea leaves.

"The best tea grows at altitudes over 4,000 feet. This plantation produces a middle grade of tea." Offered after a hearty bear hug by the rousing and robust chief of the estate, His Excellency led me on a personal guided tour. Laborers weighed moist leaves taken from bamboo baskets before placing them on porous canvas sheets to weather. Machines then process the dried leaves until varying grades of tea are produced. Once the product is delivered to big companies (Lipton, Brooke Bond), they, in turn, further blend the teas into what we drink.

Nearby, a well-known river crossing is habitually taken hostage by enormous but gentle timber elephants when taking their daily baths. A power trip of a different sort was featured in the December 1 issue of *Time*: the

137. New friends hanging in Sri Lanka's mightiest and longest river, the Mahaweli Ganga.

Pittsburgh Steelers "steel curtain" defense—L. C. Greenwood, "Mean" Joe Greene, and company.

But power trips are also relative. In Sri Lanka, Pakistan holds clout, for it is the greatest importer of Sinhalese tea. Recently, Pakistani Prime Minister Zulfikar Ali Bhutto quelled local fears by announcing that Pakistan would not make tea purchases from Bangladesh.

And speaking of drink, I tried *amsak*, Sri Lanka's version of chang. However, you cannot do so on monthly *Poya*, when, on the day of the evening of the full moon, banks, post offices, and most drinking establishments close. Thousands of candles are lit. Romantic meandering bogs of sweet smoke intrude upon celebrants and matchmakers trying to make a few bucks. Street side incense resembles early morning fog. Monthly date night for consummation?

I finally noticed. No colorful turbans in Sri Lanka. No Sikhs?

Nuwara Eliya, at 6,800 feet, is a well-groomed settlement of tea plantations and plunging waterfalls. The private estates, like those of the manors of feudal Europe, contain thousands of acres, dozens of factories, and archaic working and medical conditions. One recently opened a maternity clinic. Narrow networks of manicured motor roads, earthen trails, and maintenance sheds populate the region.

As usual, being the only sahib on most local buses including the one to Nuwara Eliya, I was surrounded by dark-skinned foreign people. A Christian cross affixed above the driver reminded me of an amusing radio program I listened to when driving to work from Queens to the South Bronx ghetto over the Triborough Bridge. One of Don Imus's satirical "Christian sermons" dealt with long hair. "Well, *he* had long hair" would inevitably lead into a sales pitch for "holy hair grooming oil, brushes and combs, and a plastic neon Jesus for the dashboard of your car"—all available from "church headquarters in Del Rio, Texas."

Constant showers in Nuwara Eliya led me to Bandarawela and the long-promised sun. Right! Jesus! I walked off the bus—into a driving rainstorm—and the charitable arms of one Ratna M. Tillekeratne. A kind and considerate spirit, this genuine *gentle*man invited me to share his tranquil valley country home, growing family, provincial values, and unbounded generosity. An accountant by trade, Ratna is presently employed in a government hospital. His wife clerks in the courts. They have adopted one child.

That same evening, a harried young woman suddenly arrived and quickly departed. A former trusted servant for some years, she had had an affair with a neighbor, had stolen money from Ratna, and had given it to her lover. Upon learning she was pregnant, the woman had returned to apologize. Trust, loving treatment as a family member, and free access to the family's strongbox had come to naught. Ratna appeared visibly shaken and hurt. Relating the story with deep sadness in his eyes, he also felt betrayed. It is doubtful he accepted her apology.

Before we were about to retire, one of Ratna's friends, a government official in charge of this region's tea-growing facilities, popped in for a night's sleep. Soon embroiled in a disagreeable chat concerning the role of America in protecting the free world, we came to little agreement despite arguing under burning incense and three glossies of Siddhartha.

Before sleep and a midnight bowl of *kriyabot* (milky-rice), I blew my nose without paper—residual behavior first practiced in Khumbu.

Bandarawela, Sri Lanka
Saturday, December 20, 1975, Morning

Moments prior to inviting me to return to Ceylon and stay with his family for some months, Ratna gave me fifty rupees to buy him shirts in Hong Kong. When I attempted to refuse a small gold antique Buddha found in a temple unearthed over two hundred years ago, Ratna would have none of it.

Madurai, India
Sunday, December 21, 1975, Morning

Via Haputone, Ratnapura, and the orange timber of the Horton Plains, Sri Lanka's highest and most desolate plateau, I returned to Colombo and checked into the YMCA. Big mistake. Even my roommate, an elderly Pakistani gentleman and devout, self-confessed "practicing Catholic," was put off by the sleazy mattresses, rusty bed frames, and one naked light bulb barely hanging from a ceiling fixture connected by a single strand of frayed, exposed wire.

I took breakfast drooling over Ingrid Bergman in a bar resembling Humphrey Bogart's Rick's Café in *Casablanca* (1942). Sidney Greenstreet refused, so Peter Lorre took my order, pointed to two gentlemen seated at a table across the room, and presented their note. "Please join us for a drink." Members of the de Silva family of Galle, these first cousins explained that their surname, commonly thought to be Portuguese, is Muslim. After they correctly guessed I was Jewish, we consumed rounds of amsak, drowning our laughter and conflicting religious politics.

Somewhat more pressing, I sought from them an explanation of the Sri Lankan calendar: rows of ten or eleven days that do not seem to correspond to weekly rows of Western calendars. When I made inquiries regarding the weather, they offered painful renditions of "Singing in the Rain."

Moments after my return to Trichy (nickname for Tiruchirappalli), India, I ran smack into Jack, alias "the major." A British bloke who first visited India six years ago, he now makes Bombay and Goa his home. Why Goa? Electric generators, guitars, sex, drugs, cheap thrills, and rock 'n' roll.

(Britons can stay in India forever. Americans can't remain for more than six months in any one calendar year, depending on the political winds.)

I had not the faintest notion where to look for a hotel. However, now and then, local street hustlers and pimps present cards. And so, it happened in Madurai. My crib? A "room by the hour" brothel!

Proudly known for its relative low fertility and high literacy rates, South India is bounded by the Bay of Bengal, the Arabian Sea, and the Indian Ocean. Contained within are Bangalore, Mysore, Madras, Hyderabad, Madurai, and the former Portuguese colony of Goa in Kerala State. Tahitian fantasies? Breadfruit and shapely brown women contrasting pristine white beaches.

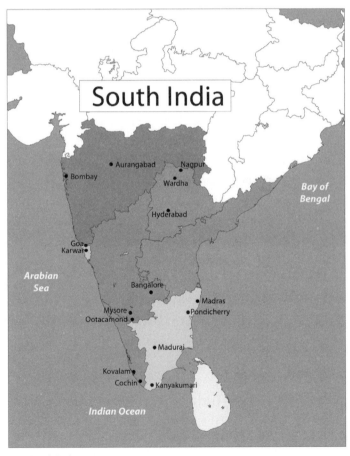

138. South India.

Injustice. My descriptions of Madurai's *thousands* of multicolored Hindu temples are futile. Maybe even insulting. Incomprehensible to imagine, the temples are priceless cultural treasures. Surely, the greatest of all is the Meenakshi Temple complex.

Although beauty is not to be compared, I would consider Madurai's architectural masterpiece to endure on the same divine plane with Jerusalem's Dome of the Rock, Granada's Alhambra, the Jameh and Great Abbasi Mosques and Ali Qapu and Hasht Behesht Palaces of Isfahan (Iran), Istanbul's Hagia Sophia and Blue Mosque, and the Hearst Castle of San Simeon, California. One can only understate the undeniable and intense depth, design, color, and workmanship of its Vedic sculptures, temple cells and red sandstone columns.

139. Street leading to the Meenakshi Temple.

Within its walls is housed an enormous subpool enclosed by four sets of ghats from which I watched children and sadhus bathe and cleanse themselves of worldly and spiritual grime. A museum harbors wooden sculptures and well-preserved murals and drawings, each depicting a melodramatic fable from rich Hindu mythology. Along outer walls, you find chai stalls, souvenir stands, cows, mother and baby elephants, and the usual chaotic informality that engulfs most temples of the East.

140. Colorful Gopuram (temple tower).

Folklore claims the Meenakshi Temple, located at the very center of the ancient temple city of Madurai, is named after a fierce, unmarried, meat-eating goddess born with three breasts. According to legend found in a Tamil text, upon her marriage to Lord Shiva, Meenakshi lost her third breast and came to symbolize women as central to Hindu family life. (Don't ask!) Or maybe ask the holy cow directing traffic.

But Madurai can also be defined by the Thirumalai Nayakkar Palace, a fifteenth-century residence of many of India's greatest Hindu rajas; the

141. Sacred cow directing traffic.

142. The Thirumalai Nayakkar Palace.

relative intactness of South India's unadulterated Hinduism; and the bustling, crowded labyrinth of streets, back alleys, incessant flower stalls, sweet
shops, and vegetarian restaurants on the banks of the mighty Vaigai River.
Paying tribute to Mahatma Gandhi's frequent visits to this most prototypic of South Indian cities is the Gandhi Memorial Museum and College.

143. Rich man.

144. Poor man. (At first, I couldn't tell the difference.)

Tens of thousands who sleep on the streets must share them with sacred cows roaming in front of garbled loudspeakers and mobile stalls where chai boys do their dance and aeration trip. Traffic is eerily quiet. Few motorized vehicles compete with bicycles, rickshaws, animals, pedestrians, and bullock carts. Many horse-drawn buggies and wagons, reminiscent of Herat and Kandahar (Afghanistan), are garlanded with flowers and bells.

That said, Madurai is the commiseration of the poor, maimed, blind, and crippled. All else pales. There are no words. No mitigation. Brutal reality. An unwanted hand is eternally in every face, at every chai stall and chapati bakery in the city. Sorrowful rickshaw "boys" toil under the weight and freight of their human-drawn vehicles. Darkness brings the pale glint of wax candles (headlights) "protected" by clear plastic flaps.

Within its schizophrenic lifestyle lies the heart of South Indian cuisine and culture: savory *masala dosa* (crepe with rice, lentils, potatoes), inescapable heat, multicolored saris, white *dhoties* (a hybrid skirt-sarong), ash-covered sadhus, saffron-robed Brahman priests, and face-painted pilgrims—all seeking Hindu salvation.

Oh, the vast majority do not queue up. People merely walk about and form their own lines to enter restaurants, bathrooms, trains, and buses, oblivious that one already exists.

Beyond the palm and horoscope readers that line most streets leading to railway and bus stations are rural bushmen, witch doctors and bus "boys" screaming "Madras," "Bangalore," and "Trivandrum." Lower profiles are maintained by many of the memsahib missionary nuns who tread among the morose masses.

Fashion. Those who do apparently dress in a linen closet. Haute couture requires white cotton shirts and pants, robes, dhoties, hats, and pastel-lined aprons and towels. "Socialites" appear as waiters in the Bahamas. Adding to the psychedelic spectacle are sheer, delicate saris wrapped around appealing female physiques.

Damn! Many South Indian women are incredibly sensuous and provocative; creamy-soft skin, youthful, healthy, and well-proportioned bodies and long silky black hair worn in a braid or left to hang naturally. Most wear nasal jewelry.

"Talkies" feature *Anne of the Thousand Days* and *With Six You Get Egg Roll*, advertised by large signs loaded onto carts pulled by day laborers. I missed the trailer for *Helga and the Sex Revolution*.

No free lunch. Took a picture of an elephant. When I refused to provide baksheesh to its mounted owner, he good-naturedly maneuvered the pachyderm to pin me against a building. As smiling crowds looked on, I placed a fistful of rupees in the elephant's trunk—and was allowed to pass.

145. Madurai.

146. Lord Ganesh, aka Ganesha, the much-loved pan-Hindu and Buddhist God of new beginnings, remover of obstacles, and patron of arts and sciences.

Indian (Asian) elephants, long ago domesticated and employed for the transport of logs and military materiel, symbolize divine knowledge, wisdom, and power. Representative trinkets, statuettes, murals, paintings, and stone and wooden carvings proliferate throughout the entire culture.

Kanyakumari (Cape Comorin), India
Tuesday, December 23, 1975
11:00 A.M.

From my elevated seat on the express bus to Kanyakumari, Tamil Nadu state, I relished views of whitewashed coastal towns. Shadowed by Spanish-like tiled roofs and stark vanilla walls, men wrapped thin dhoties around their loins. White cotton turbans covered their heads—in sharp contrast to shiny, deep-black skin. Bright green, yellow and orange wraps swathed the bodies of women balancing vegetables and baskets of hay on their heads as they sashayed down the middle of most roads.

Noisy and bristling at dawn, Tuticorin and Tiruchendur signaled another radical change. Within forty-five miles of southernmost India, the tropical earth turned rich and red, invigorating fresh air delivered by prevailing trade winds. Seafaring sailboats appeared off the southeast coast. Palm trees and sand dunes concealed all else. You could almost taste measures of salt from the briny catches yielded by fishermen who inhabit tiny, nameless bamboo villages. Rocky mountains blotted the horizon.

Kanyakumari, India
Wednesday, December 24, 1975, 6:00 A.M.

Sabah al-khair (Arabic). *Boker tov* (Hebrew). *Subprabhat* (Hindi). *Subha-bakhair* (Urdu). *Buenos dias* (Spanish). *Bonjouno* (Italian). "Good Morning Good Morning." Even the Beatles are speechless this awesome morning.

Swirling currents generated by the summit meeting of the Bay of Bengal, the Indian Ocean and the Arabian Sea became evident at sunrise. Hints of clouds turned pink and crimson above the Swami Vivekananda Rock Memorial, the final resting place of one of India's most revered sages, situated on an island one kilometer south of the mainland. Among a slew of legends, it is said that Swami Vivekananda swam to the island untouched by sharks that patrol its waters.

As the sky continued to lighten, parents in thatch huts assembled on cliffs above the beach to monitor their piglets and curious, adorable toddlers. Orange clouds turned yellow.

As I continue to write, streaks of faint purple now accent the upper reaches of these clouds above the aquamarine bay. Of various sizes and shapes, trawlers and sailboats have been put to sea. Visions of Polynesia. Ducks and chicks search for food. Young children piss ten feet to my right.

Shimmering a crimson dance, a second line of clouds lounge at the horizon, unable to conceal a brilliantly rising orange-red sun-ball. Below the boulder on which I sit, a dark-skinned boy has just taken a loose watery stool, breakfast for a murky-gray pig. Bon appetite. Sunrise in India!

147. Future maharanis of Tamil Nadu State.

Kanyakumari, India
Wednesday, December 24, 1975, 9:00 A.M.

How I long for a Northern Railway fried puri and vegetable brunch on a banana leaf.

A visit to the Vivekananda Rock Memorial confirmed that, unlike Swami V. and Ram Dass, I am not yet high enough to swim with the sharks or live on light per Therese Neumann. Who? Ms. Neumann, cited by Ram Dass, was a German Catholic mystic and stigmatist (one who exhibits wounds like those of Jesus on the cross). Some believe she ate no food for twelve years and was sustained only by the light of God.

Christmas brings an abundance of well-heeled believers to the cape, many of whom inexplicably rent rooms without beds. Not yet ready to sleep on thorns or nails, I booked a room in the leafy and clean Vivekananda Lodge. Reports of "rain and clouds" competed with "breezy and clear." The weather and beach are perfect.

Rusty browns and charcoal grays tint beige-and-white sands. Relentless waves kick up upon the shore before retiring into the navy-blue sea. Patterns and intensity of colors change—a kaleidoscopic mosaic. A hotel clerk offered, "East Coast Beach is but three furlongs away." Do I look like a horse?

Vivekananda Lodge caters to middle-class Indians on vacation, a minuscule portion of the greater Indian nation of nations. Joining families on a bus into town, I noticed similar behavior and fashion exhibited by their class-conscious cousins in Europe and North America: stylish haircuts; new, freshly pressed clothing; and sibling rivalry. Many wore the homogenous, sterile, well-scrubbed look of the American Christian fundamentalist. Had some of the young men applied greenish molasses (ZaZa hair tonic) to their hair, as I had in the 1950s? Or Wildroot? Or Vitalis? Or Brylcreem?

Mothers babied and overprotected their kids. Women looked as though they had just stepped out of the beauty parlor. Unfortunately, most of these materialistic-driven, ultraconservative souls openly display a peculiar self-righteousness and varying degrees of arrogant condescension toward most of the poor while striving to "keep up" with the Singhs and Gandhis.

A refined and educated upper middle-class Bengali couple shared their justifiable pride; their children attend university in California, Washington, and New York. Mr. A. C. Basil manages the international banking department at the headquarters of the State Bank of India in Calcutta. Having arrived at midnight, they chanted "We were attacked by the cheats" and paid twenty rupees for a stagnant, dirty, and naked room they immediately vacated this morning.

Many of my new friends express little awareness of Hinduism. Nor do they seem to grasp the essence of *The Bhagavad Gita* and the dialogues that take place between Arjuna, Hinduism's great warrior, and Lord Krishna.

It is no secret that unlike relatively narrow-focused Western religions, Hinduism encompasses a far broader realm of belief and practice. Meaning? To properly survey Hinduism, you must become well-acquainted with numerous mythologies and scriptures previously noted.

Arjuna is stuck. His predicament? As a warrior and leader pictured as a fierce chariot driver behind swift white horses, he is presented with a most symbolic ethical dilemma. Due to a series of karmic events beyond his control, he must wage war despite hatred of violence, a predicament faced by all mankind—the need to be congruent of body, mind, and spirit, the eternal, inevitable psychological battle between the animalistic id and the culture-bound, moralistic superego. In the West, the ego mediates this conflict. Hinduism fosters the transcendence of this illusory, artificial ego.

Lord Krishna, who Indian mythology tells us made love to ten thousand women at the same time is, obviously, quite a guy. A renaissance god, he comes to Arjuna's rescue by posing a series of rhetorical questions and answers that lead to the resolution of Arjuna's dilemma: the attainment of Atman (Self), spiritual enlightenment (Buddhism's nirvana) and divine consciousness. In so doing, Arjuna will come to naturally know what action to take in all circumstances.

148. A depiction of Lord Krishna and Arjuna, who is to become the hero of the great Hindu epic poem, *The Bhagavad Gita* ("*Gita*"). Their dialogue, previously noted, reflects the essence of Hinduism.

Hindus preach that through the practice of proper nutrition, meditation, yoga (discipline), *bhakti* (devotion) and *seva* (selfless service), each soul is rendered capable of escaping samsara, the perpetual life-death cycle in which all people are enslaved. When you are removed from this karmic round of birth, death, and reincarnation, you're no longer shackled by maya—illusion. Those who liberate their Selves from the chains of lower levels of consciousness grow closer to divine consciousness and Atman.

God, God consciousness, and the universe are not dualistic. Hinduism does not profess people and the material world to be distinct from God.

They are God. The integrated universe is a vibration; its sound, *"aum."* Everyone possesses the capacity, by means stated above, to discover their unique innate God consciousness. Through right action, through prescribed behavior, you can unite with the vibration of the universe, with "aum," leading to a naturally higher plane of divine consciousness where Atman is nirvana (spiritual enlightenment).

Maharishi Mahesh Yogi, maligned by the Beatles in "Sexy Sadie," makes an easy-to-understand analogy: The process to reach Atman can be symbolized by the ocean. *If* you can cause the surface waves (conscious thoughts) to be stilled, eventually you can see the ocean floor (one's true nature) leading to ongoing heightened states of atomic and molecular energy—the exact same, albeit *temporary*, effects of consciousness-altering, mind-expanding hallucinogenic drugs. Of course, as the influence of LSD, mescaline, psilocybin, and peyote subside, they are replaced by everyday emotional stressors, thoughts, and "normal" states of consciousness.

The disdain with which the Maharishi and other Indian teachers are held by many in the West speaks to our depraved focus on personality and celebrity. Too often, we reject a novel philosophy we barely understand not because of its actual value, but because of the abuse and hypocrisy of those who attach themselves to it. Is six-thousand-year-old Hinduism to be dismissed because a thirteen-year-old "guru," Prem Rawat (Guru Maharaj Ji), exploits it as justification to own a dozen Rolls-Royces? Shall we ask D. H. Lawrence, renowned English writer and poet? He warned, "Never trust the artist. Trust the tale."

Moving about India, I remain astounded at the hows and whys of local techniques. Would not a contemporary construction foreman marvel at the haphazard scaffold arrangements of wooden and bamboo toothpicks (poles) used to construct buildings? And would such "amusement" not extend to the modern American farmer's unfamiliarity with bullock carts and primeval methods employing human plows and manual irrigation?

"How did you react to the poverty you saw?" Often asked when I arrived home after my first visit to India, I do not think I was ever able to formulate and convey a truly accurate response. I will try again. In due course, most visitors develop a somewhat cold, distant, dispassionate numbness, an emotional self-protective shield. I blocked out images of those living in poverty and replaced them with faceless statistics—not dissimilar to how many of us deal with the Holocaust. Do we mentally have a choice? If I allowed myself to experience compassion and guilt all day, I would not be able to function. Kind of like reading about murders in *The New York Daily News*.

A young nurse from New Zealand, when visiting Kandy, related a sad story. Without warning, she was faced with a tragic scene on a crowded bus. A father was in tears as his daughter, about eight, sat on his lap, unable to breathe. Apparently, she was dying of diphtheria. The nurse did what she could to comfort the girl as she coughed and wheezed and vainly gulped for air—until she expired—right on that bus.

The swells of compassion that some summon for strangers, as exemplified by the Kiwi (New Zealand) nurse, contrasts my experience when meeting roadsters on the IHT. Acquaintances are immediately made, often out of need, but few become meaningful friendships. I speculate that as we age, family and friends become more important, leaving less energy to focus on strangers. A sad commentary on human nature.

Kovalam Beaches, Malabar Coast, India
Thursday, December 25, 1975, Christmas, 6:00 A.M.

I didn't expect to be greeted on Christmas morning by Santa and red-nosed reindeer, in a country where the majority of the incredibly diverse population may have never heard of Jesus. Instead, at the Kovalam Beaches, in front of the Hilton-like Kerala House, I joined a bevy of obese, extravagant, over-the-top Indian clans traveling in an entourage of polished Mercedes, conspicuously exposed baubles, oversized ghetto blasters, and uptown threads.

Kovalam Beaches, India
Thursday, December 25, 1975, Christmas, Noon

Luxuriant tropical jungle growth is bidding for my soul. Ten feet from the edge of a sprawling beige beach, tall fruit trees and thick banana leaves shade the Saleem Guest House. Neighbors include women from Sweden and Finland. One dude turned me on to three ounces of ganja. "Happy Chanukkah." "Merry Christmas." A holiday dinner party is being prepared by the boss man. Not having spent any time with Westerners in some weeks, could sex, drugs and rock 'n' roll be on the menu?

Kovalam Beaches, India
Saturday, December 27, 1975

Twenty-seven and blonde, Mikka, a refugee from a Stockholm suburb, is sensitive, soft-bodied, a current source of erotic fantasies, and surely motivated Paul McCartney to write "I've Just Seen a Face." After eight years of uncompromised freedom, my new challenge now feels she wants to hold onto something, that maybe she needs less freedom to feel complete. Homesick, she will soon return to Scandinavia.

I sense she breaks off relationships with men at the first sign of "compromise" (commitment?). But have I not felt the same way toward women I have dated? Although I seek an emotional relationship and mutual caring, I steadfastly do not wish to compromise (commit?) myself. Think Dylan's "Positively 4th Street."

On *Fiddler on the Roof*'s other hand, who can deny the attraction of ganja, bananas, chapaties, papayas, and a shower under a natural stream? Hope Eden's snake doesn't offer Mikka an apple.

And then there are the secrets of travel. Huh? I recently learned of a ten-hour sail from Quilon to Alleppey through Kerala's inland backwaters. A hidden passage leading to south Florida's Intracoastal Waterway?

More tangible is the spectacular southwest Indian surf. Incoming and outgoing indigo waves wreak thunderous, foamy white havoc. Just five feet from shore, they crash from heights far above my humble head. A body surfer's delight. After I inhaled number one Kerala weed, the surf became a fountain of youth.

Fountain of youth? Ponce de León? Who? Wasn't he the Spanish dude, *El Conquistador*, who sailed with Columbus to America, searching Florida for eternal youth? Now dig on Ponce's head. Just how grounded in reality was this joker dude?

The Beggars Banquet. As hinted, the thickly mustachioed proprietor of the Saleem, Jerry Colonna's clone entertained his esteemed guests with a multicourse dinner. In a courtyard below the veranda, assembled chairs and ironed virgin-white tablecloths complimented canopies of palm groves and beatific galaxies. Gas lanterns highlighted clean silverware, tan and smiling faces, and our don's attire—short white dhoti, starched cuffed shirt, and fresh turban.

His staff—a motley assortment of five Indians who cooked, "cleaned," and sold ganja and hashish—congregated in a neat row, hands folded at their chests, long shiny machetes attached to belts at their waists. Succulent fried fish and basmati rice and chapaties with dhal were served on large green banana leaves followed by papaya, bananas, oranges, and nectarines. On request, ever-popular *dosa*, a rice pancake often filled with potatoes and onions, and *masala*, a gritty sauce, were added to the menu. *Achchhee roochi* (Bon appétit).

Love to play with your food and eat with your hands? Visit South India, where, upon a wet banana leaf, your meal will include heaping helpings of white rice, curry, chutney, and assorted veggies. Drake's Devil Dogs and Hostess Cupcakes were not available!

Tropical Kerala State runs three hundred miles north to south and is twenty-five to one hundred miles wide. Though densely overcrowded, housing twenty-two million people, it is thought to be the most advanced state of India—a *rural* megalopolis. Equally remarkable is twilight. When the sun sits just above the horizon over the Arabian Sea, a grayish, mystical void appears on even the brightest and clearest of days.

Bus yoga. When you enter a station, on cue, "the boys" spring into action. Six to eight teenage entrepreneurs begin agitated searches for new riders—before the bus even comes to a halt. Predictably, this scenario takes place in every city and town. Often, I become swept up in a hectic mob trying to push, shove, jump—and board and exit—all at the very same time.

Those successful few who manage to arrive at silky smooth Kovalam Beaches (think South Florida, Caribbean islands, and Southern California) find them to be *the* Indian "place in the sun," so duly declared by the India Tourism Development Corporation. Marketed to the affluent Bombay crowd, the Baja Hotel and Kovalam Palace rest atop a heightened plateau sloping to the sea. It was here that I confronted the "dressed to kill" theater of the absurd.

Bombay's best and brightest men appear unsuitably attired and over-dressed in fine woolen pants, knit shirts, expensive Italian shoes, extravagant gold chains, thick-framed black sunglasses, and heavily greased "dos." Their women? Equally chic, they parade in expensive silks, saris, and wraps, 1940s netted coiffures, and spiked high heels. Cruising along the edge of the beach, most manage to get their clothing wet and dirty. But they must, for it is the vogue. One elderly woman walked with a dog attached to a golden leash. Disoriented refugees from Fort Lauderdale's Galt Mile?

An outlandish pseudo-luxurious joint, the Baja makes futile attempts to emulate Las Vegas' Sands Hotel. Glossy placards advertise a five-star bar and restaurant. Reality? No chairs, tables, or lights. It seems that when air-conditioning was installed, electrical outlets were overlooked in its nightclub. Unamused were tonight's long-haired *electric* guitar players.

Victor, a bass player originally from Calcutta, carries Western manners and a Canadian accent. Having become a high-tech freak in Toronto over the past seven years, he is frustrated by India's limited computer network. When I wondered how he adjusts to the poverty, inefficiency, chaos and timelessness that is India after leading a Western lifestyle, Victor admitted, "When I return to India, I simply put the West and technology out of my mind."

It has become readily apparent that the disparity and divergence of lifestyle and wealth may be greater in India than anywhere else: affluence versus poverty, jeweled palaces versus earthen shanties, Mercedes versus bullock carts, multimillionaires versus beggars, modern tractors versus human plows, nuclear energy versus animal energy. Perhaps the greatest difference involves *time*. When a mud villager in India visits a large town, he may be traveling more than four thousand years into the future—in a single day!

Over breakfast, a seasoned veteran of the IHP mapped a travel route: Bali to Singapore to Celebes (Indonesia) to Borneo. It would direct me to Filipino beer and available women on my way to Hong Kong, Taiwan, Korea, and Japan.

Cochin, Willingdon Island, India
Monday, December 29, 1975, Morning

> If I am not for myself, who will be for me?
> But if I am only for myself, what am I?
> If not now, when?
> —Hillel

> "Who is God?"
> "President of the Jewish people."
> —Five-year-old Sammy Glicken

John is a Briton whose father and grandfather both lived and fought for the British Raj in India. Sandy, from Chicago, has spent years in London. Enjoying their second trip to the East, they are headed to Goa for New Year's Eve after having rented a house in Kovalam for two months.

Upon checking into a four-rupee cell without bars, I joined John, Sandy, and several handsome, heavily bearded Malaysian students in an adjoining dungeon. A very stoned scene. Lying on their beds as though in opium-like trances, presumably induced by hours of smoke, the players became oblivious to twilight's yellow-and-beige sunset, Dylan's *Blood on the Tracks,* and the very first chords of Iron Butterfly's "In-A-Gadda-Da-Vida." Under the encroaching blanket of an India-ink night, the thoroughly wasted Malays could not communicate, a scene I started to avoid some years ago when frequenting the opium dens of Herat and Kabul.

"Idiot Wind" on *Blood on the Tracks* soothed me. By far the most forceful tune on the album, it is the best Dylan has made in years; the Dylan of old, of *Highway 61 Revisited* and *Blonde on Blonde.* His driving and unrelenting anger unleashes his furious genius and finest music and lyrics.

A three-pronged seaport, Cochin has been protected by its namesake fort. Save for the burial plot of Vasco da Gama and passive entertainment offered by Chinese net fishermen, only Jew Town offered any semblance of cultural stimulation. Once housing the only Jewish community in all of India, Cochin now shares that distinction with Bombay and Calcutta.

A crowded bazaar along its jetty could not conceal red signs indicating "Cochin 2—Jew Town." Such was my arrival on Willingdon Island.

149. I don't think this guy dude studies Torah!

Upon entering South India's only remaining synagogue, the sixteenth-century Paradesi Shul (synagogue), I removed my shoes to protect hundreds-year-old blue-and-white Chinese floor tiles. An interior balcony, gold-plated holy arch, and a gilded round centerpiece holding *tallesim* (prayer shawls) had not been used for some time. When a group of German tourists began, without solicitation, to explain the meaning of the Torah scroll (Jewish Law) and the Old Testament to me, I disdainfully listened, grew angry, and tried to ignore the irony.

Having donned a *tallis* (prayer shawl) and *yarmulke* (skull cap) before reciting the seminal Jewish prayer, *Shema Yisrael*, I offered *tzedakah* (charity, justice) and proceeded across a cobblestone courtyard. After the Second Temple in Jerusalem had been sacked and burned in 70 AD, the first Jews migrated to *Odhu*, the biblical name of India, in 72 AD. During the ensuing years, trade between King Solomon and Indian rajas came to include teak, ivory, spices, and peacocks.

On the eastern wall of the Paradesi Synagogue is a Hebrew-inscribed tablet from the Kochangadi Synagogue, built in the fourteenth century, but no longer standing. The tablet is the oldest known Jewish relic from any synagogue in India.

150. Tablet from the Kochangadi Synagogue.

Inquiries posed to a local Jewish gentleman led me to believe that most of Cochin's Jewish families had emigrated to Israel. After visiting so many Sikh, Buddhist, Hindu, Muslim, and Jain sanctuaries, I felt at home and at peace within this temple of my people and birth.

Nonetheless, I am no longer surprised to meet missionaries and their children. Although I had read about "Christian missionary zeal" and exploits as a child, such fervor, passion, and commitment were outside my stateside reality. They were encountered only in books and films.

It was not until I first arrived in Europe that I met missionary youth and learned European nations are often designated by American missionaries as staging areas for journeys to the "third worlds" of Africa and Asia.

Although many third world countries have intentionally or accidentally embraced occidental industry, technology, and the scientific method, when considering elements that speak to the human soul—religion, the arts, literature, music, dance, education—I am one of many who believe the tribal nations of Africa and Asia have surpassed the West. Nevertheless, to the arrogant, judgmental, condescending, and self-righteous missionary eye, there is no doubt that most indigenous black, brown, and yellow people remain raw, savage, untamed, and in need of—*Christian salvation.*

When non-Jews wish to convert to Judaism, they may approach a rabbi and state their case. In most instances, traditionally and historically, the rabbi will inform candidates of the hardships of Jewish life and, in the process, attempt to dissuade the potential convert by testing the degree of his or her resolve. If the seekers are unconvinced and their resolve unshaken, in all probability a rigorous course of study and practice will eventually lead to Talmudic conversion.

Any doubt that the conversion of the "heathen," the essential focus and goal of Christian evangelical missionary effort, is unmistakably alien to the Jewish *cup* (head/mind), must be put to rest. The Hebraic provision of care and support for those in need, *tikkun olam* (to repair the world), is essential and central to Jewish theology and is proscribed and commanded by the Torah, but it is never done for the sake of conversion.

On the lighter side, brief words on biblical animal sacrifice. It is no longer practiced. Most burnt offerings took place in Jerusalem's First Holy Temple until the Babylonians destroyed it when they sacked the city in 586 BCE, considered by many to be the salient event eventually leading, over the next millennium, to the ending of Biblical Judaism and animal sacrifice, and the start of Rabbinic Judaism. Symbolic prayer came to replace animal sacrifice.

It was with this mindset that I first encountered the international Christian missionary movement, consisting of dozens of related and unrelated denominations. Personal result? An intellectual opposition and emotional repulsion of the fundamental basis of all missionaries—their need and desire to change people who are seen as inferior to themselves. More infuriating is their absurd belief that not accepting Jesus Christ is, in itself, cause for inferior thought, behavior, and spirit.

Yet when I continue to meet outwardly gentle, generous, and kind missionaries, I grow confused. Although I'm appalled by their narrow theological glasses, are not many of these Christians also missing family and sacrificing comfortable lifestyles at home?

Bottom line. Is it not more righteous to conduct missionary work without attaching religious strings? And if there were not such strings, would these good Christians continue their mission? Have I oversimplified a complex issue? Perhaps not. You can't be half pregnant. Freud is rumored to have said, "Sometimes, a cigar is just a cigar."

We know the "chosen" people were slaves under Pharaoh prior to the Exodus from Egypt and believed in monotheism, one God, but were *not* Jewish. Abraham is referred to as the forefather of the Jewish nation, but he too was *not* Jewish. Neither were Isaac and Jacob and Joseph and his brothers. They spoke and were considered Hebrews, an ancient tribe of tribes. Biblical tradition tells us they descended from the patriarch Jacob, the grandson of Abraham.

But it was only after the Exodus, only after Moses received the Ten Commandments and the Torah on Mount Sinai, and only after they crossed the Red Sea did the Jewish people come into being. Made famous by Cecil B. DeMille in *The Ten Commandments*, these crucial events, the freeing of the Jews (then Hebrews) from slavery four thousand years ago, are considered pivotal to the establishment of Judaism, the central importance of which is impossible to overstate.

Before these cataclysmic historical events, peoples of the world were what we consider today to be pagan. All men were *not* seen as equal under God, under the law. There was no global law. Aside from the Hebrews and Ikhnaton, the first Egyptian pharaoh to embrace monotheism, there was little belief in *One God*. It was the giving and receiving of the law for the first time whereby all men came to be seen as equal—that remains significant.

Born in Israel (Palestine) and married via fixed arrangement common to the northern Israeli towns of Tzfat (Safed) and Tiberias (on the Sea of Galilee), my *babi* (grandmother) and zeyda, with their young daughter, now known as Aunt Fanny, emigrated to Buenos Aires, Argentina, and joined its large Jewish community. The desire to avoid military conscription under the Turkish control of Palestine, and a discriminatory quota system barring entry into the United States, gave them little choice. Uncle Murray was born in Buenos Aires, my dad six years later in São Paulo, Brazil. Three-year-old sister Rose died on brutal Ellis Island before the family settled in New York City.

Neither my father nor my uncle chose to join the rabbinate, breaking family lineage for over two hundred years in Israel and central Russia. And though the differences between Zeyda and his sons were pronounced and disappointing, they were eventually accepted and respected. Love was never compromised.

At this very moment, I long to see my babi and zeyda. Babi died when I was nine years old. Although I vividly recall the moment in 1972 when I learned of my zeyda's passing, a letter and notes written and mailed that day from Las Islas Canarias to Nueva York allowed me to express myself.

February 1972

Dear Mom, Dad, and Bill,

It is now 4:20 a.m. in Agaete, Grand Canary Island, about 11:20 a.m. in New York, at the cemetery where you are laying Zeyda to rest. To try to convey to you how I feel is futile. Billy had informed me of Zeyda's worsening condition—but the news over the telephone was a bit of a shock. Even now, as I grasp his nineteenth-century good luck nickel in my hand, I can't truly believe and accept that Zeyda is dead. I had planned to write Uncle Murray, Aunt Fanny, and all the family, expressing my feelings and deepest condolences. Instead, please allow them to read the words, below, so that they too will be able to better understand my grief, being so far from home.

I am immune to the beauty that surrounds me in the Canary Islands and the cliff on which I stand. I see the beauty but can't feel it. One hour ago, I learned of the passing of my zeyda, my last surviving grandparent, the patriarch of my family.

Perhaps there really is a God, as he so strongly believed. He prayed for all his children and their children, saving himself for last.

As death clouds the atmosphere, its pall engulfing my head and thoughts, I cannot separate my zeyda from Judaism. At this very moment, as my family arrives at the funeral home, my zeyda is being eulogized. And I know where I should be—in that home in Brooklyn.

Perhaps there really is a God. Is it simply coincidence that I called home this Sunday afternoon (9:00 a.m., New York time) to wish my folks a happy twenty-fifth wedding anniversary? I had already sent a card. Or was it some other force, more than just coincidental energy, that whispered to my unconscious, "Call home"? In this remarkable, remote, and neglected *pueblo* of Agaete, I never expected to hear my father say, "You called at a tough moment." And I knew. No other words were necessary. I can picture my family at the funeral home. I can picture the funeral procession. But no matter how hard I try, I can't picture my zeyda in a coffin, being laid into the cold, hard earth.

As we spoke our brief bittersweet words on the turn-of-the-century crank telephone, I was told my father shed no tears. Zeyda had been suffering on his deathbed, and passing brought release from his physical pain and relief for those viewing a loved one ready to die. Thus, it seems, some members of the family were able to understand my zeyda's death in a philosophical light, described by my mother three thousand miles away.

Yet, when is any man, any spirit, whether four or eighty-four, ready to die? The first inkling I had that my grandfather was beginning to lose a degree of his wit came sometime last year when he called me Billy. At that moment, my knees and stomach weakened and shook; my voice trembled.

I vividly remember my last visit with him in Aunt Fanny's house. He had blessed me for a safe and pleasant journey, just as he had blessed me before every *Yom Kippur* [Jewish Day of Atonement] that I can recollect. I recall my last months in New York when I would run up after work to eat and visit with him.

Just ten weeks ago, I had visited Israel and Zeyda's sisters, Razel and Dubrish. Tziporah had died. They asked about Yacov. When I assured them that he was all right, their aged, wrinkled faces broke into wide grins, expressing a joy that could only occur upon hearing of their brother, who had left Israel for France and Argentina over fifty years earlier.

I think of the holy sites I had visited in Israel: Jerusalem, Tzfat [Safed], and especially Tiberias, the birthplace of my zeyda. While I am grieved by his death, I also am enveloped by a warm internal feeling, knowing I have seen with my own eyes where he grew up and where his parents lived. It was so very poignant to see the very same picture of my great-grandparents that hung in Zeyda's apartment in the Bronx, on the Grand Concourse, also hanging in Jerusalem's Mea She'arim district in the living rooms of Razel and Dubrish.

He had given me ten one-dollar bills to distribute to his sisters, a charity, a *yeshiva* [Jewish day school], and other relatives in Israel. I distinctly recall the sisters' ecstasy when I presented them with *gelt* [money] sent by their brother.

I remember more. How Zeyda would refuse to eat in my parents' home because it was not as *glatt* [strictly] kosher as his own; how he had installed a mailbox and placed letters in the tombstone above Babi's grave; how he would examine the government checks he received with a magnifying glass; how he concluded that the first moon shot he watched on television took place in a studio; how he would put my little hands in a jar of pennies (later dimes) as a birthday gift; and how he loved and prayed for us all so very much.

Yes, perhaps God is now directly above me, driving down the rain from the black storm clouds that have just appeared overhead. I think back to the conversation I had with my parents just after seeing Zeyda for the last time. While parked on the Cross Bronx Expressway, I discussed what I had thought to be an improbable possibility—that I might not see my grandfather alive again. I did so, knowing my words would upset my mother. My father understood.

I will hold his good-luck nickel forever, perhaps one day relinquishing it to my grandchildren on their long journeys. Zeyda will no longer have to write babi letters and place them in a mail slot built into babi's tombstone. He will be with her once again.

I graphically remember my visits to their Bronx apartment on the Grand Concourse during Sunday afternoons and *yamim tovim* [holidays]. As babi rapped in the kitchen with my mother, I would read for Zeyda from the *siddur* [Hebrew daily prayer book]. We gambled and played *dreidel* [a game of chance with a Jewish top] for pennies on Chanukkah and *davened* [prayed] at the dark, brownish-red mahogany dinner table at *Pesach* [Passover] and Rosh Hashanah, the Jewish New Year ["Birthday of the World"]. Everyone would have to wait for the completion of Hebrew language programs on an RCA component radio before Zeyda's vintage television could be switched on to watch the Yankees play baseball or the Giants play football.

Where has the time gone? Has the funeral procession ended? The family must now be at the cemetery where Zeyda will be laid to rest, in peace, forever. It is only due to my zeyda and babi that I even exist; that I was brought up by a father (and mother) who love me as much as his parents loved him; that I can read and write Hebrew; and that I searched through Zurich and Venice for synagogues to celebrate the Jewish New Year and recite *Kol Nidre* on the Day of Atonement.

And now my father has no living parents, and my mother has no living parents.

As my zeyda is lowered into his grave, I am certain that God has answered his prayers for a tranquil and spiritual afterlife. At the grave site, on a cold depressing Sunday morning in New York City, in Israel, where his family is living and dead, and in Spain's Canary Islands, in Agaete, his beloved family and friends are wailing, "May he rest in peace. Amen."

P.S. At twilight, the sun dropped below the storm and appeared as a bizarre, bloated orange ball. Dulled by use, it hung suspended, inches above the horizon. No fiery rays, no rays at all. No reflections upon the ocean, save my own.

With Love,

Martin

Does the cosmos know my zeyda is dead? Surely, he recited the Shema Yisrael by rote. *The* outstanding prayer in Judaism, the Shema consists of three sections from the *Tanakh*, the Jewish Bible, each emphasizing a basic

151 and 152. Zeyda (*left*) and Babi (*right*).

aspect of Judaism. It being the classic statement of the Jewish doctrine of the Oneness of God, faith within has led to countless massacres and futile attempts at extermination over millennia.

שְׁמַע יִשְׂרָאֵל יְהֹוָה אֱלֹהֵינוּ יְהֹוָה אֶחָד:

בָּרוּךְ שֵׁם כְּבוֹד מַלְכוּתוֹ לְעוֹלָם וָעֶד:

וְאָהַבְתָּ אֵת יְהֹוָה אֱלֹהֶיךָ בְּכָל־לְבָבְךָ וּבְכָל־נַפְשְׁךָ
וּבְכָל־מְאֹדֶךָ: וְהָיוּ הַדְּבָרִים הָאֵלֶּה אֲשֶׁר אָנֹכִי מְצַוְּךָ
הַיּוֹם עַל־לְבָבֶךָ: וְשִׁנַּנְתָּם לְבָנֶיךָ וְדִבַּרְתָּ בָּם בְּשִׁבְתְּךָ
בְּבֵיתֶךָ וּבְלֶכְתְּךָ בַדֶּרֶךְ וּבְשָׁכְבְּךָ וּבְקוּמֶךָ: וּקְשַׁרְתָּם
לְאוֹת עַל־יָדֶךָ וְהָיוּ לְטֹטָפֹת בֵּין עֵינֶיךָ: וּכְתַבְתָּם עַל־
מְזֻזוֹת בֵּיתֶךָ וּבִשְׁעָרֶיךָ:

149. The Shema.

Here, O Israel: The Lord our God, the Lord is One
Blessed be the name of His glorious kingdom for ever and ever.
And thou shalt love the Lord thy God with all thy heart, with all
  thy soul, and with all thy might.
And these words which I command thee this day shall be in thy
  heart.
Thou shall teach them diligently unto thy children.

Sunset marks the start—and end—of all Jewish holidays. *Kol Nidre*
(All Vows), an Aramaic legal formulary renouncing oaths, obligations, and
pledges (made to God, *not* man), welcomes the holiest day of the Jewish
calendar, and did so in Nazi concentration camps. Kol Nidre served as the
inspiration for "A Deathless Prayer," composed in Birkenau, in 1944, by
Leon Szalet, a Jewish innocent.

A DEATHLESS PRAYER

Pain and . . . fear . . . kept us awake.

A cloudless sky, thickly set with glittering stars, looked in on our
grief-filled prison.

The moon shown through the windows.

Its light was dazzling that night and gave the pale, wasted faces of
the prisoners a ghostly appearance.

It was as if all the life had ebbed out of them.

I shuddered with dread, for it suddenly occurred to me that I was
the only living man among the corpses.

All at once, the oppressive silence was broken by a mournful tune.

It was the plaintive tones of the ancient Kol Nidre prayer.

I raised myself up to see whence it came.

There, close to the wall, the moonlight caught the uplifted face of
an old man, who, in self-forgetful pious absorption, was singing
softly to himself . . .

His prayer brought the ghostly group of seemingly insensitive human beings back to life.

Little by little, they all roused themselves and all eyes were fixed on
the moonlit-flooded faces.

We sat up very quickly, so as not to disturb the old man, and he did
not notice that we were listening. . . .

When at last he was silent, there was exaltation among us, an exaltation that people can experience only when they have fallen
as low as we had fallen and then, through the mystic power of
a deathless prayer, have awakened once more to the world of
the spirit."

The Christian Easter is subject to the lunar calendar, always falls on Sunday, and religiously overlaps the eight-day Jewish *Pesach* (Passover). A sign of divine coincidence? Come on.

Neither is the concluding song to the Passover *Seder*, an ordered, symbolic ritualized dinner depicted in the Last Supper. *"Chad Gadya"* ("One Only Kid"), believed to have first appeared in a *Haggadah* (narrative of the Exodus from Egypt, 1300 BCE) printed in Prague in 1590, is now found in every one of ten thousand different editions. Derived from a German nursery rhyme of the Middle Ages, it remains my father's favorite poem.

CHAD GADYA (ONE ONLY KID)

Only one kid, only one kid, which my father bought for two zuzim: only one kid, only one kid.

And a cat came and devoured the kid, which my father bought for two zuzim; only one kid, one only kid.

And a dog came and bit the cat, which had devoured the kid, which my father bought for two zuzim; one only kid, one only kid.

Then a staff came and smote the dog, which had bitten the cat, which had devoured the kid, which my father bought for two zuzim; one only kid, one only kid.

Then a fire came and burnt the staff, which had smitten the dog, which had bitten the cat, which had devoured the kid, which my father bought for two zuzim; one only kid, one only kid.

Then water came and extinguished the fire, which had burnt the staff, which had smitten the dog, which had bitten the cat, which had devoured the kid, which my father bought for two zuzim; one only kid, one only kid.

Then the ox came who drank the water, which had extinguished the fire, which had burnt the staff, which had smitten the dog, which had bitten the cat, which had devoured the kid, which my father bought for two zuzim; one only kid, one only kid.

Then the slaughterer came and slaughtered the ox, which had drunk the water, which had extinguished the fire, which had burnt the staff, which had smitten the dog, which had bitten the cat, which had devoured the kid, which my father bought for two zuzim; one only kid, one only kid.

Then the angel of death came which slew the slaughterer which had slaughtered the ox, which had drunk the water, which had extinguished the fire, which had burnt the staff, which had smitten the dog, which had bitten the cat, which had devoured the kid, which my father bought for two zuzim; one kid, one only kid.

Then came the Holy One, Blessed Be He, who smote the angel of death, which slew the slaughterer, which had slaughtered the ox, which had drunk the water, which had extinguished the fire, which had burnt the staff, which had smitten the dog, which had bitten the cat, which had devoured the kid, which my father bought for two zuzim, one only kid, one only kid.

Chad Gadya, Chad Gadya.

Yizkor, the Jewish memorial service for the departed, is frequently crowded with forlorn grieving souls, living and dead. Often found in prayer books dedicated to Yizkor is:

WE REMEMBER THEM

At the rising of the sun and at its going down, we remember them.

At the blowing of the wind and in the chill of winter, we remember them.

At the opening of the buds and in the birth of spring, we remember them.

At the shining of the sun and in the warmth of summer, we remember them.

At the rustling of the leaves and in the beauty of autumn, we remember them.

In the beginning of the year and at its end, we remember them.

As long as we live, they too will live;

For they are now a part of us, as we remember them.

When we are weary and in need of strength, we remember them.

When we are lost and sick at heart, we remember them.

When we have joy, we crave to share, we remember them.

When we have decisions that are difficult to make, we remember
them.
When we have achievements that are based on theirs, we remember them.
As long as we live, they too will live; for they are now a part of us,
as we remember them.

—Rabbi Sylvan Kamens and Rabbi Jack Reimer

Belief that the living, the legacies of the dead, can positively influence
the eternal souls of the dead by prayer and righteous behavior is a tenet
of Orthodox Jewish *halacha* (law). Equally practiced is the placing of life
above the violation of halacha. Examples? Although Jews are divinely
commanded not to work on Saturdays, the Sabbath (*Shabbos*), they are
commanded and *must* work on Shabbos if human survival is at stake. For
a sick person to fast on a prescribed holy day is considered a sin. Should a
person save one life, it is believed he or she saved the world. To take a life
is to destroy humankind.

While my Jewish identity has strengthened over time, more so when I
am not among other Jews, particularly in Hindu and Muslim India, I continue to struggle. How do I integrate Hinduism and Buddhism with Judaism
when the loci of God, as being internal (Eastern) versus external (Western), is diametrically opposed? Want concrete answers? Get into flatwork.

In *An Orphan in History: Retrieving a Jewish Legacy*, Paul Cowan, a
once self-proclaimed "Jewish WASP" and member of Chicago's famed Spie-
gel family, describes almost having lost his heritage and religious identity.
Genealogy and lineage are compared to a chain. If one link should loosen
and break, the two remaining ends may forever be separated, no longer
knowing they were once joined. And so it is with people and culture and
heritage and ethnicity and religion and identity.

Bangalore, India
Thursday, January 1, 1976, New Year's Day

At eight thousand feet, Ootacamund ("Ooty") boasts world-class royal
blue sky above a rampageous, whitewashed municipal marketplace filled

with animated shopkeepers. Black and white signs reflect civic pride and announce Ooty's census, number of literates, streetlamps, toilets, and permanent structures. Here, as all over India, cigarettes are sold one at a time, same as the tobacco mavens of Moroccan bazaars who uniformly chant "*casa, casa*" (only one).

Such merchants did not surprise Sanjay, a new friend and South African national attending medical school in Cairo. During the years he has tolerated Egypt's ancient city, Sanjay feels there has been no positive change in its miserable standard of living. He scapegoats defense spending.

I decided to bus to Mysore on my way to Goa via Bangalore. Long rides lead to self-entertainment—singing made difficult when I forget the words. After humming a few verses of one song accompanied by a wicked air guitar, I conclude with another. "Take It Easy" becomes "Peaceful Easy Feeling."

153. I wonder what this dude sings.

Under a fierce sunset on New Year's Eve, I made my first acquaintance with sprawling, cosmopolitan Bangalore, where, in its comfortable and clean railway station dormitory, I was able to book a room with a full-length bed, sit-down flush toilet, and *hot* running water. In the station's nonvegetarian restaurant, I shared my holiday meal with a group of beggar children.

154. Street poster for Pablo Fanque's European Circus Royal (1843). Allegedly, it served as motivation, per John Lennon, for the Beatles' "Being for the Benefit of Mr. Kite!"

Without appetite or intimate company, I tried to feel the cosmic energy of distant family and friends.

Existentially, I am always alone—born, live, and die alone. Ontological loneliness. Spiritually, I am not alone; I am with others. I am them and they are me, and we are the universe, and the universe is us, and all is One, is aum, is Krishna. Am I getting it?

Before midnight, with two British blokes, I attended a benefit circus. No, not the annual one in Times Square. Try Bangalore's Bishop's Gate. Floodlit buildings, theaters, and shops were engulfed by thousands of families and street barkers. Pimps and prostitutes worked the midway and Ferris wheel while competing for my attention, erection, and rupees. I got "high" with a little help from the celebrated Mr. Kite, the Hendersons, and Harry the Horse.

People are strange. Dreams are stranger. Last night, I watched a 707 take off, fall toward the ground, suddenly surge, and once more gain altitude before smashing into the top floor of a hotel where I was staying with friends. Ten feet above us, the twisted hulk burst into flames. Uncle Sigmund, please help!

Creating an opportunity to spend time with family and friends, I relished reading their letters on the front lawn of Bangalore's provincial capital building. Mail is a time trip that nudges me to distinguish between friends and acquaintances. To whom do I write? Who writes to me? And who doesn't? The highs are great. The lows suck.

"Want to know Bangalore, Don Martín? Get off your fucking ass and walk," a conveyance employed by India's modern youth while attending the city's rich choice of technological, commercial, trade and academic colleges and institutes. Also deemed a must-see by India's well-to-do are Bangalore's "upscale" neighborhoods: Mahatma Gandhi Road, the City Market district, and Bangalore University.

Heeding my own advice became problematic after concluding the city map is not drawn to scale. Most streets lack signs. Numbers? Sure. Number 140 is next to 32, which is next to 423. Whiskey bars, supermarkets, bookstalls, and cinemas—plus cows and beggars roaming among peddlers plying oranges and bananas—litter the sidewalks of Mahatma Gandhi Road.

City Market, the center of decrepit Bangalore, is without symmetry and concrete. Lacking the modern storefronts and generous gardens of neighboring districts, it is what urban India is all about. Merchants, shoppers, cows, dung, beggars, motorized three-wheelers, rickshaws, dust, dirt, and general havoc reign over congested street life and specialized flea markets selling fruit, auto parts, breads, sweets, religious articles, and flowers for Hindu worship.

No shit, City Market must accept its due place among the Indian subcontinent's busiest and filthiest markets. Many stalls contain nothing more than disorganized piles of loose, dirty, and seemingly useless knickknacks— frequently overseen by chubby turbaned gentlemen whose wide asses are stationed on cardboard-covered ground.

Could they possibly be franchisees of the prototypic Tangier (Morocco) flea market, where bottle caps and broken rusty screws, bolts and bent nails make up entire inventories? Before offering an informed response, take a moment and ponder the alternative. That is, not far from these ground-level "boutiques," pathetic bag men, bag women, and bag children patiently examine obsolete piles of rotting and reeking garbage, seeds, and ash.

Back on Mahatma Gandhi Road, I took brief respite in an air-conditioned movie house playing *King Elephant*. Huge man. Really huge. Second act on the bill? Hanging on the street with dudes wearing traditional, long, light cotton white dhoties they continually lift far above their knees and often tuck into their waists. As you might imagine, Karnataka State and its capital city, Bangalore, are also home to stunning light and dark-skinned women, many of whom exhibit Caucasian features and ooze erotic—but do not tuck their dhoties into their waistcoats.

Baga Beach, Goa, India
Monday, January 5, 1976, 7:30 A.M.
Seaview Cottage

Images of Jim Morrison and the Doors are found near the next whiskey bar. Don't ask why.

To better hear neighborly jazz-filled riffs harmonizing with ocean-front mantras at dawn, I placed a wooden desk and chair on the overhanging porch of my freestanding, one-room cottage.

Due to the frequent inaccurate bullshit dispersed on the IHT, I now require *two* confirmations from unreliable sources. Think fiascos at Lukla STOL Airfield in Nepal, ticketing in the Patna railway station, and finding the best dope in Goa.

Unmitigated primitive conditions were witnessed on the route from Bangalore to Goa, leaving lasting impressions of medieval Hindu society in Mysore State. Evidence? Neglected and scorned Sussi, Karwar, Margo, Kalagruba, and Sigart.

To salvage my blistered feet and sorry ass, I snaked through deep ravines and climbed over chains of mountainous terrain while inside brittle metal hulks called buses. The pigs, chickens and goats aboard did not seem to mind. In fact, I think they enjoyed watching their owners throw up. The pigs squealed and licked up every drop.

Drivers were inclined to creep along, stopping for every four-legged animal, fly, mosquito and white Brahman cow blocking the narrow, circuitous dirt-and-gravel roads. Three hours proved insufficient for the thirty-five kilometers from Jog Falls to Sussi. Still inland, when I was greeted by resident hippies of a lost European tribe in front of decrepit and abandoned redbrick stables, they turned me on to Goa's Baga Beach and the Seaview Cottage.

When the bus completely broke down between Karwar and Margo, I spoke with an unperturbed gentleman who, like most Indians, grew up with such conditions governing most aspects of life. With little encouragement, my friend shared his staunch belief that mechanical failures are the will of God and must be accepted. End of discussion. What little anxiety Indians do develop, apparently, is rarely expressed and eventually subsides.

Although Indian-Hindu culture arguably promotes the acceptance of one's fate and incarnation (caste), that such breakdowns are attributed to God's will and John Lennon's "Instant Karma" is simply beyond belief. Or is it? Who am I to judge? What do I know when imprisoned by Western logic and science? There must be a koan to apply here. *Reality is perception.*

Frustration, irritability, dust, heat, and sacred cow manure had all but baked my soul after forty-eight excruciating hours of travel to Baga Beach from Jog Falls. Finally inching past a provincial checkpoint, we entered Goa, occupied by the Portuguese until 1961. Panjim, Goa's central outpost, seemed overtly Christian when noticing Portuguese surnames, signs, churches and Western clothing. The coastal terrain is comparable to the previously described tropical paradises.

I was struck by the following notice posted in the Calangute Beach branch of the Bank of Baroda, a concept wholly unknown to legions of New York City and Indian retailers.

A customer is the most important visitor on our premises.
He is not dependent on us. We are dependent on him.
He is not an interruption of our work. He is the purpose of it.
He is not an outsider in our business. He is part of it.
We are not doing him a favor by serving him.
He is doing us a favor by giving us an opportunity to do so.
                                        —Mahatma Gandhi

Goa, India. Perhaps "It's All Too Much." Cause for George Harrison to write the song?

Scrawled on a wall in a whiskey bar: "If God is with you, who is against you?" Seated next to me listening to Rod Stewart's version of the Isley Brothers' "This Old Heart of Mine," two freaks are reminiscing over last night's stoning: grass, hashish and opium smoked in a chillum. The walls are covered with glossies of naked women above two birds "Flying United."

In addition to back-alley heroin, the Bengali Cafe also serves the same cold fruit juice drinks and shakes found in Kathmandu. Apparently, Calangute Beach and Goa are Hippie Trail resorts where you can forget the ascetic struggles of life on the road. Fact is, there are more freaks and freak cafés down here than Indians. Most resemble the prototypic Red Fish Cafe of Eilat, Israel, later Sixties, characterized by European rock music, longhairs and Middle Eastern ensembles.

Still feeling neglected? Strung out? No need. Hard drugs, chillums, pipes, joints, Western food, and loose and easy men and women cannot be avoided—all within a casual, no-hassle legal cocoon.

Calangute Beach is a scene. Weather is perfect. Warm, clear, and sunny days. Cool, brisk, and genuinely invigorating evenings. Sunrise and sunset are favored by most of the enlightened flower children.

A bit removed, Baga Beach lies about two kilometers north of Calangute, just south of The Hill. Further north is Anjuna Beach or Freak City, where electric bands and free-flowing hashish became the afternoon.

155. Anjuna Beach.

Most pass through for just a few weeks. Others, alone and in groups, including the Children of God, are encamped in thatch huts for some months. Along about sunset, escapees can be found selling Moroccan *kief* (cannabis crystals) and henna.

Lest I forget, I wish my dear brother a happily high birthday.

Baga Beach, Goa, India
Tuesday, January 6, 1976

No need to go anywhere for breakfast. The resident "milk girl," not the pregnant one, woke me for my daily ration of buffalo nectar. I was soon to learn that her friends, tender, toned, and tanned sensual maidens, have no desire to practice making children. The bread man failed to show. Their father?

January 6, 1976

Dearest Bal Yogi Prem Varni,

During the fall of 1972, I encountered a disciple of yours, an Austrian named Gerald. Upon his invitation, I traveled to Lakshman Jhula where I met his family and, over the course of many days, frequented Yoganta Academy. Due to personal obligations, I was unable to remain in Asia and so became one of your aspiring students for only a brief time.

Changing circumstances and karma have again directed me to India, rekindling my desire to live and study under your tutelage. I expect to arrive in February. As per your request, I write to you of my planned visit.

With my love,

Namaste,

Martin

Late last night I dined with German folk I had met in Hikkaduwa. By dawn, I had parked myself in one of Calangute's infamous cafés, sipped tea, blew a few numbers, and listened to old and new Dylan. Heavy shit. Shades of Kabul and Kathmandu. When too many Western dudes, dudesses, dudettes, and dizettes converge on one place, the vibes can get too weird, too tough, too cool, and too unfriendly for my taste—bizarre head trips with little communication and lots of downers and opium.

After watching a half-dozen addicts throw darts at themselves in Tito's Cafe, I'm quite certain Mr. Mandrex was responsible. A fair number couldn't keep their eyes open. Some sway to the music for days. Chillums and hash joints are passed around freely. When the joints are mixed with tobacco, as is common in northern Europe, I grow nauseous and dizzy.

Disciples of The Doors were searching for kisses before their women slipped into unconsciousness.

A sign posted above the Calangute post box: "Avoid rumors and loose talk. Do your duty."

Baga Beach, Goa, India
Wednesday, January 7, 1976, Morning

After I took a shit, and before it began to dry under the early sun, a big fat gray pig ate it. With great delight, this animated trash can chortled and "oinked" down his ecstatic breakfast.

Alberto, a long-haired Italian freak from Sardinia, born with glossy black braids, is addicted to the Stones, Nico and the Velvet Underground, and Lou Reed's "Heroin." Other immediate neighbors include four obnoxious and unfriendly French fries who arrived from Mombasa, Kenya, via Bombay. Not far are Zen Buddhists, vegetarians, uptown-ego-tripping bastards and bitches, high-fashion jet-setters, down-and-out junkies, intellectuals, and three guys from the Mani Rimdu Festival. One woman wears a pet monkey.

Zen, equality, holistic health, and fair pricing of commodities, including hashish, are concerns published by an assortment of Anjuna Beach "copy boys" in a somewhat cagey but courageous news sheet appropriately titled *The Stoned Pig*. Those well-acquainted with its popular editor-in-chief, who just returned from Penang, Malaysia, with acupuncture needles and other equipment, question whether said needles will be used to increase or decrease local opium addiction.

Found within the *Pig*'s New Year's Eve edition are horoscopic articles detailing lunar, planetary and stellar predictions. Subscription rates: two dollars to any address in India, three dollars to any address in the world. The managing editor waxed nostalgic when reminiscing about an electric band member.

The band will, of course, be the unnamed, spontaneous meeting of musical talents now in Goa. "Welsh" Mike, whose bass set the beat to last year's New Year's Eve festival, will be with us only in spirit,

as he quit his crippled body on July 23rd in Kathmandu. His music
will be sorely missed.

Buried on page 1 are lamentations upon loss of peace and freedom.
Apparently, "Brooklyn" Steve recently returned home. Below is his contri-
bution, as it appeared in volume 2, number 2, of the *Stoned Pig*.

Four Months Back from Goa
The people, all children wandering free.
Now I sit here, there is so much trouble, just to be.
My mind is moving fast, from here to there.
I want the peace I used to wear.
The game here is silly, even mad.
And all it does is make me kind of sad.
—New York, July 1974

Page two: The *Pig* held a raffle. Prizes included "chocolate cake and two
balls of pure resin shit from the Himalayas." Feeling toxic? "See Swami
Bernard for Ayurvedic Chandrodayas [Indian alternative herbs]. For gen-
eration of blood and semen and purification. Strengthens potency. Available from Bernard on Anjuna or at the flea market."

Although *The Stoned Pig* will not upstage *The Hindustan Times*, it is an
exceptional effort on the part of very few making the most of the meager
resources available to them.

Baga Beach, Goa, India
Friday, January 9, 1976

Early morning reveille? Keith Richards would laugh. "It's Only Rock 'n' Roll."

God-blessed and nature-kissed, palm-lined Anjuna Beach is home to
a prototypic hippie community. Geography prohibits many stray travelers
from reaching Anjuna, as it is separated from Calangute and Baga by The
River and The Hill. Naked, I crossed neck-high waters and joined other
nudists. Here, birthday suits are just another way of returning to nature.

Some hours later, the flea market was in full swing. Among hundreds of salt-of-the-earth milling about, an assortment of cosmic garments, trinkets, musical instruments, and prerecorded cassettes were placed on blankets. Most vendors were hippies, most buyers, Indians, a hilarious reversal of roles. Catering this affair, Indian families sold curried meals, fruits, fried and roasted bananas, and chai. Hashish, Buddha weed, opium, heroin, psilocybin, acid, and other *material de joie* were openly and inexpensively bartered.

In various modes of undress, extroverts arrived from all corners of the galaxy. Never in my life have I seen so many well-tanned and healthy tits and asses, cunts, and cocks all exposed in one place. In attendance were Goa's version of the Who's Acid Queen, classical fiddlers, rock guitarists, electric flutists, and several transvestites and burlesque "queens" in and out of costume.

Roger Daltrey, Peter Townsend, Keith Moon, and "Pinball Wizard" added unequivocal spirit to the random carnival. For the Stones' "devil"— wearing black and red robes, carrying a pitchfork with a red ribbon, and playing a get-down bluesy harp—there was no sympathy. Many high "children" emerged with high fashion; Southeast Asian, Tibetan, Nepalese, Indian, and Mid, Near, and Far Eastern regalia.

Here was a genuine exotic rendezvous of God's children set under luscious palm trees within dense jungle not more than forty feet from the beach. Roving NBC cameramen and correspondents walked about. If they came to record a cultural phenomenon, they succeeded. And still playing? "It's Only Rock 'n' Roll." Might "Tumbling Dice" be next?

Sunset signaled movement. Stumbling toward the beach, hundreds of flower children assembled in front of a fragile stage constructed above a sandy dance floor cordoned off by hemp attached to palm trees. What a beautiful sight: several hundred candles flickering in the Goan night, illuminating the faces of an international group of adventurers, hedonists, bums, and addicts as they passed the eternal chillum.

Those still conscious swayed and sang with blaring music pouring out of two humongous speakers attached to a cassette player powered by several automobile batteries. The Fillmore *East*. Awesome!

Neil Young, The Dead, Jimmy Cliff, Lee Michaels, Clapton, the Yardbirds, The Allman Brothers, Bruce Springsteen, Stevie Wonder, and Van

Morrison got down with Blackish Delta blues, "Heard It Through the Grape-vine," "96 Tears," "Do It Again," "For Your Love," "Dancing in the Street," "Bring It on Home to Me," "Don't Bring Me Down," and "While My Gui-tar Gently Weeps."

No doubt, I would be remiss if I failed to revel in the multinational an-them of the opium and heroin addicts, "Sister Morphine" off the Stones' *Sticky Fingers.* I searched in vain for her distant cousin—sweet cocaine!

On impulse, a brunette nymphette (Country Joe McDonald's "Not So Sweet Martha Lorraine"?) offered me a hit of speed. Instantaneous Wild Abandon. Of the spaced-out individual variety, no one is in need of a par-ticular partner, that is, to dance. And like most of the open sex around here, dance is a free form of physical expression. Indeed, "sweet Martha" and many souls had become psychedelicized. Yes, the Chambers Brothers' "time had come today."

Anything missing here? Sly and the Family Stone, "Dancing to the Music," and "I Want to Take You Higher."

As the local Indian mamas and *betees* (daughters) continued to feed us, the Doobie Brothers and Leon Russell welcomed the first blazing crimson streaks of dawn. White sacred Brahman cows woke to Iron Butterfly's "In-A-Gadda-Da-Vida." Morning vibes, however, did not include Hendrix's transcendent, other-worldly, psychedelic cover of "The Star-Spangled Ban-ner" per Woodstock (1969) on Max Yasgur's farm.

I knew it. I knew it. I just knew it. The Anjuna Beach freak scene re-minded me of Tom Wolfe's *The Electric Kool-Aid Acid Test.* Hard for me to fathom that while I was failing English at Flushing High School in 1964, Ken Kesey and his Merry Pranksters were gallivanting about the American South in an old school bus, stoned on acid, roof speakers blaring Martha and the Vandellas. "Fuck!" Had I been born too late? Offered below? A tease: a "Be-In" at San Francisco's Golden Gate Park:

This was a gathering of all the tribes, all the communal groups. All the freaks came and did their thing. . . . Thousands of them piled in, in high costume, ringing bells, chanting, dancing ecstatically, blowing their minds one way and another and making their favor-ite satiric gestures to the cops, handing them flowers, burying the bastards in tender fruity petals of love. . . . Oh, Christ, Tom, the thing was fantastic, a freaking mindblower, thousands of high-loving heads out there messing up the minds of the cops and everybody else in a fiesta of love and euphoria.

On one Augustus Owsley Stanley III, the legendary audio engineer and internationally renowned chemist who had been credited during the Sixties with making "righteous," world-class LSD (lysergic acid diethylamide).

After Owsley hooked up with Kesey and the Pranksters, he began a musical group called the Grateful Dead. Through the Dead's experience with the Pranksters was born the sound known as "acid rock." And it was that sound that the Beatles picked up on, after they started taking acid, to do a famous series of acid rock record albums, *Revolver, Rubber Soul,* and *Sgt. Pepper's Lonely Hearts Club Band.*

As with those who have never visited New York City, those on the IHT who have never visited Goa are the first to criticize it. To say heavy vibes, junkies, scams, and ego trips do not exist here is distortion. But to condemn the entire assemblage because of them is nonsense. Inherent in all hippie scenes are negative aspects. But like all *free* movements, no person or group is barred. In fact, it is all the more significant that this scene can take place at all, particularly in far-off, often-inhospitable India, in Goa, where many have consciously chosen to lead unbridled lifestyles. The music, behavior and free-spirited philosophies must not be summarily dismissed as "bad." Goa must cope with its problems, as do all other communities.

"Fate does not seek its victim. The victim seeks its own fate." The world and I are indebted to the philosophizing of Aleksandr Solzhenitsyn in *August 1914.* As for fate, it's like a tree. Karma determines the trunk newborns will first inhabit. But the choice of branches each will eventually climb is determined by you and me. Over time, it becomes clear that our lifestyle choices are limited by which tree trunk we find ourselves on. Alternatives for a child born to Peruvian peasants in Cuzco in the Urubamba mountains differ markedly from those of a toddler whose parents reside in technology-oriented Tokyo.

"Surrendering had proved to be even more dangerous than fighting." Such was Solzenitsyn's rueful commentary on a young Russian's attempt to capitulate to German troops in East Prussia rather than be killed in outnumbered combat. It was assumed that surrender would be easy, somewhat comparable to surrendering one's desires. The more I try, the more difficult it becomes. How ironic that surrender pertains both to belligerency and spirituality.

Bombay, India
Wednesday, January 14, 1976, 7:15 A.M.
Salvation Army Hostel

"Troubadours? Killed on the way to Bombay's Salvation Army Hostel? By whom? The Rolling Stones? Does he have a name? Can you guess? Are you pleased to meet him?" Does he deserve any sympathy?

As the love boat from Goa advanced into majestic Bombay harbor, this troubadour wailed with Mick. Sailing into this most cosmopolitan of all Indian cities may be romantic and thrilling. But at 4:30 a.m., not exactly what I had fantasized. Although we didn't slip into our berth until 5:30 a.m., Indian passengers readied their departure at 2:00 a.m.—by screaming, shoving, and fighting with one another for hours.

Buses, cabs, and sunshine didn't show for hours, but Larry Collins, Dominique Lapierre, and *Freedom at Midnight*, a violent and bloody account of India's independence from England, offered a warm welcome.

Yet, once, that vaulting Gateway of India was the Arch of Triumph of the greatest empire the world has ever known, that vast British realm on which the sun never set. . . . Soldiers and adventurers, businessmen and administrators, they had passed through its portals, come to keep the Pax Britannica in the Empire's proudest possession, to exploit a conquered continent, to take up the white man's burden with the unshakable conviction that theirs was a race born to rule, and their empire an entity destined to endure.

156. All that seems distant now. Today, the Gateway of India is just another pile of stone, at one with Nineveh and Tyre, a forgotten monument to an era that ended in its shadows barely a quarter of a century ago.

After taking a suburban rail line to Bombay's Colaba District and Church Gate Station at the historic Gateway of India, I walked to the Salvation Army Hostel on Mereweather Road, just across from the hippie-haunted Rex-Stiffles Hotel and Dipti's Juice Bar. Led to a bedroom in an airy, spacious dormitory, I observed bay windows providing obstructed views of the five-star Taj Mahal. As I passed through its gaudy lobby, opulent bookstores and pricey gift and apparel shops, I observed well-dressed American and European businessmen, Bombay financiers, and Arab sheiks in robes and *kaffiyehs* (Arab headdresses) enter black stretch limousines.

Exceedingly modern Bombay, the most European of Indian cities, appears to be a mecca of sports cars, motor-driven lorries, wide, smooth-paved, and yellow-lined boulevards, first-run movie theaters, enormous billboards, and hundreds of banks, insurance companies and textile and manufacturing concerns. London's red double-deckers pass by stock and commodity exchanges. Due north of the Electric House District, architectural style remains broadly British.

Via public bus route number 103, I was soon to discover yet other quarters of this maddening city of extremes. Bombay's western Bayshore provided sweeping views of the city's incredibly contemporary skyline.

157. Resemble Nice on the French Riviera?

Trendy Queens Shore Road, Back Bay and Tandeon provided no clue to vast expanses of sprawling residential blight and squalor, slums that extended as far as I could see. My return to the Electric House and Calabra Street wound through more networks of twisting, narrow, congested alleys, comparable to the most impoverished of Old Delhi. The noisy and endless Bhendi and Chira bazaars were thoroughly dilapidated and sordid.

No doubt, Bombay is monstrous and demands years to make its acquaintance. An enormous variety of foreign products and illicit contraband are smuggled through porous wharfs assisted by corrupt customs officials.

In addition to a great selection of English books available from *glass*-enclosed shops, the city also houses cafés, nightclubs, brothels, counterfeit currencies, and hassles of all kinds courtesy of black marketeers. Bogus train, bus, airline tickets and street drugs must be carefully inspected.

Omnipresent are beggars and street people. At night, sidewalks are littered with bodies, mostly alive.

Begging. A cold-hearted observer might conclude it to be a national pastime. Am told Bombay's beggars are unionized. All? Some? Do they pay dues? Do union leaders skim off the top? Rumors tell of mothers sending their children to target foreigners and middle-class Indians. Healthy and fit men dress in rags, place tattered bloody cloths around their hands and feet, and proceed to become one with the sidewalk.

Although the Indian government now provides food and shelter for beggars, many choose to ignore the help. Perhaps it compromises their independent street life and sense of freedom. Nevertheless, numerous street posters seen all about town speak of future economic prosperity.

THE ECONOMY IS ON THE MOVE

DISCIPLINE INCREASES THE ECONOMY

At breakfast, I met a Jew from Beersheba, Israel, one of few on the IHT. For safety, he came overland using a French passport. At a bank located within the Taj Mahal, while standing in a line of cloaked lady sheikhs, I introduced myself to Cindy, a sandy blonde from California anxiously waiting in Bombay for a wire so she could return home to attend her sister's funeral. Caught up in a designed runaround involving bank drafts, signatures, telegrams and great frustration, Cindy blamed deceitful government and bank officials who intentionally withhold the money for personal gain. She is not alone. Maybe that's why impatient visitors seem to dislike this city.

Unable to obtain today's exchange rates, several banks refused to cash my dollar-denominated travelers checks. The scapegoat? Telephone breakdowns? Computers? There are none.

To buy a railway concession at the Bombay Central Railway Station: Wait one hour for a clerk to show up, another ninety minutes for my request to be approved after filling out forms in triplicate, and wait even longer for a superintendent to sign off on it.

In the West, a secretary usually performs such clerical tasks. In India, nothing of the sort is anticipated, making a brief and simple task into a day-long quagmire. Indian bureaucracy *not* at work. It took only one more hour to learn which reservation line I must tolerate for next week's train to Udaipur in Rajasthan (state). Most trains leaving Bombay are already booked for the next two weeks. So are the planes.

God forbid emergencies: fires, heart attacks, injured cows. Somehow, someway, life's everyday problems get solved. All else becomes catastrophic. Required speed and efficiency have not yet been mastered after six thousand years.

I then attempted to ship home books, clothing, and two handwritten journals by means of McKinsie and McKenna PVT Limited. Because the firm no longer shipped parcels, the clerk recommended a former colleague's company. My strategy? My packages, especially the notebooks, might actually reach their destination if I used a shipping agent.

When Mr. Parak, a Sikh, advised me that the fees charged by boat transport are more expensive than air freight, my plan changed. We walked to a crowded yard among the buildings of the New Customs House of Bombay where I was introduced to yet another Sikh gentleman who guided me about. We soon found two corrugated boxes and purchased white cloth, and needle and thread. After sewing the cloth around the packages, which one usually does when in Iran, my accomplice, perhaps a former disgruntled postal worker, dispatched me to the post office, refusing payment for his services. Is Lord Krishna also a postal clerk?

Packages in hand, I encountered hundreds more of Bombay's "best and brightest" who make it a habit of doing nothing but looking for trouble when hanging out in front of Bombay's enormous General Post Office. Before long, I was filling out customs forms while my postal pretenders were melting and oozing orange candles to seal my packages. After "official" large cumbersome wooden customs stamps and dripping black ink pads magically materialized, the best and brightest did their duty. The orange seals were now officially stamped!

In theory, Indian customs agents are required by law to inspect freight prior to packaging, sewing, and sealing—as is done in countries throughout the world, including Iran. But here, in maniacal India, street-side messiahs serve as unofficial customs inspectors and do the required sealing themselves. You gotta laugh. Absolutely ridiculous. And there is nothing secret about it. It all takes place directly in front of the main post office of India's most modern city. When the freight arrives at its port of call, those customs agents assume proper and legal procedure has taken place in India. Or do they?

As all this was happening, I really didn't know what was happening. Who are these postal pariahs? Am I corrupting the heathen? "Hey, get real, Don." About twenty-eight seals (was I paying by the seal?) were placed on the stitching of each package with random abandonment. So were customs forms, now illegible and covered with excess glue and smudged black India ink.

Finally, I entered the post office where my parcels were weighed, metered, and registered into a yellowed encyclopedia-sized volume that probably arrived on Noah's Ark.

Continuing to go with the flow, I had no choice but to place my trust in the almighty rupee and a process that took four hours. By the time I paid eighty rupees for shipping, the white-clothed packages had been stamped, wax-sealed, registered, thoroughly blackened, and looked like they had sat in Pakistan's godforsaken Baluchi Desert for months.

And why do I keep referring to Iran? Because in Afghanistan, in 1972, I tried to send a sheepskin coat to a lady friend by post. When the postal clerk in the Kabul GPO wanted baksheesh just for giving me the *first* requisite customs form, I quickly decided to post the coat from Teheran.

Bombay, India
Thursday, January 15, 1976

One takes no risk in concluding Bombay to be standing room only. At dusk, all streets, wide and narrow, reach saturation by the faithful. India tries to feed three times as many people as the United States but has only one-third the land mass. For every American there are nine Indians. Imagine if seventy-two million people lived in New York City.

Pronouncements via posters, often instructive and directed at the "man and woman in the street," are plastered on buildings, storefronts, street corners, squares, plazas, and most public spaces. One is found in the dining hall of the Salvation Army hostel:

CHRIST IS THE HEAD OF THIS HOUSE
THE UNSEEN GUEST AT EVERY MEAL
THE SILENT LISTENER TO EVERY CONVERSATION

Double-decker buses have not been spared:

THE ONLY MAGIC
HARD WORK
CLEAR VISION
IRON WILL
STRICTEST DISCIPLINE

Bombay, India
Friday, January 16, 1976

This morning I explored the heart of Old Bombay, the infamous Bhendi Bazaar and Crawford Market. Frantic, frenzied, foul, and fucked up. Why again? Don't know. Just can't resist these magnetic, mesmerizing marketplaces.

Amusement of a different sort took place when catching *Doctor Zhivago* in the Worli District's Lotus Cinema. Less entertaining but equally stimulating was the neighborhood directly in front of it—a prototypic example of obscene Indian extremes. Not more than two hundred yards from a veritable earthen, tin, and cardboard shantytown dripping images of destitution and desolation are smooth, wide, sterile, and well-constructed blacktopped roads. Measured white concrete sidewalks introducing clean, neat, modern, and symmetrical office and apartment buildings had surely been transplanted from Atlanta, Phoenix, or Chicago.

Aurangabad, India
Saturday, January 17, 1976, Morning

No cartoons. No television. No Howdy Doody. No Buffalo Bob Smith. No Clarabell. No Mr. Bluster. No Rootie Kazootie. No Mighty Mouse. No *Andy's Gang*. And no *Ramar of the Jungle*.

Having left Bombay, I joined a "deluxe" round-trip tour bus about to pull into the Aurangabad Holiday Camp for the next two days. Aboard is an international entourage also wanting to experience the mind-numbing Ajanta and Ellora caves of Maharashtra State.

An elderly Russian couple lives in Hamburg, West Germany. Born and raised in China for twenty years, they said their goodbyes (escaped) in 1954, five years after the Chinese Communist Revolution. My assigned roommate, a Japanese seminary student, is studying Catholicism in Bangalore. Residing for six years in New Guinea, an Australian professor of engineering is traveling with his two children on a three-week tour of India.

The remaining thirty-odd passengers are well-to-do Indians: families, married couples, single (and chaperoned) young ladies and a mother-daughter team. Though bloodshot, my dream-stained eyes remain able to transcend gravity and focus on several sexy vixens. A young angel sits behind me. Another beauty with shiny black braids snuggles against her husband, causing me to ponder at least one of the Ten Commandments.

Aurangabad, India
Sunday, January 18, 1976, 7:00 P.M.

Tour members sleep in adjacent rooms, eat at a long table seating forty, and discuss a host of subjects allowing me to observe a range of personalities: courteous, loud, considerate, obnoxious, selfish, ignorant, wise—ad nauseam. A good number, Indian expatriates who now live in Kenya and other parts of East Africa, proudly and publicly confess, "I would hate to live with India's filth and chaos."

Those from Nairobi explained the city offers the balance they seek between East and West, between industry and nature. Yet even most of these prosperous and "enlightened" Indians yell instead of talk, treat women as inferior objects, and rush to eat, rush to pack, rush to walk, rush to wash, rush to sleep, rush to fornicate, rush to relax, rush to board the bus, and rush to exit the bus.

Unusually soft and understated, the approachable Russian couple is well-traveled. Attempts to brainwash them when incarcerated in Chinese communist prisons seemed too delicate a subject to explore.

Glimpses of Japan are being shared by my Japanese *sensei* (teacher).

Prior to World War II, the rails and pack animals were the predominant means of transport. Radical postwar changes have begun to infiltrate an end to Japan's centuries-old, ritualistic, class-conscious society.

We were first directed to the Buddhist, Hindu, and Jain caves of Ellora and Ajanta. *Stunning* and *spectacular* do them little justice. Equally incredible are the muted surviving frescos and stone etchings, designed between 600 and 1000 CE, that cover portions of the cave walls. The excavation of Temple/Cave 16 (the Kailasa Temple) took over seven generations to complete. Think Petra in Jordan.

Dozens of surrounding cliffs house equally implausible temples that are "guarded" by figurines of mythological Hindu deities described in the sacred *Mahabharata*. Viewing creations of such colossal magnitude and intricacy is nothing short of Ultimate Awesome!

Lost to the world for millennia, the carvings in the Ajanta Caves, not yet completely excavated, were sculpted more than two thousand years ago. Before Jesus! The caves are said to have been accidentally discovered by a British officer hunting Bengal tiger.

Having witnessed these dramatic commitments to God, you come to realize the deep extent of spiritual life in ancient India, and the great devotion and physical effort made. Virtually all human endeavor acknowledged Lords Buddha and Krishna, for spiritualism was the overriding mainstay of human existence. It was to only the gods that the ancients focused their energies and rapt attention.

Ironically, although ancient India was once prosperous and flourished, today's authentic spiritual minority has been abandoned by the mainstream of impoverished India, replaced by an obsession with material gain—or so it seems. When you do not have, you place high value on having. When you have enough, you can devote energy to the spiritual. No different than my depression–age parents who did without, and today's hippies, most of whom never went hungry. Without preoccupation to meet the needs of my organic existence, the luxury to search and question my reasons for living becomes possible.

Throughout our casual tour of Aurangabad, I often hung back with my new Russian friends. Their daughter, Ina, practices social work in India to study the treatment of diseases long extinct in Europe. She travels about

158–160. Jainism preaches that spiritual liberation is to be gained by assuming a lifestyle of harmlessness and renunciation to be focused on the health and well-being of the universe and mankind.

Indian society, often visiting construction sites. And why is that? It seems that whenever a substantial building or road is to be constructed, Indian contractors hire entire villages—men, women, and children—to work and live adjacent to the project.

The resulting shantytowns—lacking toilet facilities, decent housing, transportation, adequate medical treatment, sources of nutritious food, and basic education—are now being serviced by social welfare agencies. Given free rein to manage these agencies, Ina's benefactors have decreed that no attention will be paid to the caste of individuals—a most fantastic breakthrough in traditional, caste-iron India.

Bombay, India
Monday, January 19, 1976, 6:00 A.M.

Insight into the nature and variety of the Indian middle-class may be revealed by the predicament of one extraordinary young woman, more broad-minded, independent, and "together" than most of her Eastern *and* Western sisters.

Without question, Subhah has experienced great trouble meeting equally liberal people due to the subordinate role women play in Indian society. Given developmental space as a child and young adult by her remarkable parents, they insisted she mix with members of the opposite sex—behavior commonly frowned upon within the broader Hindu social context for fear that "some difficulties" might arise. Yet considering India's population explosion, how ironic that virtually all Indians become embarrassed and shy—and often refuse to discuss—the nature of these "difficulties."

In fact, most Indians are reticent to discuss any sexual matters. When Subhah's enlightened parents are questioned, they respond to their critics by explaining that their daughter is a person with choices. Her dad often feigns innocence. "What kind of difficulties are you referring to?" he asks, turning the conversation to "safer" subjects. Currently a medical student, Subhah (the "Brain") is enrolled in a six-year program that began when she was an undergraduate. I cannot possibly overstate her astonishing deviation from the norm. The distance between her mindset and that of the typical Indian woman (and man) is immeasurable.

In contrast is the twenty-four-year-old trophy bride (the "Beauty") who sat behind me on the tour bus and lives in a world of make-believe. Unlike most middle-class Indian women, the "Brain" was not bred to ornament her father's and husband's homes. And though the "Beauty" attended college, she confided that she does nothing all day but sleep.

In patriarchal Indian society where women are often equated with property, a distinct separation of the sexes takes place. No doubt, feminine charms are judged more valuable than feminine intelligence. And though I am aware of this sexist mentality, I would be dishonest if I declined to admit my intellectual attraction to the "Brain," and my love and lust for the face and body of the "Beauty."

When discussing marriage with my breathtaking, hurtfully sexy Fantasy, I explained that in the West, weddings are not arranged; that most modern women and men usually live together and engage in sex before marriage. The "Beauty" thought me to be crazy. "If a girl marries, she must adjust to her husband. It is her duty."

Obviously, her thoughts vary widely from the more demanding and often spoiled attitudes of many Western women—and men. Mom and Dad arranged her marriage. Separation and divorce are not—and will never be—remote considerations. *Never.* Nonetheless, placed in perspective, the "Beauty" is among India's well-educated elite. In such matters, village India is mired in the Dark Ages. Comparatively, the "Beauty" is enlightened!

Subhah does not wish to practice medicine in the villages although that is where she is most needed. As is common of most Indian (and) Western doctors, she rationalizes (rightfully so?) that there is a total lack of modern facilities in rural areas. However, when her colleagues fail to mention their priority for comfortable, inordinately profitable urban lifestyles, I must consider the variations and complications of human nature, ambivalence, and selfishness—attributes I own as well.

"Indian villagers have an aversion to modern medicine, preferring naturally balanced *ayurvedic* [traditional, alternative] and herbal practices," she noted. "Along with witchcraft, many villagers employ a hot iron rod applied to the stomach to cure bellyaches."

As we returned to Bombay earlier this morning, billboards advertised

Pond's Dry Skin Cream. As young boys, my brother and I would buy our mother a bottle of Jergens Lotion for Mother's Day—year after year after year. Mother must have thought our gestures to be cute. But I wonder what she did with all those bottles.

And for the first time during any of my overseas trips, I am receiving continuous mail from my father, his way of assuring me of his good health after recent surgery to remove malignant polyps.

Tomorrow I leave for Udaipur and Rajasthan, the "Land of Kings," where, back in the day, the bereaved wives of men lost in battle tossed themselves over cliffs into huge bonfires to protect their honor!

Bombay, India
Tuesday, January 20, 1976

With time to kill before my train, I cheerfully walked into the railway station's latrine where grimy-looking families were bathing with soap and putrid brown water in old oil drums. Gray muck covered the walls, floors, urinals, and bathers. Farther down the same platform, a *spotless* vegetarian dining hall, complete with rich oak-paneled walls, had been built by and for the British. Need I further expand on white privilege in India during and after the British Raj?

Still waiting, I could not resist visiting nearby hallowed halls of Indian justice located in the second-class booking and reservation hall of the railway station. Mellowed by a joint, I didn't even mind the two dozen Indians staring at me as I put pencil to paper in the Magistrate's Court.

A useless ceiling fan spun above the docket, the judge, black-suited attorneys, poorly clad defendants, and one white-uniformed, yawning bailiff. Beneath four dull light bulbs were a host of male prisoners crouched in a sealed wooden cage. Pinned against the perimeter were spectators, apparently enjoying the insults hurled into the courtroom by those incarcerated.

After a twenty-minute pause, one of the policemen, attired in smartly ironed, military-like pleated khaki shorts above properly folded olive knee socks, was ordered by the magistrate to prevent me from writing. Come now. How did da judge notice me—a white, bearded, blond, long-haired sahib wearing sandals—sitting in an Indian chamber of justice?

Attendant lawyers barely expressed proper degrees of grave sobriety during a half-dozen trials involving railway crimes. During one, an illiterate, itinerant woman was formally accused of something. (The proceedings are not held in English.) After she denied the allegations, the prosecution's star witness, probably a railway conductor who might have caught her without a ticket, confirmed whatever she denied. All parties yelled. And yelled. And yelled. Helpless, the judge merely looked on, trying to figure out who was shouting the truth. In short order, the court resembled a riotous, dung-dependent (for heat and fuel), rural village argument.

Moments earlier, a spectator was ejected from the gallery for falling asleep, not an uncommon occurrence. Railway cops, perhaps trained by the New York City Transit Authority, routinely banged heavy wooden batons to wake up those napping on narrow slabs of wood.

That scene in the Indian courtroom was not unique during my travels. Perhaps I had realized but never verbalized the fact that I am seeing, listening, and learning how and what poor people think about rich people. Very little, I'm afraid. Wealthy souls are automatically and contemptuously ridiculed by most, regardless of individual personality or route to fortune. Am I not guilty?

Udaipur, Rajasthan, India
Thursday, January 22, 1976

A three-hour delay in Ahmedabad would have proven to be the crowning jewel of my rail journey to Udaipur were it not for my encounter with a pleasant constable from the state of Gujarat. His smart outfit, worn over a robust black body, included pleated and cuffed khaki shorts supported by thick suspenders above brown knee socks. Between sporadic questions concerning possession of whiskey, Promit, my twenty-two-year-old civil servant, described the methods he employs when searching for contraband.

According to his testimony, he had recently beaten and arrested an African national. When revealed in court, the magistrate warned him not to intimidate and impugn foreigners while condoning the two holes Promit had placed in the African's head. Though feeling a bit uneasy carrying hashish in my rucksack, once my new friend moved on, I blew a joint on the upper berth of a darkened and abandoned carriage.

From the moment I arrived in Udaipur, I have been dazzled. My perch from the Udaipur Tourist Bungalow permits striking views of lime-shaded desert valleys surrounded by beige mountains and the marvelous "white city." A fiery desert sunset was enjoyed from its roof before walking through a mysterious pink bazaar. Palatial arches and Arabic minarets punctuated darkening horizons beneath sparkling stellar performances.

Incredible dinner service was rendered by the maître d' of the main dining hall in Udaipur's Park View Hotel. Ignoring my rusty table manners, waiters and busboys hovered over me and my new traveling companions, Tallahassee natives Gary and Linda. Recent arrivals from Singapore, they had spent a year working as city planners.

Multiple courses were prepared and cooked to our liking, served on porcelain china complemented by genuine silverware, crystal stemware and fine cloth napkins. Fabulous desserts followed our choice of savory chicken or fish *biryani* (a spicy rice dish).

The onset of wedding season in Rajasthan permitted us to crash three street processions: abundant flowers, klezmer-like sinewy music, horse-mounted grooms, dancing daddies, fluorescent fireworks, and a parade of lanterns and ladies. Lights for the procession were provided by servants carrying portable generators.

While in Calcutta, Gary and Linda attended a formal marriage ceremony lasting three days. The bridegroom's procession arrived at the girl's home ("girl" seems appropriate, as many brides are teenagers) where the wedding ceremony took place on the first night. In Western countries, mothers usually assume a major role in making such a big fucking deal about the event. In India, the groom's mother does not even attend. During the second evening, the procession traveled to the bridegroom's home. The third evening? Consummation?

Next came exploration of City Palace, Lake Palace, and hundreds of well-appointed royal residences and whitewashed homes that often created unexpected artistic plazas. Multicolored pastel murals of tigers, elephants, princes and maharajas covered many white-washed walls. Brilliant!

Thousands of mirrors and mosaics, and endless murals, archways and

161 and 162. These phenomenal artists stayed within the lines!

mazes form the enormity of City Palace. Students of historical-sexual politics might salivate (or regurgitate) over this fact: The women's wings of City Palace, one of the largest and grandest of all Rajasthan, contain no doors, outlets, passageways or windows to the outdoors. More Indian mystique!

Udaipur's scintillating lake contains several islands upon which additional palaces have been built. A glistening white diamond set against a royal blue sky and golden mountains is the Lake Palace Hotel. Immediate adjacent pools reflect the desert's prism-like spectrum of forever-changing colors, shadows, and perspectives. Blame sunrise and sunset.

163 and 164. The City Palace of Udaipur is an active complex of palaces within a palace. Current custodians, not rulers, are the *maharanas* ("king of kings") of Udaipur—on behalf of Lord Shiva.

Within and without one of a hundred Hindu temples featuring meticulously detailed stone carvings, a crowd had gathered at the lowest rung of a steep stairwell. Somehow arranged on the landing was a victim of elephantiasis (grossly enlarged, hardened limbs). *"My God."* Is it not blasphemous to conclude, as many Hindus do, that God and karma are responsible for this misery?

Despite such misfortune, I am enthralled with desert-bound Udaipur and its Moorish-Mughal architecture. My dream to experience and explore ancient and present India has not only become reality, but also provides greater insight into the Raj Singh family of Gabhana, formerly of Rajasthan. (Not by chance, the surnames of most Rajasthanians, especially those of the royal families, end with *Singh* and *Raj Singh*.) In essence, Rajasthan's exotic romance, distinct population and rugged topography characterize yet another unique nation state of India—a country of many nations.

Once owned by *maharanas*, not to be confused with lower-rung maharajas, Rajasthan's temples, palaces and fortresses define a land of enchantment, fantasy and fortitude. Daydreams prompted by literature and movies lend credence to the notion that we are limited only by the confines of our imagination. Consider the book *One Thousand and One Nights: Tales from the Arabian Nights* and the movies *Ali Baba and the Forty Thieves* (1944), *The Lives of a Bengal Lancer* (starring Gary Cooper, 1935), and "Gunga Din" (poem by Rudyard Kipling, 1890; film starring Sam Jaffe and Cary Grant, 1939).

The Amer or Amber Palace and Fort, built centuries ago near Jaipur, Rajasthan's capital city, lends credence to the above.

165. Absolutely awesome!

As I contemplate where I have been and what I have learned, I think about the arbitrary and irrational political boundaries exacted by governments. In ancient and tribal worlds, borders were set more by culture, religion, and natural geography than by power politics. Think Rajasthan, Pakistan, Afghanistan, Uzbekistan, Turkestan, Hindustan, Pashtunistan, and Baluchistan. (The suffixes *stan* and *stahan* translate as "land of.") You need not be an anthropologist to comprehend how Rajasthan was once considered to be a separate national entity.

Have just learned of the death of Chou En-lai, the Chinese Communist first premier of the People's Republic of China. Along with Mao, Chou is probably most responsible for "China for the Chinese."

Udaipur, India
Friday, January 23, 1976, 7:00 A.M.
Gary interrupted my wet dream so I could view yet another celebrated Udaipur sunrise—burning orange rays casting their strength upon gray-brown desert hues, linen-white compounds, and the kaleidoscopic stained glass of the City Palace.

Chittor, India
Saturday, January 24, 1976, Late Morning
Views from the bus on our way to Chittor: sparse, crude, rock and sandy desert villages, zinc processing plants, irrigated fields of winter wheat, and women and men in bright, multicolored shawls, saris and turbans tending to primitive wells worked by white Brahman sacred cows.

No more than a closely knit maze of commercial hovels and homely huts located below the namesake mountain and fort that strategically dominate this entire region, chaotic and sparsely populated Chittor features big bold rats that have seized the public urinals, streets, and sidewalk moats. In flagrant contrast to Chittor's trash-filled streets and clogged open sewers is an abundance of stone carvings, Moorish influence, and more rats.

Saturday, January 25, 1976, 8:00 A.M.
The Chittor Dak Bungalow is a quiet palatial estate. Amenities include spacious suites, bathrooms with *flush* toilets, electricity, fresh sheets and

mattresses, and access to landscaped gardens and grounds. Total price for three? Fifty cents!

Truthfully, booking lodging at most government tourist bungalows sucks. Usually told I can stay for only one night because a large group has reserved all beds, each evening finds many vacant bungalows. That all caretakers spout the same "one night song and dance," consistency rarely found in India, can only mean one thing: some corrupt, frustrated high official who can't get laid and is still fighting the British, decided to impose discriminatory insanity against foreigners.

Chittor*garh* refers to a renowned series of forts, palaces, ornate rock-sculptured towers and ruins of ancient bazaars and gardens situated on an immense plateau. Noted for its grandiose scale and magnitude beyond comparison with anything in the West, the former Jain stronghold still provides majestic, militarily strategic views of Chittor, the parched lands below, and the fucking rats.

If any parallel with the West can be drawn, it lies beyond random chance. That is, aged Indian fortresses and centuries-old European manors built at approximately the same time exemplify different versions of feudalism. Warriors, religions, fiefdoms, kings, and maharajas played major roles in each society. And although military might had become *the* trump card, divinity reserved a parallel if not slightly subordinate but sustaining role in the lives of all the players. These conceptual clones—self-sufficiency, architectural integrity and purpose, strategic military placement, symbiotic and hierarchical relationships, and devotion to God-kings—become more striking when considering they derive from such vastly distinct and distant cultures.

That such deeply divergent civilizations should arrive at the same methods at about the same time, to ensure the survival of their economic, political, social, and religious systems, is rather inconceivable—but surely *not* entirely coincidental. Makes me wonder: To what extent is human nature culture-bound? Did not the kernel of belief in monotheism, in a unity of one God, take place in the Middle East and in India at about the same time? More coincidence?

ॐ

Pushkar and Ajmer, Ajmer District, State of Rajasthan, India
Wednesday, January 28, 1976

Between Udaipur and Jaipur lies the city of Ajmer, a small bustling Rajasthani city that grows coffee beans for six hundred million. Across a depressed lake and over brown grassless steppes sits Pushkar, a most sacred settlement of sadhus, temples, priests, and cows. Self-appointed and self-serving, a hashish-smoking, saffron-robed priestly "guide" convinced me to burn incense—and ganja—in a temple devoted to Brahma, the Creator.

166. Pushkar and its sacrosanct namesake lake.

Jaipur, India
Wednesday, January 28, 1976

While waiting to buy a return bus ticket to Jaipur, a communal taxi hawker made me an offer I didn't want to refuse—but did—after Indians in the queue began to squirm and enlighten me: "Hey, Charlie, the taxi drivers are kidnappers and thieves."

Jaipur's City Palace, known as the Pink City—it is literally painted pink—maintains stately apartments, art museums, actively occupied royal living quarters, Moorish mosaics, and some fine-looking princesses. One of the most powerful of all Indian rajas, the reigning maharaja of Jaipur continues to retain legal custody over most of this domain. Unimpressed, herds of cows, goats, camels, and occasional elephants see to it that bicycles, pedestrians, and motor vehicles behave themselves.

Gabhana Palace, India
Wednesday, January 28, 1976

I have returned to northern India and my favorite haunt, the Gabhana Palace. Greeting me, Locki Raj wore fine black jodhpurs (full-length trousers worn for horseback riding). With his long black hair and full beard, he resembled George Harrison circa *All Things Must Pass*. As a little boy and distant blood relative of Jaipur's maharaja, Locki Raj often vacationed in Udaipur's Lake Palace as a guest of the royal family before it became a five-hundred-star hotel.

As we spent time at the palace, I focused on the many servants I witnessed on the estate. Fortunate Indians hire human servants to care for themselves, their homes, their lands, and even to provide entertainment. Europeans and Americans purchase "servants"—automobiles, radios, telephones, microwaves, refrigerators, televisions, and so on.

You may wonder about the nature of the relationships between *gurujis* (masters) and *naukars* (servants). In the West, it seems rather obvious. In India, casteism is the trump card. Dynamics between the higher castes ("masters") and the lower castes ("servants") are dictated by culture. Nevertheless, the warm, affectionate treatment of Gunda and Karala by the Raj Singh brothers demonstrates cracks in otherwise proscribed behavior.

Ravi Raj, Locki Raj, and I smoked a gun before watching laborers convert raw stalks of sugarcane into heavy blocks of brown sugar to be sold at the Gabhana market. The squeezing of freshly cut sugarcane into a pulpy liquid began the time-consuming process. After repeated boilings to ensure purification, the liquid was then transferred from one big black pot to another by extremely dark-skinned Indians wearing only loincloths. As they profusely sweated under a dispassionate sun, I recalled cartoons characters I had watched as a kid—and felt guilty.

Land ceilings. The federal government continues to limit holdings of wealthy landlords, distributing the balance to the poor. Having read of this third world practice for years, I am now able to see and feel its reality taking place in and around Gabhana. Locki Raj favors the reforms, knowing that local farmers have been made aware of modern and efficient methods of land management and conservation. No doubt, Father is of the old school.

As evening approached, I bid my hosts "Namaste." (There is no verbatim Hindi translation for good morning, good afternoon, and good night. "Namaste" is used.)

Gabhana Palace
Thursday, January 29, 1976, 6:00 A.M.

Woke to black crows chanting to Surya, the Hindu sun god. My strengthening relationships with Locki Raj and Ravi Raj are the most valuable parts of my stay at Gabhana.

Ahmad, an intern we met at the University Hospital of Aligarh, joined last night's cozy dinner party. Originally from Delhi, he came to Aligarh in 1968, completed his medical training in five years, now works for the government, and believes that his colleagues' egos are detrimental to group work. "I must acknowledge that the frequent infighting among the physicians with whom I collaborate often self-defeats the services we provide." Sound familiar?

Assisted by three paramedics from Delhi, Ahmad regularly visits Gabhana to dispense medical care at an infirmary he established. Inundated with patients suffering from varied skin rashes and ailments the very moment he arrived last night, he was not able to relax and party until quite late. (He had visited Locki Raj's folks earlier—proper protocol.)

To find parts to overhaul his tractor's engine, Ravi Raj had driven his jeep to Delhi. Had he asked his mechanic to supply parts, based on experience, they would have been old and faulty. Complete cost? Six hundred dollars. Labor? Less than one percent.

Surrounding fields, now green with winter wheat, will soon turn gold as harvest approaches. Though wheat is sown, rice is literally planted under water. Not bad for a boy raised in the "Big Apple," and who once believed milk came from cartoons "made in Brooklyn." Ha!

From medicine, Ahmad segued to politics, suggesting "democracy has come to an end in India. Emergency is not helping the poor." Officially, when the National Emergency was declared on June 25, 1975, by Indian Prime Minister Indira Gandhi, it created a shock wave throughout India. The fascist order gave the prime minister the authority to rule by decree, allowing elections to be suspended and civil liberties to be curbed. Most of Gandhi's political opponents have been imprisoned. The press is now censored. Additional human rights violations include a mandatory mass-sterilization campaign spearheaded by Sanjay Gandhi, the prime minister's son and heir apparent. This is *not* the nature of the democracy envisioned by Mahatma Gandhi and Jawaharlal Nehru, independent India's first prime minister (1947).

"I can no longer talk out against the government," Ahmad continued. Perhaps Ahmad is impatient. I paralleled Spanish history to modern India. "Forty years ago, the empty-bellied Spanish required food more than political freedom." Francisco Franco, who shamefully assumed the title of *Caudillo* (asshole), and though never referred to as a "benevolent dictator," facilitated necessary development by creating a strong central government. Today, Spain's well-fed middle class is exercising its right for political and personal freedoms.

Am I saying the price to be paid for food is fascism? Sadly, yes, but not for all. In truth, only the affluent educated minority is restrained by dictatorship because it is the only segment of society that ever actually exercises its political and civil rights. The majority, in trying to secure the basics, continue to be preoccupied with daily survival. Only when placed under a strong central government genuinely dedicated to raising everyone's standard of living can some balance between the Haves and Have-Nots begin to occur. In current form, does not India still resemble pre-Franco Spain?

That said, is the surrender of democracy, political freedom, and civil rights for material gain worth it? Ahmad does not advocate or agree with even a brief suspension of political freedom because he doesn't see such loss amounting to anything. Considering he is a member of the educated elite, might his conclusions be functions of self-protection and unconscious rationalization? Perhaps not. Perhaps he is sincere, altruistic, and ambivalent.

As a slightly informed observer, I do see improvements taking place—albeit *s-l-o-w-l-y*: enhanced train service, fewer black markets, lower prices, and initiation of new urban and rural land ceilings that will continue to limit real estate holdings of the Haves.

Bottom line? Cajoling "altruistic" politicians fool few. Despite said improvements, Indira Baby and her ilk continue to neglect and defraud the greater ninety-nine percent. Acutely shrewd, Mrs. Gandhi ensured her power station by declaring Emergency. Her timing was precise.

A political animal at heart, and no different from the entire self-serving, self-indulgent species, her attempts to placate supporters of law and democracy by plying hollow promises to uplift the lower castes play minor roles to political expediency. Although enacting Emergency may prove to be a godsend for hundreds of millions of India's wanting souls, it has already enhanced the political pulpit and legal power of the crafty prime minister. Do not be fooled. The genuine purpose of Emergency is Gandhi's political survival. The savvy woman must not be underestimated.

(Caveat: Though hard to believe, on rare occasion, political decisions taken by governments actually do have constructive consequences even if initiated by pompous, egocentric motivation. Droves of hawkish members of the US Congress became peaceful doves not because they sincerely believed the Vietnam War was wrong, but because their constituencies changed thinking, and the hypocritical schmucks chose to prostitute themselves to get reelected.)

Personally, I feel caught in a dilemmic bind. Where are Lao Tzu and Lord Krishna? Where is King Solomon? Must political freedom and civil decency be sacrificed for economic expansion? For India, the doleful answer seems to be yes. Spain wants freedom now. India cannot yet afford freedom. This is its karma, its fate. Perhaps Emergency must last two or three or five generations before enough people have adequately filled bellies to concern themselves with the freedoms of mind, heart, and spirit. Think "critical mass."

It was apparent to me when I left India in 1972 that the need for absolute central authority—to control and monitor almost all facets of life—was paramount. Nothing I have seen thus far causes me to conclude otherwise. Perhaps a Maoist government would succeed if it were radically adjusted to Indian culture. Does not the establishment of Emergency mirror these thoughts?

Locki Raj's political mantra? Though government policy may be well-intentioned, its current enactment via longstanding bureaucratic machinery is seriously impeded by deeply embedded institutional and individual corruption. Fear of disclosure and recourse to arbitrary police punishment have, thus far, proven to be virtually useless deterrents to stop and prevent such institutional graft and disparity of wealth and resources.

Rishikesh, India
Saturday, January 31, 1975

An "ashram" owned and managed by Swami Prakash Bharti is one and the same "hotel" I frequented during my previous visit to Rishikesh. Sad to say, the crib hasn't much changed, especially the chronic chillum smoking among its international hippie clientele. Though some actually refer to this place as a Hindu retreat, an ashram, I honestly don't see much difference between it and most dens of iniquity. The whimsical practice of yoga pales in comparison to far more dominant pursuits—sexual perversion and drug addiction. Although eccentric and engaging, and having once renounced the material world for the life of a sadhu, the swami is no more realized than you or I.

Before heading to bed, I walked to the Rishikesh malt shop where Archie, Jughead, Veronica and Betty had joined a group of funky Indians who passed around chillums while jamming on tablas, sitars, cymbals, and sticks. A Dutchman, carrying his own skins, got down as though he was Ali Akbar Khan, Ravi Shankar's accompanist.

Chilly drizzle continues this morning as I contemplate my navel before a fireplace located in a dreary dark chamber I share with four other stoned seekers of truth. Via mail and *Star Trek*, I'm about to astral project, one of travel's most nourishing moments. "Beam me up, Scotty."

I also turn to *Autobiography of a Yogi* by Paramahansa Yogananda, its preface written by the eminent writer and philosopher, W. Y. Evans-Wentz, equally well-known for publishing an English translation of *The Tibetan Book of the Dead* in 1927. His preface emphasizes that *Autobiography*, a book about the wise men of India, about yogis, is written not by a journalist or a foreigner, but by an actual yogi.

Perusing Paramahansa Yogananda's intimate thoughts and feelings gave rise to simultaneous rational wonder and inexplicable irrational panic as I contemplated my spiritual future. Infidels are directed to the content of a letter written by Harry Rose, Los Angeles mortuary director in 1952, *weeks after* Paramahansa Yogananda had quit his body (died). "Attendants noticed no bodily odor, decay, mold, or any sign of physical mortality!"

Rishikesh, India
Monday, February 2, 1976, Sunset

167. Bal Yogi Prem Varni:
"If you are bound to freedom, you desire freedom. How do you become free of freedom?"

168. Gautama Buddha:
"To have it all, you must give it all up."

After a long hiatus, I have returned to Yoganta Academy to ask Sri Bal Yogi Prem Varni to accept me as a serious student. Below are brief excerpts from my application.

In my late teens and early twenties, I often experimented with ganja, hashish, LSD, mescaline, psilocybin, and altered states of consciousness. Experiencing the cosmic universe for the first time, I felt naturally complete and in total touch with my naked existence, as if my mind transcended my body. I desired nothing and had everything. No limitations. *Absolute authenticity.* An out-of-body experience. I contemplated the nature of reality versus illusion. *Reality is perception.*

I believe I can best perform the ashram's most fundamental aspect, seva by serving with honesty and sincerity. By realizing that when I see others, I see myself, I must conclude that service for one is service for all. Service for the Self is nothing more than an illusion perpetrated by the selfish ego.

Unable to know the nature of my welcome, I arrived at the front gate of the ashram and recognized its gatekeeper, Bernard, who has been living at Yoganta since 1972. He appeared as he had in the past: mortal and not representative of the saintly stereotypes some hold of those cloistered in ashrams under the tutelage of masters.

For three years, I had flirted with returning to Yoganta and Bal Yogi Prem Varni; yet the reality of being conditionally "accepted" as an aspirant is now proving to be perplexing. Although I feel elated, acceptance appears to be a labile process. One hour. One day at a time. Exhilaration tempered by anxiety. Romantic notions are about to be extinguished. I feel no-nonsense vibes. Already not what I expected—an unwelcome of sorts.

And then I heard the guru speak. While in his physical presence, I am but a spellbound child, my well-guarded intimacies and defense mechanisms already known to this Realized Being.

The Tourist Bungalow, Rishikesh, India
Tuesday, February 3, 1976, 9:00 A.M.

Haven't smoked cannabis for five days. Can't fall asleep.

Noted headlines found in the censored *Times of India* reveal that Indira and her Congress Party convention delegates have declared themselves to be "bulwarks against fascism." Really? Their drivelous and frivolous proc-lamations fly in the face of political truth. Declaration of Emergency may be fine for the beginning task of improving the economy, but let's stay rooted in reality. *Emergency has transformed democratic India into a fascist dictatorship.* The convention delegates' sponsorship and support of Indira Gandhi is evidence of their exclusive motivation: political self-preservation.

When I read such rubbish, I cringe and want to wring necks. A pho-tograph of the speaker's platform includes Sanjay Gandhi, the prime min-ister's son. Nepotism lives. Fucking disgraceful!

Trivia: India's abundant labor force results in tailor-made saris costing less than those factory-made. In the West, particularly in the United States, the private sector is far more efficient than the government. In India, effi-ciency is not even relative. There is none.

And how about a rather frightening thesis formulated by one William Dufty in *Sugar Blues*. Equating sugar to poison, Mr. Dufty, a labor activist who also wrote *Lady Sings the Blues*, suggests that had the US Air Force dropped sugar pellets and candy and soda instead of bombs on North Vietnam, the United States might have won the war.

A wall poster hanging in the Rishikesh General Post Office:

COURTESY COST NOTHING
YET MAY BRING MUCH CREDIT TO YOU

Yoganta Ashram, Lakshman Jhula, India
Tuesday, February 3, 1976, 10:00 P.M.

Success means doing the best with what we have. Success is the do-ing, not the getting. In the trying, not the triumph.

—Zig Ziglar

After crossing the Lakshman Jhula Suspension Bridge from Rishikesh, I walked to Yoganta in total darkness, accompanied by the eternal rhythms of the rushing Ganges sporadically interrupted by the sounds of chanting sadhus and children singing in ubiquitous temples.

Am feeling like a newborn babe, the new kid on the block. Very awkward. Bernard's presence is supportive and comforting. All facets of my everyday life have changed. As though the structural scaffolding of the details of my basic existence is being demolished, I feel empty and naked, metaphors describing the scrubbing of my body, mind, and spirit.

For the foreseeable future, my home is Yoganta's Austerity Cottage, one hundred percent natural mud-and-thatch hut appointed with earthen floor, a prayer mat, and thin featherless mattress. Breakfast consists of a hot drink and fruit. A complete meal is taken at lunch.

I attended a brief meeting of six disciples, three women and three men. Ghiana, from Deutschland, has studied with Prem Varni for five years. An Australian mother of two has been here for six months. Having shed her cocoon, a California butterfly, "Dear Prudence," returns occasionally. Michael, here only three weeks, is French. Bernard appears to be the senior aspirant, a concept wholly blasphemous to egalitarian ashram sociology and theology. Or is it? What do I know?

We sat on floor mats next to burning candles and dense incense. The morning's discussion (unusually casual and lighthearted with much laughter) turned into a talk on how the pigs of Goa eat breakfast. (How did Prem Varni know of my morning in Goa?) Jesus, I never thought the first thing I would hear from this guru—or any guru—would be how pigs eat shit! Swamiji continued, "If you have diarrhea, pigs think you are a great man."

Knowing I had also taken a taxi from Rishikesh to the Lakshman Jhula Bridge (how did he possibly know?), Swamiji described the day the Maharishi and the Beatles helicoptered to Rishikesh. He mocked their arrival by indicating that the small earthen circle immediately outside Yoganta's entrance could accommodate a heliport. Smiling broadly, he continued to satirize Maharishi's flirtations with rich and famous seekers. "When the Beatles came to Rishikesh, the Maharishi created three tiers, the Maharishi, the Beatles and the Hippies." Jesus, Moses, Krishna. This dude is spaced.

I rise at 5:00 a.m. with the aid of a mechanical alarm clock; other aspirants naturally rise before sunrise. Required equipment includes a Neti Lota, a tubular, rubber nasal catheter/apparatus; a white handkerchief for straining water, salt, rosewater, almond oil, and incense; matches and candles; a broom and dustpan; straw mat; and personal items. Swamiji granted me permission to continue to keep my diary. He suggested I entitle a chapter "From Goa to the Ganga."

169 and 170. Located at the feet of Himalayan foothills, and bisected by the teal and flowing sacred Ganga, Rishikesh is a pilgrimage destination for seekers of Supreme Truth. "Rishi" is Sanskrit for sage or great sadhu. The sacred township, a center for spiritual study over the centuries, stores hundreds of ashrams. (Parmarth means "greatest ultimate truth.")

Wednesday, February 4, 1976

The sun is setting. (I share the Hindu belief that sunrise and sunset emit spiritual vibrations.) My day is drawing to a close. With Bernard, I bathed in the brutally cold but gorgeous Ganga. Submerged in clear turquoise waters passing through kelly-green Himalayan foothills, I felt a deep, almost enjoyable pain. My hair and skin turned baby soft.

Early evening clouds continue to reflect pink and crimson as they float above divinely secure Rishikesh. Each cloud holds a unique and fleeting existence somehow bound to the flow of one another and the pace of The River.

At dusk, I washed dishes with cold water, sand, and pieces of bark from coconut trees. Body wash is a concoction of biodegradable ingredients.

After reading the first chapters of the *Ramayana* (Hindu scripture), I now fully realize that I'm living in the realm of a true saint, untainted spiritualism, and no-nonsense concentration on Atman, the Self. Bernard again led me to a white sand beach along the east bank of the Sacred River. Oh, how beautiful it was . . . and is . . . and will be.

I suppose, in due time, Swamiji will assign me tasks and I will begin my ashram work. Yet, perhaps, it has already begun—through nonaction. *Nothing is something is Zen.*

Yoganta Academy, Lakshman Jhula, India
Wednesday, February 4, 1976, After Dinner

Realization. My entire life has changed. All activity and habits are different: the way I shit, eat, sit, talk, sleep, think, feel, and breathe. Everything is natural. But not natural for me. No added chemicals whatsoever. And so, without alternative, I have come to realize that I totally overestimated my desire for the spiritual path. For this spiritual path. *Personal Failure City?*

Already? Some correctly say that a guru destroys one's dreams and desires, particularly if they are momentary illusions that are impossible to grasp over time. Surely, I am not the man I imagined my Self to be—unable to lead the life of an ascetic. My days are filled with anxiety and mental and physical distress. Everything is done in a specific way. Any variance is wrong. Absolutely *no nonsense* permeates the atmosphere. What is natural is not yet natural for me.

Am deeply disappointed and disillusioned. People here are aloof and spaced-out over Krishna, Rama, and Swamiji. Not really knowing what I am doing, I hum along when the women sing beautiful devotionals. While attempting to adapt my empty behavior and expectations to that of the other aspirants, I've been taught almost nothing and spend most of my days uncomfortably wondering about what it is I am to do.

While everyone else has his or her program, I have nothing. And isn't it ironic that I use high tech "program" to describe cosmic and spiritual matters? Nothing is what I thought it would be. *Absolutely nothing.* After I use the "wrong" bucket or forget someone's name (I have committed many "minor offenses"), Swamiji tells me I lack common sense.

During a walk to Lakshman Jhula with The Master and Bernard, Bal Yogi Prem Varni more than intimated that I am not ready for his ashram, the "ashram of a yogi." Swamiji believes I do not know how to live at Yoganta and feels I should try a different one.

Dreams are broken here—very quickly. Perhaps, at first, I should not have been so meek and hesitant. But I wanted to follow, possibly too blindly, the dictates of a Realized Savant. Truth is, this beautiful Astral Being has reached into my inner Self, my deepest levels of consciousness, and found them wanting for whatever it is he feels I need to possess to remain in his ashram.

I had long planned to study here, and now my scheme seems to have been shattered. Yet it is all meant to be. You must go with the flow. To stay here for months as originally intended would ignore today's reality. Rationalization? Perhaps.

Sagacious Bernard, far wiser than his thirty years, opines that Swamiji is testing my resolve. Yes, I think he is. At last evening's meeting, I begged Prem Varni for permission to remain, and believe he will acquiesce. However, a visa problem must first be resolved by going to Jammu to obtain a three-month extension. Perhaps I should heed Swamiji's suggestion: stay some days at Vivekananda Ashram just across the River Ganga, and sporadically visit Yoganta.

I guess what I really want is an integration of East and West, not the life (even temporarily) of a sadhu. Wishing to learn physical (hatha) yoga and other meditative techniques, I have been concentrating on chanting "Rama." (Rama, a Hindu God, is considered an avatar descended from Lord Shiva.) And even if I remain and hack the physically strenuous regimen, the psychological strain may well be beyond my present capacity. Nevertheless, I desperately want to stick out this experience for three months.

Surely, it will facilitate discovery of my true, absolute, cosmic Self. But at what price? My sanity?

Unwilling to bullshit myself, I simply cannot pretend to feign interest in much of the Hindu mythology and divine chanting to which I am now exposed. But how do I pointedly focus on yoga, meditation, and consciousness to the exclusion of all else when everything is integrated? Within the depths of my soul, I can't help but recognize that I am deceiving myself when paying homage to symbolic picture gods (Krishna, Shiva, Vishnu, Brahma, et al.), knowing I sincerely believe the eternal, blissful, all-knowing spirit lies within, not without.

I have neither developed a strong emotional affinity for bhakti (devotional) yoga in which Yoganta is steeped, nor found a coveted balance of study and gratification despite the constant ridicules I have tolerated. Bal Yogi Prem Varni believes I am senseless. In *his* way, he may be right, but my ego is too sensitive, too fragile, too vulnerable, and too damaged to handle all this shit at once.

While I concede I am not yet prepared to relinquish the desires and baggage lashed to my ego by the tentacles of Western insecurity and vanity, I must also acknowledge and own my delusions regarding how "spiritual" I have (not) become. Being taught little, perhaps I have learned much, particularly when painfully assuming, for more than an hour at a time, the full lotus position. But have I not gained increased perspective on myself, my Self, my needs, my wants, the differences, what I want out of life, and what I am willing to do to find and achieve them?

Though feeling dazed and confused, I still believe that we all possess the potential to spiritually realize ourselves: to feel, to think, to do, to simply be. How far I will go to transcend those tentacles is probably hidden somewhere in my karmic past and future. Today, total austerity and devotion *ain't* my Tao. I repeat. Balance and integration of East and West suit me to a far greater extent than all-encompassing bhakti.

However, having reached these mutable conclusions, I experience nagging disconcertment and bewilderment throughout. I still fiercely want to receive a mantra from this blessed, omniscient yogi, understanding that it takes Swamiji about two to three months for him to feel my nature.

Until then, he can teach me little in the way of vibrational techniques.

But how can I remain here when I want *satsang* (spiritual gathering with a realized being) to end, when I am unable to concentrate on and understand his wisdom because my legs are aching as I sit in the full lotus position? Surely, much of what I have written contains feeble rationalizations of the fact that my ego refuses to accept crushing defeat.

At least, as regards seva, service for others, *the* focal point of this ashram, I feel headed in the right direction. As for enlightenment, I have no doubt that those genuinely spaced-out, devotional seekers who are well on the austere, yogic path to nirvana, and whose actions speak more forcefully than words, thoughts, and feelings, do not believe the balance of which I speak is an authentic path to realization. Am I deluding myself in thinking that such a balance can take me to the same place? But are there not infinite paths leading to like destinations? Is the attainment of enlightenment prevented by use of a "wrong" bucket? Yet I recognize that awareness is a consequence of inconsequential detail.

All appears weird and paradoxical. Though the Blessed One is understandably teaching me in his own way, it is beyond my understanding. Apparently, the process goes against the grain of my Western-based ego/self. From what I can thus far glean, to know humbleness and humility, you first must learn to serve. For if you are to be a master, how can you do so until you know what it is to be a servant?

Growing up in New York City provided no alternative but to hurry or be run over. Now that I have finally slowed my pace, the All-Knowing One wants everything to be done immediately, right now, yesterday. During other moments of silent ambivalent reflection, I *am* able to place all this into a broader context; my longing to experience a genuine Vedic ashram is being sated.

Before satsang, I accompanied Swamiji and Bernard on a walk near the Ganga, passing the spot where, in 1972, I ecstatically witnessed a legendary sadhu lying on a veritable bed of thorns. Also known as the "The Monkey Man," and though able to speak, he has now posted a sign indicating his silence since 1973—and his intention to remain so—until 1985!

As the sun set during satsang, I freaked when my orange-robed guru began a deep long nasal vibration: "Aaauuuummmm." Seated to his left and right were his devoted disciples. Offerings of incense and natural fragrances were placed in a small charcoal fire. Flames burst high. All chanted, "Aum Shanti Aum." (God bless us with peace.)

After satsang, Bal Yogi Prem Varni made another unveiled comment directed toward my departure before allowing Bernard to walk with me in the forest. Convinced that Swamiji can cure Michael's paralyzed right hand, Bernard spoke of the Bal Yogi's glorious abilities—that it can be done if Michael allows Swamiji into his heart, permitting Michael himself to cure his own malady. Such are the workings of the Tao.

Upon returning to the ashram for a spot of warm goat's milk, I felt elated and hoped Swamiji would ask me to remain. But this did not happen. And, in hindsight, I was foolish to even entertain such wishful thinking. Realized beings are not like mothers, fathers, Western clergy, and school-teachers who change their mind if you are good.

Lakshman Junction, India
Some Days Later

Am waiting on a deserted platform for a train to Jammu and the material world so that I can extend my Indian visa. First stop? Venerated Hardwar, home of the spectacular Kumbh Mela, the Great Gathering and Pilgrimage made by *twenty million people* every twelve years.

Actually, a Mela is held every three years, is rotated among four hallowed river junctions, and attracts a massive gathering: soulful teachers, seekers of spiritual purification, genuine and knockoff gurus, sadhus, Brahman priests, Untouchables, witch doctors, snake charmers, astrologers, Zoroastrians, palm readers, monks, the faithful, and the not-so-faithful. However, today, Hardwar's Railway Station is the domain of dozens of screeching, swinging monkeys.

Surprisingly unable to buy any spiritual literature at the station's kiosk, I purchased a copy of the *Times of India* dated Saturday, February 7, 1976 (not necessarily today's edition), and was immediately confronted by the depths of India's desolation in contrast to the spiritual beauty of ethereal and sublime Yoganta and Rishikesh.

Beyond ugly, selfish, and seamy political intrigues, cops shooting robbers, and railway ambushes was this headline:

SALES OF EGGS BANNED

The Rishikesh municipal board decided on Friday to ban public sale and purchase of eggs, fish, and meat within the municipal limits. Those who violate the ban selling these articles will be fined rupees 500. The buyers will be required to pay a fine of rupees 250.

Rishikesh, "the place where saints dwell," one of India's most sacred spiritual communities and considered the birthplace of yoga, annually draws millions of sadhus and fervent Hindu faithful into its many ashrams. However, it is doubtful their presence will deter black marketeers from making a killing. Surely, the ruling will have absolutely no effect on the *rajasic* (non-stimulating) and *sattvic* (pure, balanced, spiritually healthy) diet of Yoganta Ashram.

Jammu and Kashmir, India
Sunday, February 8, 1976

Glacial peaks of the distant Kashmiri Himalayas punctuate the horizon of an enormous snowless plain. This surreal vista is shared by armed Indian troops who now occupy Jammu and Kashmir, an Indian territory also claimed by Pakistan and Led Zeppelin on *Physical Graffiti* (1975).

Jammu, the winter capital, is populated by Muslim street vendors adept at creating a carnivore's delight, frying chicken, beef, and fish kabobs in makeshift black woks. Ironically, Jammu and Kashmir is ninety percent Muslim, a fact not lost on those who live in this unsettled territory.

So often, it is merely the simple, unpredictable whim of an official that dictates the outcome of events. Hence, I offer exhibit A, my two-hour ordeal at the Central Intelligence Department (CID), a study in inconsistency and misinterpretation. After filling out triplicate copies of a visa application while enduring verification of my passport, visa, name, rank, serial number—and my Aunt Fanny's recipe for *latkes* (potato pancakes)—I was subjected to the ever-scrutinizing eyes of a puritanical zealot and protector of the Hindu homeland.

He paid special note to the entry and exit stamps of Indian, Nep-

171. Jammu and Kashmir is the only Indian state populated by a majority of Muslims (90 percent). Under Indian administration since the British occupation ended in 1947, the political situation has been an irritant to Pakistan and cause for sporadic bloodshed.

alese and Sri Lankan customs officials. Obviously unimpressed, he also required I produce the equivalent of a John Dewey doctoral dissertation to prove my contention that I was a teacher.

And then, seemingly on cue without warning, Mr. Secret Agent Man suddenly became animated and friendly, and smiling and curious, asking me to exchange some rumpled rupees for his one-dollar bill. A series of introductions to colleagues, more than a few beers, and a serious discussion of Indian whores followed. Finally, with preliminaries aside and evidence accepted that I was an "OK guy," we reached the crux of the matter.

While in Madras in December, I had reported to the Foreigners Registration Office and requested a visa extension. I did so because, according to the original wording of my Indian visa issued in New York, I had been allotted ninety days to remain in India from my first date of entry, October 12, 1975. Told by the woman in Madras that I did not yet need a visa extension because only those days actually spent in India are "debited from my account" (meaning the time I remained in Nepal and Ceylon was exempt) proved cause for a denial of my requested extension.

Based on the Madras official's calculations, my visa will expire on February 24, 1976, causing me to visit this visa office at least one week prior, as directed by Indian law. Additionally, I explained that the female agent in Madras had refused to put anything in writing, assuring me her interpretation was standard policy throughout India.

Barely allowing me to finish, the G-men immediately declared my visa to be null and void, informed me it had expired on January 12, 1976, began to recognize I was in the country illegally, lined me up, and put me before a firing squad. Kidding.

However, they accepted my word as a "gentleman" that I had been fooled in Madras. In unison, they responded, "Fucked stupid woman." Because this matter was a bit unusual, we waited for the junior chief to show up.

Their articulate and well-dressed boss quickly bought my alibi: an American history teacher exploring material for a ninth-grade unit on Kashmir. After further explaining that "my journey might help to correct bizarre notions held by American students regarding Indian lifestyles," I learned that his son, a former engineering student in California, had often been asked if roads existed in India. Instant karma. In less than two minutes, the visa extension was granted, inexplicably to April 18. Smiling broadly, a Sikh agent exposed a mouthful of rotting teeth before repeating, "Fucked, stupid woman."

And so, it appears that my stay at Yoganta Academy has been, remains, and will continue to be beyond my control. I suffered under the illusion that I initiate and cause actions to happen rather than perceiving reality as it is—the intertwining of events and people usually reacting to circumstances and situations beyond their control.

That part of me that is perseverant, that prevented me from turning back on the Everest trek, now longs to return to the ashram. That part of me that seeks wine, women and song wants to run away. An existential predicament, it represents the perpetual inevitable struggle among id, ego, superego, and Self that Vedic yoga purports to successfully resolve.

Yoganta Ashram, Lakshman Jhula, India
Wednesday, February 11, 1976

Excerpts from a letter written to brother Bill:

What is time anyway? Nothing more than a vague concept that some allow to rule their lives. Forget the schedule of life that society arbitrarily places on us. It's nonsense.

No matter what you do, life is imperfect. If you decide to try law school, you may get depressed. Barbara B., my friend and mentor at Hofstra University, would often counsel, "Once in a while, depression is healthy." Regardless of the outcome of your decision, be mindful that life is too often a series of compromises. Sometimes we must accept our limitations as they are and act accordingly. Don't get down because you are comparing yourself to a Billy that does not exist. Whatever you decide will be the right choice. Expect nothing and you will achieve something great.

Please know you are not alone when undergoing mental gymnastics. During December and January, I trucked, encountering cycles of rugged travel, relaxation, and heavy smoke, punctuated by periods of spirituality and renouncement.

After I spent a brief time at the ashram described in my previous letter, Bal Yogi Prem Varni requested I go elsewhere, explaining I wasn't ready for *kundalini* (spinal energy) yoga.

Heartbroken and about to depart, a senior disciple speculated that Swamiji was probably testing my resolve. And so, the torturous matter remained unresolved. When Swamiji again mentioned I try another retreat, I chose to ignore his insulting remarks.

During that panic-stricken day, I asked myself if my desire for yoga and enlightenment was great enough to tolerate and accept the rigorous and stern life of Yoganta, one that breaks a man's ego and is so physically and emotionally trying. All the while, I recognized that my hedonistic id and ego were battling against my spiritual Self, that part of me that seeks eternal bliss and liberation.

This morning, I returned from Jammu on the night train, picked up your letter at *post restante* [general delivery], and rang up the ashram. Resigned to the reality that I could not return to Yoganta, I learned otherwise and found a vacancy in its Austerity Cottage.

A genuine Indian mystic, Bal Yogi Prem Varni possesses psychic powers, the nature of which he would never exhibit. Unable to comprehend his cosmic Tao, I am lost. Although his ways seem loving, they also seem harsh. He teaches that the ego is to be unmasked and reduced before finally being accepted, not destroyed, as I originally thought. A minor player, ego becomes subordinate to Absolute Self, to Brahma, to eternal Truth, Love, and God.

Yoganta is permitting me to live in the presence of one devoted to Realization and Truth. Swamiji's metaphoric talks at satsang draw comparisons to plant nature, animal nature, and levels of self-realization. Apparently, hatha yoga (*asanas,* physical positions) plays a lesser, secondary role to the evolution of consciousness as depicted in the *Ramayana*, the story of Lord Rama, and *The Bhagavad Gita*, the "Celestial Song of Lord Krishna."

Sitting at his feet before a small fire, the Bal Yogi's students emulate their guru's long nasal incantation "Aaauuuumm" before they go into deep meditation and feel Atman's universal truth vibrate throughout their bodies and souls.

Swamiji is enlightened truth in human form. If he sleeps, he does so in *samadhi*, a meditative, trance-like state, the final stage of spiritual attainment and enlightenment. By opening my heart to him, he will forever be with me.

Feeling impossible to ignore the karmic reality of the material world, Swamiji preaches yoga to be the vehicle that allows us to live half in and half out. Radha Krishna, a known and published Indian theologian, believes yoga is discipline, which, in turn, conveys an inherent suffering that leads to and is necessary for eventual spiritual enlightenment.

Is ashram living capable of teaching me more than I can possibly imagine? It already has. To know that God is love—to feel it beyond the intellect—is to achieve it. Grasping for same has caused me to become vegetarian.

Well, dear William David, the night is passing, my eyelids are closing. I have fallen in love with India: this diverse, incomprehensible realm of beauty within a sea of madness. So much more than a physical entity, perhaps only China can compare to India's lengthy, multitudinous civilization, its scope and magnitude dwarfing most Western nations.

Of epic proportion, sleepy and static textbook history has become a living, breathing series of never-ending, in-my-face, all-encompassing events and people. And though I marvel at humankind's evolutionary achievements, I am saddened by its repetitious cycles of progress and relapse. Yet so unpredictable and resilient are the tribes of the Earth that I prefer to remain optimistic and believe that one day, universal Truth and Love and God will broadly manifest themselves.

Love,

Namaste,

Martin

According to anonymous sources, my zoned-out angst happens to everybody and, sometimes, for quite a long time. "So, this is part of Swamiji's technique; that there is no structure. Once I study here for a time, and am accepted, all will be cool," so says Don Martín.

But that is the fucking problem. I'm always first wanting and needing acceptance and approval—to know where I stand—*before* proceeding. But that does not happen here. I must not allow my emotional need for a sense of belonging to remain a barrier to be hurdled before I take action. When feeling insecure, I lack confidence. When I get depressed, I want to withdraw. Or have I placed the cart before the horse?

The cadence and chanting of a Sanskrit mantra are especially beneficial for the neophyte Westerner who is attempting to develop bhakti. Activities involving vibrational use of Sanskrit are *nonintellectual*. They bypass our cerebral shit and so naturally lead to bhakti and nirvana—so the story goes.

Earlier today I overheard Swamiji say to Sharona, "I went into the kitchen and freaked out." (It was dirty). He then told me, "Freaks stay at Swami Prakesh." (I had never told him.)

Yoganta Ashram, India
Thursday, February 12, 1976

My need for approval and acceptance before taking action is but one manifestation of a greater need. If I can just complete this, or do that, or accomplish one more anything, all else will flow. True? Sometimes.

My neuroses hinder my psychic growth. According to Swamiji, "A thought always travels. You can't hold onto thoughts, so how can they disturb you? We are not the thoughts and delude ourselves that they stay with us. They must be worked through and solved before we can go on to something else."

I have been officially registered and accepted as an aspirant in Yoganta Academy. Whatever else follows is karma. If it comes to pass that I must leave prematurely, it is all *bashert* (preordained, meant to be).

My legs ached so much during last night's satsang that I almost walked out. Had to constantly change position. Truth is, sitting "improperly" troubles me more than it upsets Swamiji. I desperately seek his approval. After having finally been instructed in *pranayama* (breathing) techniques and asanas, the ashram, located at the edge of the jungle, was attacked by a vicious gang of adolescent chimpanzees. Hidden karmic meaning?

The following reconstructed quotes and paraphrases are derived from notes made during satsang. I believe Swamiji's comments and the rhetorical questions he poses are to be understood on several levels: simplistic and complex, material and spiritual, mortal and immortal. Take your pick. It's *The Only Dance There Is*, writes Ram Dass.

(At the risk of repetition, my attraction to Hinduism, Buddhism, Zen, Taoism, and Eastern philosophy is, for the moment, far more intellectual than emotional. If the spiritual lies somewhere between, it may explain my enthusiasm more for states of consciousness and less for Hindu prayers, chanting, methodology, and bhakti.)

Brahma created the mountains, rivers. and the Earth. Krishna brings love to the cosmic universe. Vishnu brings light to the cosmic universe. Shiva brings pure wisdom and enlightenment to the cosmic universe.

Guru is a remover of darkness, a teacher of consciousness. Awareness leads to the wakened condition. But awareness is not enough. People keep their eyes open but still sleep. Watchful awareness also means a sense of duty.

The nature of nature is change. Watch how people put things down. It reveals their nature.

People are the flowers of the Earth. Love is the fruit of the tree. Flowers accept sunlight according to their capacity. The sun is the flower of the sky. Buds open and awake. As human beings, we must do the same.

The ego is not really destroyed. Rather, it eventually just is, existing as part of one's being, to be subservient and not master of Absolute Self.

Pigs are bored in a garden of flowers.

Mantra sound. All movement creates sound. A man who can track sound maintains intuition. Concentrate on sound vibration; *faith* is necessary for *mantra* to work. Brainwaves are changed and the mind can then open to the flow of the heart. Mantra acts as the filter on the mind's thoughts and brainwaves. This is why it can take effect without the user knowing its meaning. A good seed put in fertile soil will grow whether or not the planter has known what kind of plant he has sown.

Asato Ma Sad Gamaya: Lead us from Unreal to Real.
Tamaso Ma Iyotir Gamaya: Lead us from Darkness to Light.
Mrtyor Ma Amrtam Gamaya: Lead us from Death to Immortality.

Shanti Mantra
Aum Dhyoyha Shanti: Peace for the sky
Antareksham Dhyna Shanti: Peace for the earth
Apoha Shanti: Peace for the waters
Osha Dyayaha Shanti: Peace for the trees

Vanashpa Dyayana Shanti: Peace for the plants
Vishwa Devaha Shanti: Peace for the Gods
Brahma Shanti: Peace for the Brahma
Aum Shanti Shanti Shanti: May that peace come unto me.

Sound is the spiritual sense. Sound comes from ether. The seed of ether and container of ether is the sound of reality. If you touch sound, you can join and absorb reality. Each of us has his own sound in this creation. The Ganga, the oceans, all have unique sounds.

The sound of Atman is aum. All mantras come from aum. Aum is the sound of reality. You touch reality from aum. All existence is aum. Aum is carried by the Ganga.

Where there is sound, light is the creator. The source of light and the source of sound is the source of consciousness.

Inner spiritual music, the sound of Atman, is only heard by intuition. Opera is mortal music. Follow the sound of Atman. Live in it. Become it. Join your real nature. Join your existence.

Sound is more subtle than light. You can hear sound in a room, but you cannot see it. You can hear sound through a wall, but still can't see it.

Each sense has its own speed. You can hear from one-half mile away but can't taste from one-half mile away. You can smell from one-half mile away. You can hear a barking dog, but don't know what it is eating.

Freedom. If you are bound to freedom, you want freedom. How do you become free from freedom if you are attached to freedom? Freedom is your rope. It is complex. You must follow the real nature of your existence, of your Atman. This is the purpose of life. Flow with your nature, your consciousness.

Guru nature takes risks and sacrifices love. Friends' nature takes no risks and enjoys love. Friendship supports you. Guru clarifies you, shakes you awake.

Gita. *The Bhagavad Gita* is scripture, a great friend. Without it, without love, you cannot serve properly. The path is faith and devotion. Who guides? Who gives direction? The guru.

The difference between light and enlightenment. Light is objective. Enlightenment is subjective.

The way of love. If you don't have love, how can you give love? Without love, you can give nothing. You can only take.

The tree gives all it has: flowers, fruits, wood, leaves, and shade. And all the time it just stands. It never leaves you. The tree is rooted in love. We are rooted in desire. That is our reality. If the tree is separated from earth, it dies. We are rooted in pure Self. If we are separated from it, we die.

The way of energy and life force. Pranayama is not respiration. It is the yogic breath control of life energy. It is aimed at cleansing the nervous system so that each individual system can tolerate divine (God) energy. If no preparation takes place, the attempt to open our selves could be damaging and lead to insanity. We clean our vital system through kriya (a type of breathing technique). We cleanse our sympathetic (gross) and parasympathetic (subtle) nervous systems.

The center of prana (life force) and sheath (body) is the navel. The umbilicus represents communication with life before and after birth. We wish to go beyond prana. We wish to reach realization. But we must use it and understand it to touch pure consciousness.

We must learn purity and humility. This is the space we need for cosmic energy. The ego occupies this space, so we want to get rid of ego. This cleanses ourselves.

Preparation. If we are not properly prepared, we freak out. Preparation leads to purification which leads to transformation which leads to transcendation which leads to space out!

The third eye. There is name and form. Beyond name and form is the third eye, reality.

Attachment. If you want light, you must first have darkness. If you want to enjoy peace through yoga, there are many problems at first. Objectivity is not bad, but you must give up attachment. Attachment is the problem. Attachment is the source of pain and sorrow. Enjoyment of pleasure is not bad. But attachment to pleasure is bad.

Dreams. At night, during sleep, we have many dreams. You may dream that Swamiji made your sleeping bad. Only when you awake do you realize the dream was a dream. During the dream it all seemed real. If you see the world as a dream, you will remain attached unless you can awaken and detach from the dream.

A dream can fix a dream problem. If someone cuts off your head in the Ganga, you must wake up. The duty of Shiva is to wake you up. Awareness.

Yoga and discipline. Yoga balances the intellect, brain, heart, spirit, and prana. Through yoga discipline you can balance the system. If your body has balance, you can enjoy life. The mind is not a problem. An unbalanced mind is the problem. If a nostril is blocked, it can't smell perfume. If the system is blocked, it needs openness and cleaning. You must be open and clean to receive anything from yoga.

If you dig near the Ganga or ocean, it is easy and quick to find water. If you dig on a mountain, it will take a long time to find water. If you practice seva near a realized saint, your servitude will take less time than if you practice it somewhere else.

The mind is ten times quicker than the senses. The intellect is ten times quicker than the mind. The mind needs experience and discipline. Animals have an instinctual, sensual energy. Humans have psychic energy. Through discipline, yogis have special powers. The monkey has a great body for hatha yoga. But the monkey has no clear mind. Animals are cunning but have no discipline.

Realization. Philosophers depend on attainment and realization. Scientists depend on experimentation and achievement. Philosophers have more understanding than scientists—through realization.

Atman is omnipresent in the omniscient.

In meditation, first try to open body consciousness. You create change by uttering "Krishna" and "Rama." Their nature and vibrations reflect on your consciousness. They lead to realization.

Coal to diamonds. When trees die, they become gradually buried under the earth by dust, rock, other trees, and animal bones. As eons pass, the remnants of each previous age are gradually pushed deeper and deeper under the surface of the earth. Each level or stratum builds on top of the one before, causing great pressure to be exerted on those strata thousands of years old.

It is the nature of trees to turn to coal once they have been buried by future earth and debris. The resulting natural pressure forces the coal deep into the earth, where diamonds are created from extremely compressed coal.

In a similar way, via discipline, the ego also must yield to the process of nature, that being change. The ego, when under pressure in the form of discipline (yoga), must endure and change. The mind must eventually still itself and, as it does, it will become obvious that the desires of the ego are merely illusions. Through this natural process, the confusions, desires, and delusions of the ego shall end. The mind will reach understanding. A balance of heart, brain, spirit, and prana will take place.

The way of learning. It is a matter of common experience that, on hearing from his elders the glory of learning, a person tries to pursue his studies. But having no real experience of the glory of learning, he finds it most unpleasant and difficult to continue his studies to the exclusion of play and recreation. Learning is poison in the beginning. It means exclusion of worldly pleasures. When you feel the joy of working in meditation, it tastes like nectar. Don't get caught in the trap of raja (powerful) and tamasic (selfish) joys.

Yoganta Ashram, India
Sunday, February 15, 1976

"Freak out" are the words Swamiji uses to describe what happens to his aspirants when they find life here a bit too much. And so, after spending some weeks at the ashram, I "freaked out," packed my rucksack, told Swamiji and Bernard that I wished to leave, and asked Ghiana to return my passport, documents, and camera. When I had almost reached this point some days earlier, Swamiji removed a small piece of Swiss chocolate from his stash (Can you believe this guy?) and shared a sliver with each aspirant. I laughed—and cried—and returned to the Austerity Cottage.

> On one occasion I also had the experience of seeing one of my comrades entertain doubts; he renounced his vow and relapsed into disbelief . . . this unfortunate man, who had seemed sad and restless for some time . . . came back to our camp in a dreadful state of excitement and with a distorted countenance. He made a commotion outside the leaders' tent, and when the Speaker came out, he shouted at him angrily that he had had enough of this ridiculous expedition which would never bring us to the East. . . .

He had had enough of the journey being interrupted for days because of stupid astrological considerations; he was more than tired of idleness, of childish wanderings, of floral ceremonies, of attaching importance to magic, of the intermingling of life and poetry; he would throw the ring at the leaders' feet, take his leave, and return by the trusty railway to his home and his useful work. It was an ugly and lamentable sight. We were filled with shame and yet at the same time pitied the misguided man. The Speaker listened to him kindly, stooped with a smile for the discarded ring, and said in a quiet, cheerful voice, which must have put the blustering man to shame: "You have said good-bye to us and want to return to the railway, to common-sense and useful work. You have said good-bye to the League, to the expedition to the East, good-bye to magic, to floral festivals, to poetry. You are absolved from your vow."

—Herman Hesse

True. I too had felt shame and guilt and humiliation. I had embarrassed myself every day until the feelings came to overwhelm me. I felt I had no alternative but to physically escape from the "prison" I had created in my own head, full well-knowing to do so was an illusion.

Gabhana Palace, India
Late February, 1976

I have returned to the palace once again, my fourth and final visit, spending most of my time with Locki Raj, sharing his room. Still smoking guns, the brothers are more determined than ever to, as they say, "go out" from India. Locki Raj must wait for his sister to get married. An arranged affair, she'll meet the boy once or twice, with the option to back out.

Excerpts from brother Joel's letter:

You will notice that I have enclosed the standings, as of today (Christmas Eve, 1975), of the NBA, ABA, and NHL. The ABA has condensed into one division after three teams folded earlier this season. The Knicks have won four of their last five.

And one last sports item. The baseball owners fired the impartial arbitrator who ruled in Catfish Hunter's favor last year. The reason is clear. After ruling that the standard baseball contract does not bind the player to a team "in perpetuity" (a ruling that merely reflects fundamental principles of contract law), the owners realized they had hired a man more interested in protecting and preserving the law than their money. Firing him is truly the American way.

My take? All hail Curt Flood, New Age labor reformer and former center fielder for the St. Louis Cardinals. His refusal to accept a trade after the 1969 baseball season led to the Supreme Court, the death of the reserve clause, and the establishment of free agency in all professional sports. I propose all professional athletes, today and in the future, donate ten percent of their salaries to Curt Flood and his eventual estate.

Other matters discussed at the palace? Does this make any sense? We questioned whether our sense of self is compromised when in the company of others? Are we able to behave naturally, without anxiety, within most situations and with most people? In an ideal setting, yes. Reality, however, strikes a somewhat less resonant chord.

Most of us are basically fearful of being ourselves because deep down inside we believe that if we really allow our true selves to emerge, other people will not like us. A heavy fear-of-rejection trip? *My* heavy fear-of-rejection trip? *My* projection trip?

Self-confidence is the other side of the coin. One regulates the other. Umm, I need to think this through before I continue.

Next up? My contention that fishermen in Maine, Japan and India have more in common by means of their shared vocation than differences resulting from their diverse cultures. I am convinced that occupation holds greater sway over people than nationality, religion, ancestry and heritage. Ravi Raj agrees that the changes experienced in the lives of farmers and those tied to the land (and sea) are, for the most part, more induced by adaptations to nature than by the traditions of the society in which they live.

It appears that people whose work has little to do with nature will be least affected by it and, consequently, social, religious, racial, ancestral, and political influences will dominate their lives. Bottom line determinant?

Economics. Those who are most alienated from nature, who appreciate it the least, and who take it most for granted are the first to lose awareness of its very existence and will eventually destroy it.

And speaking of influences, it is not difficult to list well-known, larger-than-life personages who accomplished great deeds: FDR, Churchill, Napoleon, Lincoln, Jefferson, and Mao among them. Unfortunately, all of them also committed monumental brutalities, some of which may have been "necessary" to achieve the greater "good." Accordingly, their acts against humanity and morality balance and tarnish their "greatness."

Is there one man who has *not* committed any atrocities against mankind, who does not fit into this "balanced'" category, and who stands uniquely above all the "greats"? And surely, would he be the first to deny it? I nominate Mohandas K. Gandhi.

Application of the forces of good and evil, of course, is not limited to the famous and infamous. Just take a look in the mirror!

I now turn my thoughts to my Self—to my enormously growing zest for free-spirited living, truth, and spontaneity, all dulled by the mechanically scheduled and manipulated life I previously led in New York City for two and a half years between global travels.

Although my existential freedom, by definition, cannot be absolute and *must* be compromised by the needs of my physical body and insecure psychology, it still allows me wide spaces to explore. Conscious and unconscious intrigues make travel richly rewarding and entertaining—the joy and dance and song of life. Living and breathing in the *now* involves dragging your past shit and luggage with you, understanding your present, and dealing with both in the immediate moment.

Lord Buddha's "*wa*" (balance/harmony) has become the key to *my* peace of mind—for I am coming to realize that I am fulfilled by a balance of work and play, study and stoning, material and spiritual pursuits. Wa does not inherently imply compromise, but compromise must be made to live within society. *Absolute freedom is impossible.*

I do not wish to do without the material advantages of the industrial and technological revolutions: home, car, nutrition, adequate medical care, and so on. In fact, most remarkable, this is the very first time I feel comfortable enough to accept my material desires as congruent with my Self—a lesson never thought to be gained while attending an ashram. Fucking far out, man!

Have I integrated my "real" and "ideal" Selves while compromising my "purist" and "natural" longing? If so, have I not transformed my "ideal" self-image? Are not the mental constructs of my stereotypic hippie values (for example, materialism is bad) being adapted to new experience? *Reality is perception.* Nothing takes place randomly. Everything is linked and interdependent. Nothing is sheer coincidence. Ironically, again, it appears that my new realization regarding materialism cannot be divorced from Swamiji and the Yoganta Ashram. (One definition of mental *health* is the ability to adapt to a changing environment. One definition of mental *illness* is the inability to adapt to a changing environment.)

Sadly noted, some days ago I painfully and ambivalently walked away from the ashram. Heavy. Very fucking heavy. I would like to think I departed with a clear mind, certain of having convinced myself I seek that balance previously discussed. Must I become a yogi's slave to develop humbling humility? My ego and psyche suffered too much to believe it was worthwhile to stay. Hedonism at work? No matter. Expanding knowledge of my capabilities and limitations assure that such life experiences will lead to greater personal truth. That said, I can now give myself permission to confess that Yoganta was beyond me, that my rationalizations had taken charge.

Swamiji made leaving difficult, wishing me to return for my passport and parcel of valuables the following morning. But I felt certain of my decision and did not want the opportunity to painfully reexamine my thoughts and feelings. Only after, "Please, Swamiji, don't torture me like this" was I provided my possessions. Escorting me to the front gate, Bernard spoke with me for some minutes before bidding each other "*hari om,*" with mutual hopes to meet again one day.

During those last moments, as I blamed Swamiji for causing me intense emotional anguish, I could not hate him or get angry at him. Were not his efforts made for my benefit? After expressing his love, "You take your head wherever you go" were his parting words—or so I thought.

Dejectedly walking toward the Ganga, I impulsively checked post restante for mail. Karma? The appearance of a telegram caused fear of a family tragedy. Wildly ripping it open, I discovered it contained a message from Jared and Bonnie, friends I had originally met in Colombia, South America, during a trip I had made during the summer of 1974. They had arrived in Delhi on their way to Agra and would leave a message at the tourist office. Which one?

I ferried across the river, joined a communal taxi to Hardwar, and boarded the night train to Delhi. Jared and Bonnie were nowhere to be found. By 10:45 a.m., I was on a bus to Agra, acutely aware of how much distance I had put between myself and the ashram in such a brief time.

J and B and I met up at the Taj and explored the South Gate Bazaar before visiting too many ganja and bong shops. Deep personal embarrassment and emotional exhaustion made it impossible for me to convey my ashram experience.

My feelings for Swamiji and his devotees (Archeva, Padmina, Sharona, Bernard, Michael, and Ghiana) appear in a letter I wrote to them.

Dear Shri Bal Yogi Prem Varni and Aspirants of Yoganta Academy,

I send you greetings of love and peace, the little that can be found in the material world, and wish to apologize and offer heartfelt regrets for the brief interval of time I spent at Yoganta. My spreading of "poison" and negativity was as unintentional as was my profound sincerity and honesty with which I first came to the ashram.

Perhaps one day I will genuinely *feel* the love and knowledge of Self that I find so easy to relate to on an intellectual basis. I had wished to depart with the blessing rather than the anger of Swamiji. Instead, I left with a vague but somewhat open invitation to return to Yoganta when I "wake up."

Perhaps one day I shall really open my eyes and mind and heart and allow Vedic divinity to manifest within me. I have nothing in my heart but great love for you all.

Hari om,

Martin

From Richard Lannoy's *The Speaking Tree*:

One of the commonest features in a Hindu ashram is the compulsive need of the disciples and supplicants not merely to have *darshan*— the "blessing" of the guru's presence—but also to ensure that they are each, personally, seen by the guru.

Considerable amounts of time and energy are spent in devising ways to achieve this end. . . . In an ashram, personal attachments are rigorously discouraged. But rapport with the guru is another matter. The depersonalized gaze of the guru directed upon the disciple is unattached, disinterested; it is therapeutic if the disciple can respond in similar fashion without hunger for recognition and attachment. In one sense this means that he is more terribly alone than in the outside world. In another, the unflinching mutual "plumbing of the depths" of the depersonalized gaze is an exchange of disinterested love. If the disciple is "not ready," it is said that the guru cannot really look at him; hence the dual anxiety—fear at being seen, fear at not being seen.

A poem I composed and read at satsang.

IN THE SPACE OF FAITH

In the space of faith
Is not a trace of hate
Dharma reigns supreme
When body and mind are clean

To escape delusion and confusion
Is to leave the world of maya illusion
He who evolves to Atman
Is assured the joys of Brahman

Of ego we must beware
It wants to live unaware

It seeks its own desire
But must vanish for something higher.

Pain and sorrow we bare
For we are filled with fear
Of what we do not know
But ego says it's so

Material reality is fraud
Confusion resembles a sword
They cut our Selves in two
Separating us from what is true.

During my return to the palace, Locki Raj had suggested I invite J and B to Gabhana. They declined. By deciding to run around India, Burma, Thailand, and Hong Kong for two weeks rather than concentrate on any one country, J and B are in harmony with their Tao, certainly not mine. Their style precludes spontaneity and, as far as I am concerned, is an utter waste of time. Declining to meet the Raj Singh family is their loss. (Is being nonjudgmental no more than keeping one's judgments to oneself?)

During my brief stay in Agra with J and B, I endured the Taj Guest House, a flop house of sorts located along the Taj's Southern Gate. Habitually waking in the early a.m., I unintentionally witnessed a desert convocation, the likes of Afghanistan's "lost" tribes. Scattered about open concrete courtyards, stairs and balconies were hundreds of village Indians eating, singing, and totally decimating what little serenity existed before their arrival.

At dawn, when the colorful faithful departed for places unknown, I felt repulsed at the amount of trash that could be produced in five hours. The mess, not cleaned up for two days, was attended to by a young, educated woman who told me that neighboring modern apartments rent for eighty rupees (nine American dollars) per month!

To leave Agra for Gabhana via New Delhi and Aligarh, I was obliged, in Delhi, to trespass within the Palace House Bus Station near the Red Fort—and freaked. For before my bedazzled eyes again appeared the masses of the East: fouled and frantic. An untamed assemblage of flesh and turbans was seemingly trying to escape the bubonic plague. Marauding mobsters posing as mortal men stood on top of others' shoulders, futilely attempting to push their bodies through wire mesh grids protecting inquiry and ticket sellers. A gracious, poorly clothed gentleman deposited me within the protective womb of the Aligarh bus.

But reaching Aligarh is not reaching Gabhana. Within an hour of my arrival in Aligarh, I boarded another vehicular tragedy together with an army of poor and tattered unfortunates, crying infants, grain sacks, chickens, goats, and flies. Blocking all floors and aisles while the bus creaked and crawled, legs, arms, shoulders, necks, and heads made it impossible to discern where my body ended and that of another began.

Arriving at the palace after traveling fourteen miles in ninety minutes, my incredulity regarding the heat, filth and crowding was noted and good-naturedly joked about by the now familiar, good people of Gabhana. B and J had missed a thrill and experience of a lifetime, often so perceived in retrospect.

Delhi, India
Tuesday, February 24, 1976

After final farewells to mom and dad, Gunda and Karala, to the Gabhana Palace, and to Ravi Raj and Locki Raj, both of whom I hope to see in New York next year, I boarded the now familiar 5:00 a.m. bus to Delhi.

My brief and relatively shallow glimpse into their lives has been historically and culturally rewarding, but it pales in comparison to having made friendships based on elements that transcend politics and culture—love, music, and ganja. In addition, I have witnessed the protracted effects of current events on a former royal family and the contrasting ways in which its individual members react to the pressures of the declared Emergency and obligatory land reform.

Father doesn't work, or so it seems. Laboring over his own fields, Ravi Raj feels he is entitled to keep them. However, says Locki Raj, "More production will occur if our property is parceled out to landless villagers and peasants."

In opposition, Ravi Raj retorted, "The resulting parcels will be too small for profitability."

Don Martín's two cents? "Is it not a moral and economic injustice to allow land barons to own vast tracts, parts of which lay fallow, particularly in a country where people equate land with life and sustenance? But is it also not criminal to take active farmland from the wealthy and distribute it to the ignorant poor who don't know how to use it?"

Responding to my ambiguity, Locki Raj assured me that the peasants know well enough about land. In fact, "it is the peasants who actually work the fields owned by the rich."

Viciously designed, a cruel system of eternal indebtedness has bound these serfs to acreage they would never own if not for government intervention. The youngest of the four brothers, Vijay Raj, feels that if the family's land is confiscated by the government, unemployment will rise. He reasons that those formerly hired by the barons will lose their jobs.

I was fascinated as I listened to the Raj Singhs grapple with these issues. Unlike Locki Raj, the eternal socialist, Vijay Raj feels he is being raped by the government. Ravi Raj stands somewhere between the two.

That same morning, on page 1 of *The Times of India*, an article reported legislative passage of new urban land ceilings. Consequence? Further reduced holdings of the Raj Singh family in Delhi and the Dehradun District near Rishikesh.

Pissed, Ravi Raj continued to blame government "bums" for failing to uplift the poor, implying that the people and those they elect are not one and the same. Insisting that legislators of a republic and their electorates are one and the same, Locki Raj emphasized that through the interface of the people with government via bribery, apathy, and inefficiency, it is families like theirs that continue to delay unfavorable reforms by taking every adverse decision to court. More accurately, it is the Raj Singh clan as a unit, not the individual brothers, that institutes litigation. (It was unclear if the Raj Singh family will be compensated for the mandatory forfeiture of their property.)

Setting politics aside, I see Locki Raj, Ravi Raj, and Hare Raj (who "went out" to Afghanistan) as possessing compassionate, warm hearts—the very reason I feel so fortunate to have met them. Righteous Indian *men-*

schen (plural of *mensch*, the highest compliment a Jew can give another human being).

Delhi, India
Wednesday, February 25, 1976

After I walk along Chandni Chowk and whiz crosstown on a Harley carriage, it finally dawns on me. Views of the phenomenal red sandstone Red Fort (1639) and Jami Masjid Mosque (1656) are the last I will see of them for some time.

172. Built by the Mughals, the Red Fort had been sacked and plundered by the usual suspects—Sikhs, Marathas, Persians, and Afghans—before the British arrived. Every August 15, Indian Independence Day, the fort serves as a backdrop for pretentious presidential proclamations and pathetic political prophecy.

Miraculously, the immediate slum engulfing Arabic and Urdu scriptural prophecy etched into the mosque's white marble walls has "disappeared." In place of squalid huts, filth, beggars and generalized decay, local government has installed grassy walks, clean open space, neatly trimmed hedges, and freshly cut sod fronting rectangular reflecting pools. Above the dull static of an electric sound system, the drones of the *muezzin*, the dude (not dudette) who calls Muslims to prayer from the minaret of a mosque, have just drawn a crowd to the great arch for prayer.

173. The Jami Masjid Mosque or "The Mosque of the Celestial Sphere." Its courtyard can accommodate 25,000 worshippers of Allah.

To my meager mind, the deeply rooted Hindu and Muslim concepts of male superiority and fixed marriages are equally abhorrent, and cause for countless millions around the globe to value male babies more than female babies. While I condemn such ingrained belief—that marriage should be decided by parents because it is too important to be left to children to decide—I better understand how and why such cultures engage in these practices. But really. How do you judge one culture by the values of another? But not to do so is equally impossible.

As I continued my final walk, I could not avoid highlights of Indira's Twenty-Point Program for economic improvement splashed on a humongous billboard in the center of New Delhi: price reduction, land and homeless reform, development of the handloom industry, increased energy and irrigation, and tax and educational reform.

As I spend my last days in Delhi obtaining Burmese and Thai visas, I see more street posters encouraging discipline and hard work. The latest and greatest, plastered everywhere, literally pictures the prime minister above:

SHE STOOD BETWEEN ORDER AND CHAOS

SHE SAVED THE NATION

In attempting to build a political and public image equating herself with the Indian government, Emergency, the twenty points, and indispensability, it appears Mrs. Gandhi is also seeking to establish a personality cult among the ignorant and uneducated. "What is good for the P.M. is good for India" smacks of "My country, right or wrong, my country." Can "Love it or leave it" bumper stickers for bullock carts be far behind? The Chinese Communist Party developed and exploited such practices in Mao Tse-tung's China. Will India's future, its school children, join the cadres of the Red Guard?

Sanjay Gandhi now attends all political functions with his mother, is head of the Indian Youth Congress, is being groomed for a future role as heir apparent and represents dire confusion as to the ultimate future of Indian democracy. Though a great deal of fluff is currently paid to "life, liberty, and the pursuit of happiness," deceptive speeches by cagey politicos persist in the spreading of the illusion of separate political parties and justice for all.

Ironically, unlike the polished hypocrites of the American political scene—who, historically, have been self-serving—twentieth-century Indian leaders have practiced compassion and altruism. To accept that their authenticity has been contaminated by Mrs. Gandhi's fascist behavior is difficult and perplexing.

The timing and implementation of Emergency reveals the extent of her need and desire for political power. She *loves* her political power. She *craves* her political power. She is *addicted* to her political power. Perhaps the prime minister really believes that "what is good for Mrs. Gandhi is good for India." Perhaps she really feels she is indispensable for Indian progress. If so, most historians and I highly doubt Indira's commitment to India's democratic legacy.

Today, Village India is little influenced by the government in Delhi. As in most poor, rural regions, people of the land are tied to it and usually preoccupied with pressing concerns far greater than those brought up for votes by politicians in their capital cities. And although the extent to which Urban India has accepted Indira and Emergency remains in doubt, the policy's true litmus test hinges on whether Village India will benefit from the twenty points.

Communication, distribution, and efficiency must reach new levels for Emergency to work. *If* the twenty points can eventually uplift impoverished lifestyles and increase demand for economic and political freedom, it will have succeeded. Spanish fascism taught us that economic cries lead to political tears. As to how many decades India will require to achieve these ends and whether, indeed, it is a fruitless task is, well, blowing in the wind.

Too lazy to peruse *The Bhagavad Gita* and get down with Lord Krishna, Arjuna, and his chariot? Refuse to read the *Tripitaka* (discourses of the Buddha) and the *Sutras* (earliest Buddhist writings) and hang with Siddhartha on the Eightfold Path? Try the decapitated, two-by-three-inch versions of these fundamental texts found in the Thus Spake series. And who knows? Perhaps the next title will be *Thus Spake Indira!*

171. Thus Spake book series.

Calcutta, India
Sunday, February 29, 1976

Capital of West Bengal and featuring grand colonial architecture and rich art galleries dispersed among staid headquarters of the Indian Corporate State, Calcutta, population ten million, is one terminus of the Grand Trunk Road that ends in Kabul.

The twenty-four-hour train to this former British capital of India is my last during this journey to India. Am feeling down. Have no idea when I will return. With the polite assistance of a thickly bearded Sikh travel agent, I am confirmed on Thai International Airlines to Rangoon, Burma.

A day in the life of Calcutta. Not easily forgotten. Witnessed the city's hungry, poor, and downtrodden queue up to be fed (as they do every Sunday morning) in front of my current residence, the Salvation Army Red Shield Hostel located on Sudder Street. Not far is the home of the Missionaries of Charity congregation, founded and supervised by Mother Teresa.

As the day progressed, I roamed about Dalhousie Square and walked over the Howrah Bridge before reaching Chowringhee (Nehru) Road and the "New" (Hogg) Market at Park Street. Although I did not see the Biafran-like emaciates huddled outside the Howrah Railway Station as I did in 1972, it became impossible to enjoy the clusters of bananas, layered flatbread, thin slices of French toast, and chai located across the street. All was donated to the beggars.

Calcutta, India
Monday, March 1, 1976

My last night in India. Thick dust and pollution were swept into bogs of stifling hot and humid air by noisy, horn-blowing cars, trucks, and buses swollen with people, some barely clinging to the back and sides of certifiable jalopies. High-energy street urchins, hawkers, beggar children, merchants and office workers electrified dispassionate streets. Literal streams of flesh, blood, perspiration, and sacred cows gridlocked honking lorries, immobile buses and explosive tempers. Calmly smoking a hash joint, I was soon enmeshed in this engulfing masquerade of absolute urban anarchy, chaos, and confusion immorally posing as sanity.

Relentless in their pursuit were hog-farm hawkers and rickshaw "boys" pulling their awesome loads through such tense streets of urban blight. "Please, sahib, just look. Just look." And so it struck me that most of India's bicycle-rickshaw drivers, who's dreadful work has always saddened me, had it relatively "easy" when compared to the staunch rickshaw men of Calcutta—who propel their burdens with bare, sinewy legs.

Perhaps the most astonishing scene I have ever witnessed and joined was tonight's bus station activity on Chowringhee Road. As foul rings of perpetual dust and bluish pollution became increasingly visible under dim, yellow streetlights, commuters lunged, jumped, and fought their way onto all means of mechanical and animal conveyance, most of which never stopped. Already stunted with burlap sacks, human missiles hurled themselves into crawling vehicular cracks and crannies.

Calcutta's gloomiest reality? The millions who literally live on the streets, and the early morning trucks charged with only one purpose—the collection of their corpses.

When I witness such inhumane conditions, I question the existence of a benevolent, all-loving God. Think holocausts, including the Turkish slaughter of three million Armenians in Eastern Turkey in 1915—still denied by all Turkish governments. Causes me to wonder if religion is a man-made contrivance. The conundrum gnaws at me. Which is more fundamental? Psychology or religion? Which came first? Did one invent the other?

Compassion. Hard to exactly pin it down. Part sympathy? Part empathy? Part love? Part guilt?

Voluntary? Mandatory? Each of us defines and expresses it differently. It seems easy to dispense compassion to those who have truly earned it: the downtrodden, disabled and have-nots of society who have become so through no fault of their own—by means of birth, accident, sickness, war and the like. But what about those unfortunates—and their children—who caused their own misfortune via crime, violence, lethargy, ad nauseam? Do you extend compassion to those who have made their own bed? Is the bottom line one of deservedness?

One final question. Had Rod Serling lived in India before producing and directing *The Twilight Zone?*

The palaces, maharajas, and deserts of Rajasthan, the verdant carpets, white beaches, and palmyra palms of tropical Kerala, the glacial-capped spiritual Himalayas of Kashmir and Uttar Pradesh, the magnificent ancient stone temples and art forms of Madurai, the primitive tribal life in the jungles of Bihar, the incredulous caves of Ajanta and Ellora, the great meccas and bursting bazaars of Calcutta, Delhi, Bombay and Madras, the Gabhana Palace and the loving Raj Singh family, the Taj, and the legacy of Mahatma Gandhi.

Tomorrow, I leave this fantastic country of euphoria and misery, of vast wealth and dire poverty. India spans the descriptive dictionary, the spiritual dictionary, the impoverished dictionary. It represents great paradox, where hippies wearing white, sun-bleached pajamas, dhoties and sandals molded out of tires walk among middle-class Indians in Western suits recently dry-cleaned.

Is India a state of mind, a condition of consciousness, a geographic amalgamation, or an assimilation of God's children? India is a nation of carts, castes, turbans, dung, diseases (tuberculosis, smallpox, diphtheria) and people struggling in cities and in the fields, in great heat and greater humility, for basic survival. It is Benares and Bangalore where tin huts and mud shacks share sidewalks with skyscrapers. It is the ill-paid, resigned, and complacent servant and the inescapable, omnipresent rickshaw driver who lives on, sleeps under, and torturously drives his burden, multiplied by the hundreds of millions.

India is a vast train network, an enduring world in itself. India is hard sell. It is the adverse and depleted forever hawking something to eat, to wear, to barter. It is an infernal, twenty-four–hour marketplace where the conflict between life and death is often obscure.

India is corruption and extortion—from its highest officials to its lowest railway redcoats. It is the legacy of the British Raj and the bastardization of justice, democracy, and the principles of Mahatma Gandhi—under Emergency.

India is Rishikesh, the physical and spiritual convergence of ashrams and painted sadhus searching for salvation, escape from samsara, or a chillum. It is a country unlike all others, affirmed to the death of the illusionary ego leading to realization and enlightenment. It is the Ganga, and it is the yogi and his disciples of all ages and colors, searching for Truth and Knowledge and the Wisdom of the *Vedas, Upanishads,* and *Bhagavad Gita.*

India is spiritualism—Buddhism, Jainism, Mohammedanism, Zoroastrianism, Christianity, Judaism and, of course, Hinduism. Perhaps it is this realm more than any other that compels believers to view India as essential, as unique, as paramount, as Home. And though encyclopedic volumes have been written to accurately portray Hinduism, perhaps the following symbolic narration briefly defines its essence.

It is said that in the late nineteenth century, one of India's greatest sages, Swami Vivekananda, journeyed around the world so that people might be able to distinguish a purer form of Hinduism from the diluted version that so upset the Swami. To accomplish his goal, he would narrate the tale of a man who drove a coach through the countryside, choosing to ignore voices heard from within. "How could someone be inside the coach when I am its only master?" he asked himself. Eventually acknowledging the presence of a "passenger" after years of denial and internal conflict, the driver brought the coach to a halt.

Vivekananda's metaphor is rather enlightening. Symbolizing our conscious, rational ego—which believes *it* is responsible for human motivation and behavior, and which the Hindus refer to as illusionary in nature—is the "driver" of the coach. Our true nature, or Self (Atman), the "passenger," is represented in Western psychological terms by the unconscious. Until the "driver" recognizes his illusionary nature and acknowledges the dictates of his "passenger," he will forever suffer and be fated to never escape painful samsara, the life-death cycle. It is the experience of meditation and yoga, disciplines of mind and body, that will eventually free one to attain higher states of consciousness.

India is all these things. Above all, India is six hundred million souls— trying to find a vacant seat on a second-class train at the same time!

The soundtrack of India? Please consider George Harrison's "Isn't It a Pity." It is the mood set by George Harrison's musical brilliance that is the mantra of India.

India is a realm of beauty within a sea of madness.

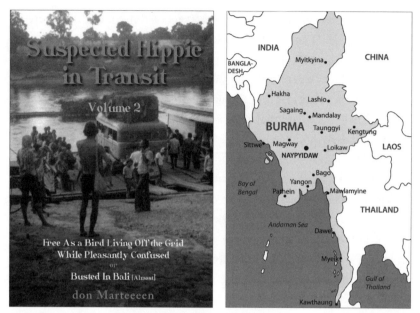

175 and 176. *Left*: cover of volume 2; *right*: map of Burma.

Excerpts from *Suspected Hippie in Transit*, volume 2:

Rangoon, Burma
Wednesday, March 3, 1976, Early Morning

Only a one-week travel visa is issued by the Burmese government, barely enough time to realize I've left India. But seven days are better than no days. Is the glass of life half full or half empty? Are you an optimist or a pessimist? Do you focus on what you have or what you don't have?

Hanging in the "refreshment room" of the Rangoon Central Railway Station, waiting for the 7:00 a.m., twelve-hour express to Mandalay, I can't believe I'm not in India. Am I finally east of the subcontinent? All about is soft, light skin stretched over faces of oriental features and bone structure. Thai International Airlines graced its service and superb reputation with excellent cuisine, complimentary French wine, and beautiful Thai women.

Last evening, while walking the streets of Rangoon, I discovered a marvelous pagoda complex generously sprinkled with golden meditating Buddhas, and crowds of kneeling Burmese paying penitence as they meditated at the lotus feet of their deity. Of the Hirayana (Southern) School of Buddhism, they contrast the Himalayan or Mahayana (Northern) School. Is it unfair to speculate that the radical, cultural, and climatic variances between densely populated tropical Southeast Asia and the isolated, forbidding Himalayas of Northern India, Nepal, Tibet, Sikkim, Bhutan, and China played a role in the evolution of these two Buddhist sects?

The Burmese appear honest, reserved, and meditative without continually hawking everything under the sun. Very friendly, many seem naive and childlike. Those few Burmese who speak any English do so without an Indian accent, are fun to meet, and lack the aggressiveness so prevalent in the personalities of their northern neighbors.

Strange days. When is the music over? The doors to the foreigner's trip once within Burma is revealing but atypical, the result of severe time restraints imposed by the government. Nevertheless, a "hippie trail" does exist: Rangoon to Mandalay to Pagan to Rangoon.

The value of Burmese currency is determined by the absurdly wide variance between the official bank rate of exchange and the unofficial, illegal, but predominant black-market rate. In contrast to thirty chat per US dollar everywhere else, the bank rate stands at a miserly 6.3 chat. Consequently, when leaving Calcutta, most buy the allowable one bottle of Johnny Walker Red or Dewars and one carton of Triple Five cigarettes. Purchased with foreign currency, the contraband costs $8.50.

In Rangoon, such valuable black-market commodities will fetch 275 chat—enough to live in Burma for one week. But it is deemed wise to exchange some dollars at the official rate so one's currency declaration will look kosher. Five dollars is acceptable.

ॐ

Booked solid, Rangoon's YMCA offered no solace. And when the only other flophouse in the city, specifically dedicated to accept foreign guests, didn't, I purchased a railway ticket for Mandalay, checked my pack into the luggage storeroom, carried my sleeping bag, and resigned myself to sack out on a train station platform. As things worked out, I slurped noodle soup at the YMCA, slept on a dusty floor with newly encountered speed freaks, Michael and Bob, smoked a pinch of Thai grass, and reacquainted myself with mosquitoes imported from Hikkaduwa. For the remainder of the evening, all was cool in hot, sticky Burma.

Acknowledgments

No book is an island. Rather, *Suspected Hippie in Transit* is the result of an aggregation of skilled and talented professional accomplices to whom simple thanks does not cut it. Regardless, I will try.

The following people provided invaluable strategy and support while protecting the author from himself: Don Marco Z., "Mohank" Schweitert, publisher Perry White (of the *Daily Planet*), and Don Ronaldo. They joined Mademoiselle Alexa Raider and Monsieur Pierre on my unpaid editorial board.

First to assist me to discover themes outside of my awareness was shaman Melanie Mulhall, award-winning editor and author. Even-keeled renaissance woman Sandra Jonas (Sandra Jonas Publishing) designed *Suspected*'s interior and front and back covers and continues to serve as my prescient project manager and marketing consultant.

Deserved special notes of praise belong to my editors, Alice Levine, Thomas Locke, and Sandra Jonas. Daily technological struggles were amicably resolved by my administrative assistant par excellence, "The Fabulous Miss L.,"w Leah Frumkin. Her twin sister, JoniRoni, assured I attended workshops offered by My Word Publishing and its founder, Polly Letofsky. Had I not done so, I might still be looking for a traditional publisher.

Suspected's long, strange journey, from raw notes to final product, also owes much to CIPA (Colorado Independent Publishers Association) and those nameless individuals who founded and maintain this awesome trade group. Without it, at this very moment, you might be reading your Bible.

The countless ethnic and aboriginal peoples I met on the road remain treasures. When invited into their homes, I was taught how to share, how to host, and how to love.

Lastly, I wish to thank Aurora S. Berman, my friend and the daughter of Frank Stiffel, survivor of Treblinka and Auschwitz, and author of *The Tale of the Ring: A Kaddish* (1984). Their combined experiences provided priceless inspiration during the final drafts of *Suspected*.

Bibliography

Benedek. Laslo, dir. *The Wild One.* Stanley Kramer Productions, 1953.

Bezruchka, Stephen. *A Guide to Trekking in Nepal.* Kathmandu: Sahayogi Press, 1972.

Buber, Martin. *Legend of the Bal-Shem.* New York: Princeton University Press, 1955.

Cassady, Neal. *The First Third.* San Francisco: City Lights Books, 1971.

Collins, Larry, and Dominique Lapierre. *Freedom at Midnight.* New York: Avon Books, 1975.

Conrad, Joseph. *The Rescue.* London: J. M. Dent, 1946.

Cowan, Paul. *An Orphan in History.* New York: Bantam Books, 1982.

Dalai Lama. *My Land and My People.* New York: Potala Corporation, 1962.

Dupree, Nancy Hatch. *The Valley of Bamiyan.* Kabul: Afghan Tourist Organization, 1967.

Dylan, Bob. "Gotta Serve Somebody," track 1 on *Slow Train Coming.* Columbia Records, 1979, vinyl.

Dylan, Bob. "Precious Angel," track 2 on *Slow Train Coming.* Columbia Records, 1979, vinyl.

Furer-Haimendorf, Christoph von. *The Sherpas of Nepal: Buddhist Highlanders.* Transatlantic Arts, 1972.

Gandhi, Mohandas K. *Third Class in Indian Railways.* Lahore: Gandhi Publications League, 1917.

Gauba, Khalid Latif. *The Assassination of Mahatma Gandhi.* Bombay: Jaico Publishing House, 1969.

Goldberg, Natalie. *Writing Down the Bones*. Boston: Shambala, 1986.

Goodspeed, Bennett W. *The Tao Jones Averages: A Guide to Whole-Brained Investing*. New York: Viking Penguin, 1983.

Gurdjieff, G. I. *Meetings with Remarkable Men*. New York: E. P. Dutton, 1969.

Harrer, Heinrich. *Seven Years in Tibet*. London: Rupert Hart-Davis, 1953.

Hesse, Hermann. *The Journey to the East*. New York: Farrar, Straus, and Giroux, 1956.

Huxley, Aldous. *The Doors of Perception*. New York: Harper and Row, 1954.

James, William. *The Varieties of Religious Experience*. New York: Macmillan, 1961.

Lanoy, Richard. *The Speaking Tree*. London: Oxford University Press, 1971.

Mascaro, Juan. *The Upanishads*. Harmondsworth: Penguin Books, 1965.

Maslow, Abraham. *Religion, Values, and Peak Experiences*. Viking Press, 1964, 1970.

Mathur, Barkha. "Naga Panchami: A Mix of Faith and Superstition." *The Times of India*, August 11, 2013. https://timesofindia.indiatimes.com /city/nagpur/nag-panchami-a-mix-of-faith-and-superstition/article show/21751648.cms.

Michener, James. *Caravans*. New York: Random House, 1963.

Rabbi Sylvan Kamens and Rabbi Jack Weimer. "A Litany of Remembrance." In *Gates of Prayer: A New Union Prayerbook*. New York: Central Conference of American Rabbis, 1975.

Shirer, William L. *Gandhi: A Memoir*. New York: Simon and Schuster, 1979.

Solzhenitsyn, Aleksandr. *August 1914*. New York: Farrar, Straus, and Giroux, 1971.

Solzhenitsyn, Aleksander. *One Day in the Life of Ivan Denisovich*. New York: E. P. Dutton, 1963.

Snow, Edgar. "The Message of Gandhi." *Saturday Evening Post*. March 27, 1948.

Stiffel, Frank. *The Tale of the Rings: A Kaddish*. New York: Bantam Books, 1984.

Swami Suddhasatwanada. *Thus Spake The Buddha*. Madras: Sri Ramakrishna Math, 1964, 1968.

Szalet, Leon. "A Deathless Prayer." In *Experiment "E,"* trans. by Catherine Bland Williams. New York: Didier Press, 1945.

Theroux, Paul. *Happy Isles of Oceania: Paddling the Pacific.* New York: Putnam, 1992.

Trungpa, Chogyam. *Cutting Through Spiritual Materialism.* Berkeley: Shambala Publications, 1973.

Watts, Alan W. *Psychotherapy East and West.* New York: Ballantine Books, 1961.

Watts, Alan W. *The Way of Zen.* New York: Pantheon Books, 1957.

Vasto, Lanza del. *Return to the Source.* London: Rider, 1943.

Vyasa. *The Mahabharata.* India. 300 BCE.

Wolfe, Tom. *The Electric Kool-Aid Acid Test.* New York: Farrar, Straus, and Giroux, 1968.

Yogananda, Paramahansa. *Autobiography of a Yogi.* London: Rider, 1969.

Zaehner, R. C. *Hinduism.* London: Oxford University Press, 1962.

Photography Credits

Every effort has been made to obtain permissions for photographs and text quoted or adapted in this work. If any required acknowledgments have been omitted or any rights overlooked, it is unintentional. Please notify the publisher of any omission, and it will be rectified in future editions.

Some images captured before, during, and after 1971–1977 were not taken by the author. They are included to provide readers with a broader, historical visual experience. Throughout this list, the following abbreviation is used: MF (Martin Frumkin, author).

Map of Asia: Olli/Adobe Stock
Map of Hippie Trail: Public domain

1. Map of India: Peter H. Furian/Getty
2. Benares, Ghats: L. Pallen (Lucas the Nomad)/Flickr
3. Benares, Cows: MF
4. Chillum: MF
5. Sadhu: Siraj Ahmad/Getty
6. Map of Nepal (#1): Peter H. Furian/Getty
7. Gadhimai, kot: Nur Photo/Getty
8. Gadhimai, field: Robert Schmidt/Getty
9. Kathmandu, Durbar Square: Public domain
10. Kathmandu, Durbar Square: MF
11. Kathmandu, hashish dispensary: MF
12. Durbar Square, subpools: MF

13. Bhairavaka (Mahakala): Maureen Barlin/Flickr
14. Pashupatinath(bridge): Sergio and GabriellaFlickr
15. Pashupatinath (temple): Sergio and GabriellaFlickr
16. Map of Afghanistan: Peter H. Furian/Getty
17. Band-i-Amir Blue Lake: Maximillian Clark/Getty
18. Gatekeepers: MF
19. Bamyan,Big Buddha: MF
20. Mountain village: ToghkoNorband/Afghan's Photography/ Flickr
21. Mountain village: David Kohl/Flickr
22. Cat Kabob Man and Son of Cat Kabob Man: MF
23. Delicious Friends: MF
24. Express Bus: MF
25. Kabul Garment Center: MF
26. Kabul75: Jean-Paul Blanc/Flickr
27. Kabul Hill: David Kohl/Flickr
28. Caravan: Max Desfor/AP photo
29. Inside Kabul market: AP photo
30. Kabul street scene: AP photo
31. Kabul traffic light: Henry Burroughs/AP photo
32. Balloons: AP photo
33. Trucks: Henry Bradsher/AP photo
34. Kandahar City: Fabrizio Foschini Archives/Afghan Analysis Network
35. Kandahar: David Kohl/Flickr
36. Drawing of Herat Citadel: Alamy
37. Herat 3 shops: David Kohl/Flickr
38. Herat shop and camel: David Kohl/Flickr
39. Herat women wearing burqas: Na'eem/Flickr
40. Herat street life: David Kohl/Flickr
41. Herat market and minarets: David Kohl/Flickr
42. Herat, baked-mud homes: Na'eem/Flickr
43. Herat horse carriage: David Tapsell/Flickr
44. Herat Panorama: Fabrizio Foschini Archives/Afghan Analysis Network

45. GhazniFort: Annemarie Schwarenbach

46. Ghazni homes: Jon Arnold/Alamy

47. Hindu hotties: Subha Addy

48. Birth control street poster: MF

49. Pan Am: MF

50. Map of Israel: Peter H. Furian/Getty

51. Jerusalem, Wailing Wall: Lucky-photo/Adobe Stock

52. Jerusalem, Dome of the Rock shrine: Cunaplus/Adobe Stock

53. Frumkin Street: Craig Eagle

54. Map of Turkey: Peter H. Furian/Getty

55. Music Festival poster: Isle of Wight Music Festival, 1969

56. Third Class in Indian Railways: Gandhi Publications
    League, 1917

57. Crowded platform: Robbie/Flickr

58. Eclipse Asia: Ajay Verma/Reuters

59. India: K. K. Arora/Reuters

60. Harley Davidson taxi: Jeffrey Taunton/Alamy

61. Three-wheel rickshaw: MF

62. Gabhana Palace royal welcome (top): MF

63. Gabhana Palace royal welcome (bottom): MF

64. Palace interior (top): MF

65. Palace interior (bottom): MF

66. Raj Singh family jeep: MF

67. Gabhana Unified School District: MF

68. "Biblical" oxen: MF

69. Brahma: Public domain

70. Vishnu: Public domain

71. Shiva: Sorayuth 26/Getty

72. Nataraja: F9 Photos/Getty

73. Kerala, sister, and bullock cart: MF

74. Fatepuhr Sikri: Stefano Ravali/Getty

75. Longhand notes: MF

76. Nepalese customs man: MF

77. Trek Map, Kathmandu to Everest: Steven Bezruchka

78. Daman in the Early Morning: Walter Callen/Flickr

79. Inn Eden: MF
80. Business cards: MF
81. Kathmandu, Durbar Square (Guardian): MF
82. Kathmandu: MF
83. Kathmandu Pagoda: MF
84. Patan (oil): Khatri Chetrri family
85. Patan, Tibetan rug: MF
86. Bhaktapur, Durbar Square: Satish Parashar/Getty
87. Nyatapola Pagoda: John Guest/Flickr
88. Swayambhunath Stupas: Suziinnepal/Flickr
89. Swayambhunath: Sergio and Gabriella/Flickr
90. Everest trek permit: MF
91. Guide to Trekking in Nepal. 1970: Steven Bezruchka
92. Bridge: chains and planks: MF
93. Nepalese rural mountain hut: MF
94. Personal trek map: George Zirfas
95. Mountain stupa: MF
96. Tibetan butcher: MF
97. Baby in basket: MF
98. Pasang Sherpa of Ringmo: MF
99. Mountain porters (oil): Khatri Chetrri family
100. Green sweater: MF
101. Hotel/Altitude sickness: MF
102. Tengboche Monastery: Alan Fairbank/Nepal photo history project/Peace Corps photo history
103. Ama Dablam: Boyloso/Getty
104. Ama Dablam: Daniel Prudek/Getty
105. Ama DablamPanorama: Clive Griffiths/Flickr
106. Ama Dablam: Daniel Prudek/Getty
107. Pangboche(1): MF
108. Pangboche(2): MF
109. Pheriche hut: MF
110. Free Tibet: Annette Dugan
111. Mt. Everest (top): MF
112. Mt. Everest (bottom): MF

113. Mandala (top): Getty
114. Mandala (bottom): Getty
115. Grand Lama: MF
116. Mani Rimdu: mask/procession: MF
117. Mani Rimdu: horn section: MF
118. Mani Rimdu: congregants: MF
119. Mani Rimdu: congregants and stupa: MF
120. Mani Rimdu (depth and perspective): MF
121. Mani Rimdu: monks dancing: MF
122. Lukla airfield: Dave O'Connor/Rounds Imaging Services
123. Tenzing: Hilliary Airport: Frank Overbeck/Flickr
124. People on train tracks: Jitendra Prakesh/Reuters
125. Shore Temple at Mahabalipuram: Vikas Rana/Flickr
126. Madras sidestreet temple and beggar: MF
127. Madraschai stall: L. Parry (Lucas the Nomad)/Flickr
128. Map of Sri Lanka: Peter H. Furian/Getty
129. Handwritten notes: MF
130. Hikkaduwa sunset: MF
131. Sri Lankan tropical temple: MF
132. Helga and the Sex Revolution: MF
133. Galle municipal parking: MF
134. Galle meat market: MF
135. Galle fish market: MF
136. The Weerashingghe family: MF
137. Three elephants bathing: MF
138. Map of South India: George Zirpas
139. Street to MeenakshiTemple: Wesley Rosenblum/Flickr
140. Gopuram: Victoria Bergeson/Flickr
141. Cow in Madurai St.: MF
142. ThirumalaiNayakkarPalace: Saiko 3p/Getty
143. Rich man: MF
144. Poor man: MF
145. Mounted elephant: MF
146. Ganesh: Naushaud Siddiqui/Getty
147. Kids/Sunrise at the southern tip of India: MF

148. Arjuna and Lord Krishna on chariot: Reddees/Getty

149. Cochin, JewTown: MF

150. Synagogue: MF

151. Zeyda: Frumkin family

152. Babi: Frumkin family

153. Sh'ma: public domain

154. Tropical oxcart: Manfred Sommer/Flickr

155. Circus poster, 1843: Pablo Fanque/Public domain

156. Anjuna Beach, Goa: Amit Rane/Getty

157. Gateway of India, Bombay: L. Parry (Lucas the Nomad)/Flickr

158. Bombay Bayshore: MF

159. Ajanta Caves (top): MF

160. ElloraCaves (middle): Adobe Stock

161. Ajanta Caves (bottom): Getty

162. Udaipur wall mural: L. Parry (Lucas the Nomad)/Flickr

163. Udaipur wall mural: Manakin-Manfred Sommer/Flickr

164. UdaipurCity Palace facade: Mr. Kartik (Roving Eye)/Flickr

165. Udaipur City Palace: Manfred Sommer/Flickr

166. Amber Palace: Javi M. Braco/Getty

167. Pushkar: Anujak/Getty

168. Bal Yogi Prem Varni ("Swamiji"): Yoganta Academy

169. Gautama Buddha: Dawid Markiewicz/Getty

170. Rishikesh/Lakshman Jhula: Elena

171. Rishikesh ashram: DMS

172. Map of Jammu and Kashmir: Rainer Leshiewski/Getty

173. Red Fort: Roop Dey/Getty

174. Jami Masjid Mosque: Poltushyamal/Getty

175. Thus Spake: MF

176. Volume 2, front cover image: MF

177. Map of Burma: George Zirpas

Author photo: Jane Frumkin

Front cover: MF

Back cover photo: Elena Volkova/Adobe Stock

Permissions

Grateful acknowledgment is given to the following publishers and authors for permission to reprint the material from their books:

Although permissions for copyrighted material were not required, upon written requests, blessings were provided by Stephen Bezruchka; Neal and Carolyn Cassady's middle child, daughter Jami Cassady; and Jack Kerouac's estate:

Bezruchka, Stephen. *A Guide to Trekking in Nepal*. Seattle: Mountaineers Books, 1985.

Cassady, Neal. *The First Third*. San Francisco: City Lights Books, 1971.

Kerouac, Jack. *On the Road*. New York: Viking Press, 1957.

About the Author

MARTIN FRUMKIN, born a boomer in Lower Manhattan, escaped middle-class morality and malaise in his travels throughout North America, Europe, Asia, and South America. His journals became his compass—a guru of sorts—often in conflict with his own attempts at self-discovery while wrestling with God.

Five years of open-ended, spontaneous backpack travel morphed into a career in the trenches of psychiatric social work. By serving society's have-nots and homeless, Martin found the balance he sought, Buddhism's *wa*, a compromise between American corporate tyranny and Timothy Leary's psychedelic mantra.

First called "Don Martín" by fishermen in the Canary Islands, and later by friends and enemies, he lives with his wife in Colorado.